The Carmen Chronicle

The Carmen Chronicle

THE MAKING OF AN OPERA

Harvey E. Phillips

STEIN AND DAY/*Publishers*/New York

First published in 1973

Library of Congress Catalog Card No. 73-80797

Designed by David Miller
Printed in the United States of America
Stein and Day/*Publishers*/Scarborough House, Briarcliff Manor, New York 10510
ISBN 0-8128-1609-9

For the two opera-goers who agreed
to keep a seven-year-old company
at his first visit to the Met (yes,
it was a performance of Carmen*):*
my mother and father.

*

Introduction

When Goeran Gentele died in a meaningless automobile accident while vacationing in Sardinia with his family two months before his Metropolitan Opera debut as both General Manager and stage director, the music world found itself thrown into profound shock. When the initial disbelief at such horror befalling a man and his loved ones (two daughters also died in the crash) whom New York had taken to its heart in the little time he had already spent in that city could be pared down to the proportions of manageable tragedy, one overriding question remained: What would happen to *Carmen,* the work scheduled for opening night, 1972?

Of course, this was meant to be no ordinary opening night. Gentele's arrival on the scene had been counted on to write an upbeat *finis* to the Bing regime, twenty-two years of often brilliant productions and growth, especially as represented by the move from Thirty-Ninth Street to Lincoln Center, but also a period of acrimony, bad public relations, management-artist feuds, and most unhappily, an impregnable conviction that refused any deviation from a sacred, pre-1939 Central European faith that opera is and should be as opera was, and that nothing should or could change.

In Gentele one had reason to hope that all this was to be, perhaps not swept away, but at least examined in a clean, honest light. The man was affable, genuinely warm, and charming. He was as adept behind the footlights as behind the manager's desk, having personally directed many of the Swedish Royal Opera's most successful productions. In his few public statements in New York he demonstrated awareness of a possible opera-television alliance, of the vast audiences beyond the atrophied Manhattan black-tie stereotype, of the necessity of linking the Metropolitan's activities with operatic ventures all over the country, of getting young people into the theater, of establishing a stage for chamber opera. In short, many expectations, perhaps some quite unreasonable and certainly some to be disappointed, were riding on Gentele's assumption of power.

Sir Rudolf Bing had originally saddled Gentele's American bow with possibly the Metropolitan's weakest production, an ancient, dusty *Tannhäuser* that was sure to get his successor off to a creeping start, even if the cast did include two international superstars, Marilyn Horne and James McCracken, both in their first major Wagnerian ventures. The Swedish impresario immediately saw the danger in this choice and prevailed to the extent that a new *Carmen* was substituted, still with the same major singers, but in addition Leonard Bernstein in the pit and with sets by one of Europe's most respected designers, Josef Svoboda. As for the director, Gentele also aimed for the top. Rumors abounded. Giorgio Strehler was mentioned, even Broadway's Tom O'Horgan, but for one reason or another (Strehler was alternately said to be in poor health or unwilling to work with singers of Horne's and McCracken's physical, as opposed to vocal, stature) no one was found for the assignment, and Gentele decided to do it himself.

Preliminary meetings and thinking took place, but after Gentele's death, the new *Carmen* was left without a captain. It was known that Bernstein would conduct a version that restored many traditional cuts, one based on the researches of Fritz Oeser which had resulted in the Alkor-Bärenreiter edition of 1964 and in the tangible East Berlin Komische Oper production of Walter Felsenstein in 1971. Even more of a departure for this *Carmen,* it was to be performed with the original *opéra-comique* dialogue, as opposed to the grand-opera score everyone had taken for granted, especially in America, since Guiraud added those recitatives for Vienna in 1875. But what was to be done with all this novelty remained a question. Gentele's ideas, as reported by Bernstein, Svobada, and others who had talked with him or even participated in a past Stockholm production of the work, were but generally known. (A rather strange exception to the vagueness was an intention to graft on a ballet to Act Four, a practice long fallen into disrepute.) There remained the beginnings of a prompt book, and good faith, the best of intentions, and most of all, the necessity of putting on a *Carmen* on September 19, 1972, that would justify the attention the entire operatic world was focusing on the event; for event, not only performance, it had to be.

Again the search for a director got under way, this time the investigation headed by Schuyler Chapin, a Gentele-appointed deputy who was then named Acting General Manager. In a curiously unspectacular decision for the unnewsworthy, instead of bringing in a widely recognized name (Jerome Robbins, with whom Bernstein has been working on a ballet project, was much mentioned), the choice fell on Bodo Igesz, the thirty-seven-year-old Metropolitan staff director who had been slated to be, under Gentele, *Carmen's* second-in-command. Now the job belonged to him alone. Not only would this have amounted to a nerve-racking assignment for the most glittering personality in the business, but it was also Igesz's first solo-flight production with the company. Few envied him the pressure this burden brought with it.

Forces realigned, sadness thrust into the background, *Carmen* and the new Metropolitan era prepared for their launching. What *The Carmen Chronicle,* the book that follows, attempts is a blow-by-blow (nonliteral) account of how it all happened. It is meant to be as unbiased a job of reportage as is possible when only one brain and one set of eyes and ears are available to register and record. Naturally, I could not be everywhere at once (sometimes I was not allowed *anywhere*), but I have treated the subject as it was revealed to me. What can be construed as judgments are there to put in relief the reality of a moment—musical or dramatic or purely visual—as anyone with some critical faculties would have to interpret it. I apologize to anyone whose feelings may be hurt by my candor, but I have reported events as honestly as a flying felt-tipped pen and a yellow pad would permit.

I have sought, in this log of rehearsals and performance and the recording sessions that followed, to reproduce the world of work that goes into opera. There *was* drama, there *were* jokes, and, yes, there *was* tedium, and it would be a falsification if any of these elements was slighted. The *Carmen* people were all dedicated, in many cases brilliant, and I thank them for letting me observe them in their difficult process of creation. It was my belief in setting out on this journey that the great audience for opera should have a clearer idea of what transpires before one enters the theater, switches on a broadcast, or places a record on the turntable. To do this was only part of the chronicle, I felt, the other being to put together a detailed documentation of one of the most important operatic productions in American musical history.

Besides the cast of *Carmen* and every musician and artisan that worked for its success, I would like to thank in particular, for their cooperation, Schuyler Chapin, Francis Robinson, Charles Riecker, and Anne Gordon of the Metropolitan Opera Association, Thomas Mowrey and Lloyd Gelassen of Deutsche Grammophon, and Margaret Carson of Amberson Productions. Gratitude, too, goes to Jane Fluegel and Audré Proctor for their practical assistance.

HARVEY E. PHILLIPS

New York
April 1973

THE REHEARSALS AND PERFORMANCE

*

August 10

Although preparations for *Carmen* had been going on for many months, and in some ways years before, in the minds of Goeran Gentele, Leonard Bernstein, Josef Svoboda, and Alvin Ailey, this observer's introduction to the production came on August 10, exactly forty days before the curtain was scheduled to rise.

The day sparkled coolly for August and light poured in through the broad windows of Francis Robinson's memorabilia-rich office as the Assistant General Manager, the only top-level survivor of both the Johnson and Bing regimes, discussed the upcoming rehearsal schedule. The important sessions were not slated to begin until August 21, when Bernstein and three of the four principals—Horne, McCracken, and Stratas—would first be available (Krause was not expected until later because of long-standing commitments at the Salzburg Festival). Nevertheless, rehearsals were under way—ballet, chorus, supporting singers, and covers—and the physical production was taking shape. In fact, a technical rehearsal was in progress that day on the enormous stage. Without lighting, however, it was easier at that point to get an idea of designer Svoboda's intention from the maquettes on display in the design shop on the fifth floor: the stark black and white abstraction of a cavernously deep Act One, the contrast of undulating bamboo screens and a deep platform runway for Act Two, the startlingly Spartan bisected black tube for Act Three, and the combination of strong geometry and strong natural materials (the redwood of the arena gate) for Act Four.

Robinson proudly exhibited these models, and indeed they immediately suggested a firm stylization, a spacious antitraditional approach that promised a keen-willed production (one made possible by a gift from the Gramma Fisher Foundation) if this was any indication of what was to emerge musically and dramatically. The day did not finish, however, without encountering the first reactions of some of the singers to the sets, reactions that grew to the point that, for those working in them, the sets never stopped being controversial. On the main stage Robinson gazed at the stagehands struggling to erect the awesome Act Three mountain pass which rose at a steep angle, like a gray section of a toboggan run, to a height of approximately seventy feet. At the top the smooth curves ended in a rough-cut line meant to suggest distant peaks. Singers returning from summer engagements, singers, conductors, and their assistants reporting for the start of rehearsals of one of the season's early scheduled performances, and just plain curious members of the company passed by.

"Jesus, is it the *Ring?*" one inquired.

"Wait till they [the Carmen cast] see that carpet," said another. "Will there be howling!"

Yes, the tube on closer inspection proved to be made of ordinary acrylic carpeting. Indeed, the floor for all acts, for the entire performance, was to be covered with this fabric. "Svoboda must have a brother-in-law in the business," someone else cracked. Of course the worry of any singer seeing so much material around him was that it would absorb too much sound, making his job to reach and wow the thousands out front just that much more difficult.

The first musical sound heard that day, however, did not originate on the stage, produced by a contemporary golden-throated immortal, but in the steeply raked chorus rehearsal room known as List Hall, the small theater within a theater, from which the Saturday intermission features are broadcast, to the left on the parquet level. The voice belonged to a croaking adolescent auditioning for the chorus of *Carmen* urchins, and he was being told with gentle finality by David Stivender, the assistant chorus master, that his days as a Metropolitan soprano were over. He was thirteen and through. Rudolf Bing never found a diva this obliging, for the boy, although downcast, left without an argument. The first musical rehearsal of the day was to begin, and personal tragedy was not going to cause delay.

The urchins, in reality, are totally hard-working moppets—often the children of orchestra members—who are capable of larking about the Met's labyrinthine corridors, bouncing balls against a star's dressing room, and carrying on like kids generally are expected to do, except that when work is demanded, their attention is absolute. They sing their little heads off. This morning session was more of a brush-up session than anything else, since most of the boys had sung in the Met's last production—the disastrous Jean-Louis Barrault version—but since the Bernstein-Gentele concept reintroduced the original *opéra-comique* dialogue (in drastically reduced form) as well as much resurrected music and since Bernstein also had already communicated some of his interpretive stresses to those who would be assisting him, new and veteran children had to reexamine their parts.

David Stivender as the urchins' mentor, resembling more a camp counselor than a maestro (although he and every other assistant conductor at the company *are* formally addressed and referred to as "maestro"), was taking them through their Act Four paces—the "Les voici!" cries greeting the arrival of the corrida and set to the same music as the Prelude. Heads bobbed with effort as Stivender checked them on pronunciation, feminine and masculine articles being continually up for grabs. Then they intoned a passage that had just been rhythmically recited, Stivender making sure all were counting, the boys not exactly singing, but sort of cheering at one dynamic level. They usually hit lines that really pleased them; it always seemed that their comment on the picadors, on a nice repeated middle A—"Ah! comme ils sont beaux!"—found them particularly lusty in their steaming along.

After this brief run-through for what was really only about half the full children's complement, the kids were paid off on the spot for the rehearsal. Their lineup in front of the assistant exchequer who commandeered a piano top for an office was as orderly as any end-of-week General Motors payroll line.

In contrast, the afternoon chorus rehearsal, again in List Hall, was an entirely adult affair, Stivender now relegated to accompanying at the piano while chorus master Kurt Adler took charge. The first scene considered was the first in the opera, that in which the soldiers laze in front of the guardhouse, commenting on the passing Seville scene. Curiously, in this production no one passed or came, the idea of the set (supposedly originating with Gentele himself) being that the guardhouse was located in a fenced-off compound along with the tobacco factory. Adler, a plump, owlish, usually soft-spoken but rarely mirthful man, was perched in front of the chorus, which filled every seat in the room, the *Carmen* score in front of him. He stopped them almost as soon as they started: "The maestro [Bernstein] wants it slower, more 'dolce far niente.'" Adler had received his instructions. When the smokers' chorus was eventually reached, his orders were for everyone to try to sound like a soloist. "It has to sound rich, but on pitch too. And don't cut off the endings. The maestro wants them all a little longer."

Spending some time among this large group of voices, one wondered sometimes about the egos of these people who at best could receive only anonymous credit if a production were a success. A partial answer was given during that day's break by one lively lady who looked like she might like to talk. "Oh, you're writing a book about *Carmen.* I have a writer in my family, too, my cousin Philip Roth. I've often thought I'd write a book about my experiences at the Met. I already have the title: *The View from an Ant Hill."* Another part of the answer, however, was supplied by some of the mezzos who, when the men in the chorus were rehearsing their concerted exchange with Carmen on her entrance, mouthed the heroine's responses. Designs on a career? Regrets for a career?

The fight between the factory girls in Act One is a very tricky business. How do you pull hair and sing together at the same time? At this stage, however, the passage was just worked through concert-style, coiffures intact. The din, nevertheless, in the confines of List Hall was terrific.

The entrance of Escamillo in Act Two was looked at, Adler remarking that the tenors were coming in "like bullets, but late ones." His problem with *Carmen,* of course, was that hardly a chorus member felt that he had to consult the score, much less approach the material with his mind open to a new treatment. In preparing a work like *Carmen,* to forget is almost as important as to learn.

A difficult spot in Act Three comes just when the curtain rises and the chorus of smugglers begin the "Ecoute, compagnon" ensemble. There is an octave jump on a G at the repeat of those words, and Adler was telling his forces not to actually sing the high note. "Just throw it away, at least don't sing it with an honest-to-goodness voice. But also stay on pitch. And altos, always sing with big moustaches. Think of Katina Paxinou in *For Whom the Bell Tolls* when you get to the 'Quant au douanier' section" (Bernstein's favorite *morceau,* incidentally).

One of those matters of long and ineradicable habit came to light in Act Four on the chorus's very first words: "A deux cuartos." For some reason they had got into the habit of saying "A dos quartos," translating the whole phrase into Spanish. Whenever this moment was reached in rehearsal, almost until opening night itself, there was sure to be some voice coming from somewhere being purer Andalusian than Bizet. "But why one word in French and one in Spanish?" came the question, and "Don't ask us, the maestro wants to be faithful to the text," the answer. And Stivender or Adler would grunt a weary, automatic corrective "deux!" in fact so often that it seemed like an involuntary reflex.

But on the whole the chorus appeared to be looking forward to this production, largely welcoming the opening up of cuts, reacting to the excitement Bernstein managed to get from people, symbolized for them by his insistence that every eighth note become a sixteenth, every sixteenth a thirty-second. This was his way not of exaggerating but of ensuring a sharpness of attack that kept everyone's antennae working at peak receptivity. "Oh, he just draws it out of you!" beamed a mezzo, while a crustier tenor, demonstrating his imperturbability at the whims of so-called genius, remarked, "Every conductor wants something different. We're used to that."

*

August 14

Alvin Ailey preferred that no outsiders attend his very first meeting with the corps de ballet, so a second visit backstage was spent observing some of the effort being expended on the question of diction. This, at least in French, comes under the supervision of Mme. Danielle Valin, an attractive, auburn-haired woman with Piaf-style penciled eyebrows, in her early thirties, who has spent six of her twelve years in the United States working for the Metropolitan, specifically on their productions of *Faust, Roméo et Juliette, Les Contes d'Hoffman, Pelléas et Mélisande,* and now this, her second, *Carmen.* An acting student in France, she has translated her talents to some off-Broadway work and several films and to the emphasis on dramatic intelligibility she tries to bring to her diction drilling. She rarely corrects pronunciation without developing for the singers some sense of a histrionic delivery of these words.

The first dialogue stretch that mid-August day was with Russell Christopher, the Dancaïre, in one of the dressing rooms not being used by any early returning singer and his or her repertory pianist coach. "Monsieur Christopher, you must concentrate more on the vowels. Stress the 'a' in 'allez,'" Mme. Valin was saying.

"I guess I sound too American," sighed baritone Christopher as he tried to get an authoritative purchase on such resistant phrases as "Ce n'est pas une raison, cela."

"Non, non, Monsieur Christopher. You are not angry here. You are trying to reason with her," and then Valin repeated the phrase with a typically Gallic puckering of the lips, raising of thin eyebrows, and a deprecatory shrug of the shoulders.

The eager and cooperative Christopher was not only worried about his diction but about the effect his vocal production in speaking on stage might have on his singing. He was also apparently uncertain whether to accept Mme. Valin's "interpretations" since at this point he had not met with either conductor or director. This question of the extent of Mme. Valin's authority came up many times over the next few weeks, but she claimed that it was impossible not to get into interpretation, in fact to separate elocution from meaning.

"More weight, more vowels, Monsieur Christopher," she repeated with a quite readable look of "Oh well, he's not French" in her eyes. "Now 'je vous assure' must be done more on the lower lip, less on the tongue." Christopher duly repeated the phrase, as he had so many times with tape recorder aid since June when, along with the rest of the cast, he had been sent the dialogue segments. "Do you understand, Monsieur Christopher? Yes? Oh, I'm afraid I've indulged in being too French."

In one of the bigger second-floor studios, meanwhile, assistant conductor Alberta Masiello, officially credited with the musical preparation for this *Carmen*, was taking a second cover for Frasquita, Christine Weidinger, through her paces. Miss Masiello—fifteen years with the company—whose deep voice, witty comments, and deft fingers are known to Saturday intermission broadcast listeners throughout the country, and Miss Weidinger, winner of the 1972 National Auditions and a very young woman who was not actually to make her debut until she appeared as a Valkyrie later in the season, were huddled around an upright piano, looking lost in this large space.

"Make sure those releases are clean," said the blond-haired Masiello, her pearl earrings shaking as she suppressed a persistent smoker's cough, "and no *portamento,* [*Portamento:* carrying tone smoothly from one note to another by sounding all intermediary notes.] God forbid!"

The rather fiendish Act Two quintet was being studied. The piece had now become even more of a problem because over the years, through some tradition, many lines had been transferred from Frasquita to Mercédès and vice versa. (All

G. Schirmer scores proved useless for these preparations, but not everyone was as yet equipped with the German Alkor-Bärenreiter edition.) The quintet gone through once, the somewhat Melina Mercouri-ish Masiello nodded a "That's fine."

"I don't believe it," replied the nervous soprano, who nevertheless was showing that she had a pleasantly light, well-schooled voice.

"Now in the Act Three trio, give us a really sexy crescendo on 'et maintenant.' It must—what is the word?—dovetail with Mercédès," continued Masiello, "and remember you are the gold digger, Mercédès the sentimental one. I assume you have a translation of all these words?"

"Yes, but what about 'mais il'? Is there an elision or not?"

"Ah, you must ask Mme. Valin about that. Now let's try that *piano* again. I will never let you go until you give me that *piano*."

*

August 15

Some members of the ballet corps were willing to report on what had happened at their initial session with the visiting choreographer, Alvin Ailey. For three hours he had laid the groundwork of his conception, that is, that the Act Two Lillas Pastia scene would reflect the primitive, erotic side of Moorish-Gypsy Spain. He had played strongly rhythmic Cuban music to get the dancers in the mood, at the same time setting, in general terms, the dance to be executed barefoot and indicating that most of the small group—about twelve dancers in all at this stage—would each be given an individual characterization. They would dance as a group, but it was to be a group of identities.

In the big mirrored basement (C level) ballet practice room this second day of dance work, Ailey was smoking and thinking, his dancers, some in practice skirts or leotards and kerchiefs, in attendance to dimensionalize his improvisations. Not much was getting done, and Ailey, after a little pacing and a few slow turns on the floor, with his cigarette describing wide arcs, stopped and announced: "Take five so I can figure where I'm at."

Dancers, at least at the Met, are a talkative bunch, and they like to air gripes in about equal measure to expressions of enthusiasm. "Hell, in the last production," one chorine remarked, "all we did was stand around and smoke in Act One and do some heel tapping in Act Two. Now we're out of Act One completely, but in Act Two we'll be integrated into the action, a part of the opera, the way Gentele wanted it, without a real feel of choreography."

Ailey was ready to resume, a slight twitch in one eye betraying his concentration. He slunk around the room in a most convincing fashion. "Jesus, look at him move. He should do Carmen himself," whispered one lady of the corps. He snaked his way among the patient dancers, some of the girls already looking properly saucy, camping it up ("What did you say your name was, soldier?"), building the right mood. The room itself was set up to the proportions of the stage, with chairs marking the placement of that almost Hilton Hotel-style serpentine bar. Some of the cover dancers stood in for Carmen, Frasquita, and Mercédès, about whom the working dancers had to whirl. The rehearsal pianist mechanically plunked out the beginning of the "Chanson Bohémienne" again and again, but during the many breaks he copped a read from a lap-held paperback. In case he got too involved, there was always a voice to summon him back to work: "Come on, Irving. Trala-la!"

"Now the idea, kids," Ailey instructed, "is that it is very late. You've been dancing all night, and now it's four in the morning and Carmen wants everybody to dance one more time. You're thinking you want the soldiers to go home and 'oh that same song'—you know—'la même chanson.'" His delivery was pure Pearl Bailey.

The girls, some quite young, some obviously veterans, looked in the mirrored wall, studying their poses—a narcissistic-appearing practice but, of course, necessary to the step-building process—as Ailey and his assistant, a tiny German lady who helps him translate his wishes into terms classically trained dancers can most easily understand, tried to figure out what to do during the "fill" after the second verse. A rather sullen, black-eyed dancer standing on the sidelines, having been assigned as a cover to the ballet, was growing bitter at the lack of action. "I tell you I'd rather dance for four hours than just stand around. I suppose they'll make us put moleskin on our hands so we don't make any noise when we clap. We had to put moleskin over our finger cymbals in *Aïda* when Steinberg conducted. He couldn't stand the noise." She went on: "This whole thing is all wrong. They get the cast. Then they pick the opera." Movement was starting up again. "OK,

Vera Ellen," she hissed at a gung-ho colleague with a part to play, "do your stuff." This other girl was suggestively wiggling about, a cigarette between her lips. "And don't forget to blow smoke in Miss Horne's face. She'll love it."

What was being done now was called "the explosion" that section after the singing gypsies have trilled their last E-natural "la" and the stage erupts into about twenty measures of furious dance. Ailey had concentrated all the dancers around the stand-in Carmen, instructing them to burst away from her at this point, the boys twirling off with upraised chairs. On this run-through they were working with the voice of Maria Callas on a portable record player, her intensity eliciting a heartfelt "Shit!" from Ailey when she came to the climax. Once again, and Ailey himself was standing in for Carmen. "OK, everybody watch Carmen. What's Carmen going to do? Come on, Tania, shake your hips." For the explosion this second time he directed the boys to hook the girls under the armpits, and the husky choreographer demonstrated the facility of this one-arm maneuver with his petite assistant. Easy, yes, but the men of the corps are only marginally heavier than their partners, and counting madly—"eight, two, three, four, five, six—nine, two, three, four, five, six"—they staggered under their burdens. Not one was able to make the final hoist to his shoulders. "Oh, it's easy," sighed Ailey, "and with your other hand snap your fingers. I guess it's Wheaties time. Don't worry, we'll figure out a way to get them up. John Simon will go out of his mind."

*

August 16

This morning meant, in part, a return visit to List Hall to watch Stivender at work with the boys for their important part in the beginning of Act Four. "Come on, guys, we gotta hear the little notes," he was urging, also correcting pronunciation, especially that coming from a Tom Sawyer blond head that was insisting on "toot" for *tout.* Stivender, however, with all his vehemence, was not innocent of a few bloopers of his own: "*la* dernier coup," for example. When everyone, including adults, was to be *tutti* on the reprise of the Toreador Song chorus, Stivender cheered on the kids (none of whom was reading from a score): "It's not a commercial for Mother's Baked Bread. Let's hear some Spanish pride. Come on. Don't worry about that G-sharp. Take it high or low. Everybody's singing. You won't be heard anyway. But keep counting. Those numbers gotta burn on your brain, guys, cause if they don't, that's when we get into trouble. They've got to flash by like oranges and lemons on the slot machine. And now this is big. It needs a big breath. This isn't kid stuff."

The children responded, giving, as usual, a full, easy breath on the phrase "comme ils sont beaux," grabbing greedily and sitting on that friendly middle A. "Keep counting," commanded their leader. "If he doesn't give you a cue, you're up the creek, and you know what creek."

One of the little ones raised a point about a change in Act One. Stivender replied that that was the way "the man wrote it. And after all, this is the Metropolitan and everybody thinks we're pretty good, even if we know better." Another minor star asked who was going to be the conductor. Stivender and most of his colleagues turned to him with a surprised look. "Bernstein!" they shouted.

"Oh, he's a nice man," the lad replied quietly.

Meanwhile in an otherwise darkened auditorium, a lighting rehearsal was in progress. Rudolph Kuntner, the Metropolitan's lighting chief, seated for the moment at a command table set up halfway back in the orchestra, was giving his stage crew commands, either shouted raw or over a microphone. "Come on, fellows. Let's get on the ball!" his voice barked as a serious Josef Svoboda looked on at the illuminations being devised for Act One. Kuntner had his hands full coping with Svoboda in German and his staff in very New York–accented English. Svoboda occasionally, in his eagerness, tried to bypass his translator and address the technicians directly. But their blank faces quickly put a stop to that.

The set at this juncture looked particularly stark—the white, white walls of the factory and the guardhouse reflecting the brilliant basic lighting. Projections of leaves, somewhat mitigating the harshness, were being bounced on the *toldo*—a saillike canvas flying above the guardhouse—against the back wall behind the gates of the compound and against the front of the factory. (Most of these projections—fifty had been prepared—were eventually eliminated when the walls were repainted a very light gray.)

Kuntner was trying to get the rear-wall foliage in focus. "Joe, can you hear me?"

"Rudi, the projection *ist zu eng.*"

"*Bitte,* Herr Svoboda, patience! For Christ's sake, Frank. Where ya hittin'?"

Kurt Adler to the full chorus about the "douanier" chorus: "You will pay heavily if you don't pay attention. Forget what you've been doing for the last twenty-five years. This maestro wants it differently."

Act Four, for the chorus, however, was getting most attention today because, according to the schedule, it was to be the first segment that director Bodo Igesz would stage the following Monday. Actually that honor fell logically to Act One, but Adler was drilling them, especially on that "A deux cuartos" (to one girl stubbornly sticking to "A dos cuartos": "The brain doesn't last that long?"), and on the newly restored music that accompanies the processional appearance of the Alcade. He also reminded them that, in contrast to previous productions, they would be seen during the final duet. "But don't worry about having to stay in costume later than usual. It will be the same, because Acts Three and Four are being done without a break."

Russell Christopher, Andrea Velis (Remendado) and his cover, Charles Anthony, were holding a dressing room conference with Mme. Valin, but before they got very far, Miss Masiello looked in to request a two-hour session with the diction coach to establish firmly the succession of music and dialogue. Mme. Valin nodded assent.

"You know," commented Christopher, as the blond, limping maestra (she had suffered a broken ankle the previous winter, and the recovery was proving slow) departed, "Miss Masiello is clearing up fifteen years of my bad habits."

"Now, Monsieur Velis, it is '*de* jolis hommes' and not 'des.' Please keep in mind the French ear."

The subject of elision came up in time, and Mme. Valin informed the singers that since they were portraying low, nonacademic types, they would of course make elisions whenever possible.

"Five years ago we would have been killed for it," noted character tenor Velis, probably the best known of his breed, at least at the Metropolitan, since the days of Alessio DePaolis.

"I know about my predecessors," replied Mme. Valin. "When I told the man who first coached diction for *Roméo et Juliette* that I was doing this *Carmen,* he wished me good luck as if I was going to my death. Now, Monsieur Velis, can we try that 'Ça ne m'empêche pas' again?"

"It always sounds like 'son-of-a-bitch' to me," Christopher contributed. For his part, he was still having trouble with vowels and getting his lips from one place to another fast enough. The second "e" in Velis's "certainement" was coming out like a broad "a."

"Oh, Monsieur Velis and Monsieur Christopher, I will give

you a beautiful line through the vowels," promised Mme. Valin as some mezzo in a neighboring room was heard via radiator-pipe communication singing her lungs out in the Judgment Scene from *Aïda.* "Monsieur Velis, you are doing much better, but it could be more so if you colored the vowels more. Of course, it will ultimately be your interpretation, but you cannot abuse the line. For instance, your inflection on 'utile' I find childish and obvious. And, Monsieur Christopher, you will never say to me 'Ce n'est pas une raison, cela'?"

The men left Mme. Valin's domain, to be replaced by diminutive Miss Weidinger, who, it turned out, was not only covering Frasquita but also charged with covering the cover for Micaela. That character's letter scene with Don José in Act One was under scrutiny, with Mme. Valin reading the soldier's lines. "Miss Weidinger, look at me. Don't be afraid. I'm not making love to you."

"I can't. I can't look in people's eyes. I get lost."

"Eine Minute, Herr Svoboda. *Bitte!"* Kuntner, looked in on two hours later, was still struggling with Act One. He was on the phone to the technicians on the bridge, but seeing a couple of workers not blending with the scenery, he erupted. "Will you two guys get off the stage?"

"Certainly will, chief."

A photographer for *Fortune,* which was preparing a portfolio of pictures on backstage activity for the November issue, pointed out that the 280,000 watts of light being used—so strong that it could make black read as a soft gray-white—was just short of tropical-sun intensity.

This day also marked a first encounter with two of the Metropolitan's more venerable institutions, Louis Mélançon, the organization's official photographer, and Stanley Levine, its stage manager. These two were the source of hugely amusing anecdotes about the company and its personalities, for most of which they exacted assurance that they never be repeated. (Not, however, the one Stanley Levine tells about his first meeting with conductor James Levine. "I am the serene Levine," said Stanley. Riposted James: "I am the devine Levine. You are the obscene Levine.") On this occasion it seemed that their barbed, albeit not forked, tongues were directed against the inadequacies and peccadilloes of, in turn, the orchestra, the chorus, and the ballet. Presumably they too were warming to their tasks.

"Go up on five. Talk to them on six." Alvin Ailey was building the individual parts of his corps. Just one day later, and already the routines looked very different. For one thing, more boys had been added. But Ailey still used his educated slink to project the presence of Carmen, and the girl who had been given a sultry cigarette (and some piddling-in-palm gestures to match) was wondering whether she would be able to flick ashes on the stage carpet.

"Laura," Ailey implored as he went through some lascivious turns with a chair, "give it sex, like Carmen Amaya, like you hate everyone. Now, Jacques, while you're in that impossible position, clap your hands. Skiles, I like the way you scratch your ass. Keep it in."

Audrey Keene, the ballet mistress, came into the rehearsal room to pick a few girls for the first costume fittings. "My God," she whispered, "everybody looks like a real bitch. It can finally come out." The new routine had one further run-through that day, and when it ended, the corps applauded its choreographer. Then it was up to the wardrobe room with two of the girls, Tania and Skiles, where long tables were covered with materials and lots of English voices seemed to emanate from every corner. Tania was the first to emerge for the scrutiny of David Walker, the costume designer who was also making his Metropolitan debut. It was his first day in New York.

"I think I look too distinguished." Tania sounded disappointed. "I thought we would be half nude."

"Don't worry, love," piped Walker, "the skirts will be made ragged, dipped in water, and bleached."

Ailey came in. "And she should be covered with crosses, because she's a witch."

"I want to be nude on top and have a wig."

"By the time these awful dancers will be through with my costumes, there won't be anything left."

"What was that adjective?"

"Gisela, love," continued Walker, unperturbed, turning to an aide, "can we get more tit? Oh, Alvin, I wish you'd bring in a fashion for big women. All the dancers I dress are *this* thin."

"She needs boobs too," remarked Ailey as Skiles appeared. "She's a nympho, and her costume should be full of holes. Can you move your rib cage in that? Side to side? Now back and forth. OK."

Tania rued that she was then seven pounds overweight, and Ailey allowed that he had chosen slightly heavier dancers on purpose to get the idea of a zaftig Spanish type. "Besides, I don't want to surround Miss Horne with a lot of bean poles."

Orange underskirts were swished about to observe the effect and to decide where they should be cut (just above the ankle), and then the procession of dancers, Ailey, Walker, Keene, and various assistants crossed the floor to the wig department, the ballet mistress lamenting on the way that because of the union ruling that dancers must be allowed a half-hour dressing and a half-hour undressing time, rehearsals in costume had to be kept to a minimum.

Ailey's first comment to wig stylist Nina Lawson was that his prime concern was for variety. "That's no problem," responded the lady, pointing to the dummy heads of tumbling curls and falls, indicating how Skiles's red, for example, would be balanced by the odd red wig in the chorus. No gray was to be used, however, because gray, unless it is almost white, will not look like gray in the vastness of the Metropolitan.

"Charlie [Charles Caine, costume coordinator], we need a stock of tortoise-shell combs with brilliants."

"Right, David. No problem." At this stage, apparently, nothing seemed to be a problem.

"But by variety, I mean I want some of them to look Moorish."

"Oh yes, Alvin, but no Afros, love. That would look too

1972." And Walker brought out his book of Gustave Doré sketches made during that artist's travels through Spain and found a particular drawing of a slightly Negroid figure.

"Oh yes. That's my people."

"And of course, Alvin, we won't allow anyone to have spit curls. The hairdos will have a fallen-down look, won't they, Nina, love? And the makeup will be brown, a real brown, a Spanish brown."

Ailey definitely looked satisfied. "I guess I'll just sneak away and say it's *gorgeous!*"

*

August 17

This new day in the life of *Carmen* began with Masiello coaching Velis and Christopher. "Now, Andy, let's work on that balance of legato and staccato on the phrase 'Vous viendrez avec nous?' you sing to Zuniga after he becomes your prisoner in Act Two. I love it that way. Bernstein suggested it." (He later changed his mind.) And she played the phrase a few times, the first part insinuatingly smooth, the second half—"avec nous"—sharp and mocking.

"Now, you two," she went on, "in the quintet you must not count the 'de vous,' but the bars. I will breathe better if you do it that way. Don't fight with me."

This rhythmically tricky bit was practiced, although perforce rather tentatively since Masiello admitted she had as yet not received tempo indications from the maestro. "Now those tied-over grace notes are written in for the mute 'e's.' Sing. Always sing. Don't chop-chop-chop. Andy, that's the wrong note."

"I'm glad, Andy, you've been making the same mistakes as I."

"Naturally, Russell. We've been in this opera together for years."

Four-fifths of a quintet materialized with the arrival of mezzo Marcia Baldwin (Mercédès) and Weidinger, who was subbing for the not-as-yet-on-the-scene Colette Boky.

"Now let's talk through the quintet to get the rhythms." (Masiello herself supplied Carmen's lines, not an unlikely solution at all, since she had sung the role many years ago with the New York City Opera.)

Mezzo Baldwin appeared to be counting her "de vous" by bumping her slacks-encased hips rather than using real numbers, but the four came out right.

"Once more. That was an accident." This time it was a shambles.

"We better get this right. There's not going to be a prompter," Velis informed them.

Masiello produced a big sigh of satisfaction. "Good! At last!"

"Yes, but what happens when the fourth cover has to go on?" the tenor asked.

"I'll rehearse the fourth cover. Now, once again. *Ancora, un'altra volta.* What's the matter, Russell? You don't enjoy it?"

"You know it."

Masiello growled, and in her biggest, huskiest voice, confessed. "I hate this opera! I'm sick of it! I can't stand it! Now, everybody, once again."

The quintet was sung this time, with Masiello stopping to correct Christopher's overemphatic approach. "Don't bang, you're not angry" (a point also made by Mme. Valin).

"We know you can sing."

"Well, Marcia, you're one, at least."

"And, Russell, will you say 'ce ne' instead of 'ce n'est' until you die?"

"I blame Julius Rudel. I did my first Dancaïre with him."

"Also, Russell, *non voglio mai un portamento.*"

"Alberich does lots of *portamento.*" (Christopher was also then beginning his preparation as a cover for Gustav Neidlinger, the Alberich for the *Siegfried* unveiled on November 17, the only other new production of the season.)

Any rehearsing of the quintet needs frequent, psychologically spaced breaks if the singers are not to tie themselves into knots. Masiello supplied one by reminiscing about past performances of the opera under the conductor Jean Morel. Evidently Morel was something of a prude, and he was profoundly shocked not only at the offstage dalliance of the leading mezzo and her tenor but at all the kissing and hugging Tyrone Guthrie got into the final "la liberté" chorus at the end of Act Two. "Ladies and gentlemen," said the maestro, laying down his baton, " 'la liberté' does not mean *sexual* liberty!"

The quintet suffered another sweep-through, Masiello

stopping only once at a mistake she blamed on baritone Christopher ("Where the hell did you get that?"). "Very good, ladies and gentlemen. But remember, I need triplets and *niente portamento!*" Velis then remarked that the tempo of the quintet was always a giveaway as to a conductor's experience; the young ones doing it too fast, the old ones too slow.

"Bernstein, I think, will be just right," Masiello assured as the men left, leaving her to work on the Act Three card trio (without Carmen) with Baldwin and Weidinger. Apparently it was the first time the mezzo had heard the soprano, because she got so excited listening to the fresh timbre of the youngster that she forgot her entrance. However, Masiello was not perturbed. In fact, she even allowed Baldwin one of those *portamenti* in singing "l'amour" just before Carmen's entrance. "Of course, my dear, a *portamento.* It's schmaltzy."

He stood onstage, legs spread for solid anchorage; his mouth was open. Kuntner was taking on Act Two. "Kill those work lights!" Done. The bamboo-like slats that gracefully roofed Lillas Pastia's tavern were dotted with green, red, and yellow lights, a somewhat tawdry, Christmasy effect if not counteracted by strong light emphases elsewhere. The carpet sweepers, brought out every time a new act was set up, kept up a constant short-barred background accompaniment.

Svoboda was slated to return to Prague the next day and not to reappear until September 1, then to stay only one week in New York before departing for Hamburg. He was to miss opening night completely. Today was therefore, perhaps, more crucial for him than for anyone else.

Back at the mid-parquet console, Kuntner broadcast from a telephone, his voice echoing throughout the house several seconds after speaking. Otherwise there was silence as blue border lights came up. Stage director Igesz, thin, sharp-featured, long-haired, and pale, had just arrived from Santa Fe, where he had staged a contemporary German opera, *Melusine.* He was mostly silent too, observing the Act Two layout, exchanging a few quick comments in German with Svoboda.

The slats themselves got a spotlight play, light added to the projections over them, the twinkling random lamps and a lone super giving the stage picture a human dimension. Michael Bronson, the Met's young technical administrator, looked in, introduced himself to Svoboda, and decided that the set looked intimate; no mean achievement on a stage as gargantuan as this one.

"Herr Svo-bo-da!" Kuntner was calling for an opinion on an effect.

"Rudi, we need more light on the bar. Like that. Yes. Only broader, broader."

"OK. Up there on the bridge. Number ten and number six. No, that's too bright. That's fine."

"No, Rudi, it's too *giftig,* too poisonous."

An argument ensued ("Es tut mir leid, Rudi, aber. . . ." "Es tut *mir* leid, Herr Svoboda."), but the basic light pattern for Act Two was eventually set, patience having been called for by Kuntner ("Just a minute. The switchboard has to set this up. It isn't done with mirrors!") and warnings uttered concerning the possibility of blowing the circuit breaker and the fragility of the angle lamps, five or six of which had already been shattered.

Igesz then decided he wanted to see for himself how the stage looked as a bare entity. "George, please get off the stage," he called out.

"Just a minute, Bodo. I'm working with him!"

Svoboda took a picture.

"Oh, I think it's remarkable." Now David Walker was exercising his eye. This had to be done quickly, for Act Two was being dismantled and Act One set up so that Igesz could get an impression of it, now that its lighting too was set. The designer, slight and energetically chirrupy, finding a moment free from his duties in the costume department, hunched down in one of the parquet seats and chatted about his career and his involvement with *Carmen*.

"It was last Christmas that I first discussed the possibility of my doing the costumes. Originally Gentele had an Italian design team in mind [reportedly the one including Strehler], but when that didn't work out and he decided to direct, he got in touch with Svoboda and then with me. Our idea, beyond the Doré look, was to strip away everything that wasn't necessary. We felt the drama was strong enough not to be decorated. I had worked in Stockholm for Gentele, but never when Gentele was actually directing himself, and other than a small *Carmen* I once did in Dublin, this is my first go at the opera. I must say I find the greatest goodwill here at the Metropolitan. Everybody modestly works.

"My career? Well, I'm freelance, for opera, ballet, films, and plays. I've done the costumes for *The Charge of the Light Brigade* and *The Great Waltz* [films], *Hamlet* with Richard Chamberlain [stage], *Così fan Tutte* and *Suor Angelica* at Covent Garden [opera], *A Midsummer Night's Dream* and a *Cinderella* for Ashton [ballet]. The *Cinderella* is hideous. I suppose that for the last eleven years I've averaged five productions a season.

"I began my 'artistic life' at the Sadlers Wells ballet school at nine. I played with making costumes and wigs. I even posed for artists. I rather kicked around a lot in a feckless sort of way until Lila de Nobili, who's a great friend, took me in hand and encouraged me to design. Zeffirelli also encouraged me, although I've never worked with him. I was twenty-six when I really started to do it seriously.

"I'd rather work in opera than in anything else, even if very few productions get on as planned. And I'd rather dress a singer like Marilyn Horne than a dancer with no tits. Her size is no problem. In fact, in this production she will have a wonderful eighteen-eighties voluptuous Victorian quality I quite like. Designs have to be adapted. You have to use the quality of the person. Oh, I've worked with marvelous artists, people of the first talent, every one of the sirs.

"When you design clothes—I prefer 'clothes' to 'costumes'—you begin with a shape and then destroy it, like the dresses for the ballet, but, of course, I like ideally to do the whole piece, the *La Traviata,* for example, for which I did both sets and costumes, at Sadlers Wells. Here I must adapt my ideas to Svoboda's, be prepared to fit in. That's my job. As a result I've put no color in the clothes. I use false blacks, textures, soft textures for the clothes, and like the carpet, they will absorb the light. The lighting is the atmosphere, and the atmosphere is everything. In Act One I try to make real people existing in a void. Act Two is the most difficult to do because the color is punched up and you risk getting a lot of cabaret. The materials, however, are not realistic. Act Three, as it is done here, reminds me of the pyramid in *Antony and Cleopatra,* a moment in eternity."

Walker continued to scattershoot. "I love the music of *Carmen,* and I love Regina Resnik in it and listening to Conchita Supervia's recordings. I have many idols—Helpmann and Fonteyn for years, even before I worked with them. My admiration, fortunately, doesn't interfere with my work. What I admire is seriousness in people—not earnestness. I deplore earnestness. That's something quite different. I like the lack of earnestness in the eighteenth century. Take Giulini, for example. He is serious but definitely not earnest. I remember an exchange of telegrams we had when he was doing *Don Giovanni* at the Holland Festival. He cabled me 'El Greco,' and I replied 'Velazquez.'

"Ah, but the Italians. Their theater is so decorative, their visual knowledge so perfect, so instinctive, that their emotions never get involved. I mean, look at Visconti in *Death in Venice.* I think he went quite over the top. . . ."

Act One stood before us, fully lit and waiting. Kuntner looked around him. "Where's Bodo? He's holdin' up the works."

The week ended with this set inspection and with much speculation in opera circles about the existence of a Gentele prompt book with written indications of the details of staging. "There is no book," someone flatly stated. "Igesz has been getting the staging from Ragnar Ulfung, Gentele's Don José years ago in Stockholm. Fortunately he has a photographic memory. But how it can be applied to this production remains a mystery, at least in the case of Don José, since Ulfung is five-ten and weighs one hundred fifty pounds. He's practically an acrobat. Besides, Horne herself will have her own ideas about the staging since she too talked with Gentele." Someone else reported that Svoboda was very unhappy with the lighting, stating quite openly that the Metropolitan, contemporary plant that it is, lacked the right kind of equipment to achieve the effects he was after.

*

August 21

These negative notions, however, took a very background position in one's mind when Monday brought with it the real major opening event of these preparations: a piano rehearsal in a large second-floor studio that would greet not only Marilyn Horne, James McCracken, and Colette Boky, on hand at last, but also the maestro, Leonard Bernstein himself. Only Tom Krause and the still-scheduled Teresa Stratas remained among the missing.

The room hummed to the exchange of greetings, joshes, reminiscences, talk of summer activities. Since all covers and the indispensable Masiello, Valin, and associate conductor Ignace Strasfogel (Bernstein's own cover) were present, it was a full house. Horne, in slacks, her favorite working attire, and the startlingly white-haired McCracken contrasted with the scarfed and leather-jacketed Bernstein and with the chicly leather-hatted and pants-suited Boky. (Speculating on her day's attire choice became rather a game after a time.)

Bernstein, taking his place at a music stand at the front of the room, with Masiello at the piano, uttered his first words of command: "Good morning, class. Alberta and I are smoking fiends. Who objects? Is everyone here, including D and R and F and M, as I call them? Let's start with Zuniga's entrance in Act Two. Have you been Frenching it, Donald?" (Bass Donald Gramm took over the role of Zuniga after James Morris, a most promising bass still in his twenties who was originally announced for the lieutenant, withdrew. It was judged that a more experienced artist was needed in this far from principal but quite crucial—especially in the *comique* version—part.)

"Now, Carmen and Don José, you should sound out of breath. It should be spastic," Bernstein continued. "All this requires tastefulness and style. It should be flexible, light, have a pulse that moves." The section through the Zuniga-José duel was run. "Now, Jackie [Horne's nickname], the 'Bel officer' bit should have a gavotte feeling." Repeated, the "Bel officer" came out as he wanted it. "A quick study is what we call Jackie Horne. Don't slow up on the legatos."

Then the "Vous viendrez avec nous?" of Dancaïre and Remendado came into view, and Christopher and Velis faithfully did their carefully worked-out legato-staccato thing, to which Bernstein reacted immediately. "I'm not cuckoo about that. Remember, you're making a farce of Louis Fourteenth behavior in this little campy scene. Now at the *tempswechsel* [an LB coinage] at 'gare a vous,' what does your Schirmer say, Donald? 'In a merry tone!' I don't believe it. 'Mais gare à vous'—that should be in a merry tone?"

Onward. "Jimmy, when you sing 'Il le faut bien,' it's the fate thing. You know, like Beethoven's Fifth." The ensemble continued until one of the most musically controversial moments of this production was reached: that passage when Horne rides the crest on a climactic "La liberté!" taking the optional soprano line (invented, like the now-suppressed recitatives by Guiraud) up to a high B, then swooping down an octave and a half to the standard mezzo E above middle C. In the room the effect was spectacular, a real ear-piercing show stopper that put on display Horne's command of a high tessitura usually not available to mezzos and her powerful chest tones—and all in two measures. Bernstein looked nonplussed. "Jackie, you have five hours of music already. We'll talk about that later." He turned his attention quickly to other matters. "Now, everyone must get the mute 'e's' in the same way."

Coming to the very end of the final ensemble of the act where everyone—including chorus—sings of the benefits of "la liberté," Bernstein pointed out the spot where the time changes from 6/8 to 2/4 and announced, "We're going to slow down on that, all five hundred of us on the stage and in the pit together. We're going to do it just to show we can. It will be tuhrrific!"

The finale was repeated, with interruptions because Bernstein found someone making a *fermata,* because Boky did not know about the changes in the apportionment of her lines with respect to Mercédès, and because the thorny question of elision came up again, this time whether or not it should be done for sung French. Bernstein solved it, in one case at least, by advising that if it was easier to sing the elision ("vous à travers" here), to do it.

Act Three was turned to, McCracken starting the commentary by stating how uncomfortable he thought it was for Don José to sing along in the "Notre métier" sextet, to which Bernstein replied, giving him a dramatic clue, "As long as you know it." The "Ecoute, compagnon" octave leap gave the three women the same brand of trouble that the chorus had discovered—how to keep it light, together, up front, and on pitch. The card trio was passed over and the "douanier" ensemble begun. Sixteen bars went by without interruption ("Fantastic!" Bernstein exclaimed), and then on to the point where Bizet wrote a descending sixth figuration that takes the ensemble back to G-flat Major after a brief visit to B-flat by modulating through F. "It's a thriller, that moment," Bernstein exulted, and to show he meant it he got up from his stool to conduct it, stamping his feet in the marked rhythmic ritard, his gray locks shaking with every emphasis. "Oh God, what a piece! I'm always sorry when it's over and Micaela comes on."

This *morceau* ends on the words "en avant!"—the clue today for a new final-consonant elision dispute to break out, the problem greater here because a breath has to be taken between the two words. Bernstein thought it ridiculous to sing "e ' navant," while Valin insisted that it would be very un-French to have it come out "en ' avant." This yes-no argument got nowhere, even with Mme. Valin calling on Boky for colloquial support.

Bernstein, moving on, indicated some innovations. For one thing, there would be no gunshot after Micaela's aria ("so that the laugh this usually gets won't seem like a reaction to the soprano"), and too, the fight scene (Don José vs. Escamillo) would, with restorations (the concerted section now cut, however), last twice as long. John Reardon, covering the toreador but scheduled to sing him during the June 1973 series, was taking over today. The versatile baritone immediately showed his good command of French and his ability to establish the atmosphere of a character, only warned by Bernstein not to make any ritards in his music after the duel with José because "this is not top-drawer Bizet at this point, and you'll put everybody to sleep."

This section ends with the discovery of Micaela. The line—"Halte! quelqu'un est là qui cherche à se cacher"—was written for Remendado, but when Velis's light tenor attempted to detour the ensemble at this new development, the incongruity caused much laughter. Bernstein theorized that the line had been given to the original Remendado because elsewhere he only had "gay" jokes to utter. (Gentele, according to Velis, had decided that the tenor smuggler was to be played as a mincing homosexual, a perhaps more logical burden for the outlaw than it is for King Gustave III in the late director's much-talked-about *Un Ballo in Maschera.*) It was decided, since she has the next line ("Une femme!"), to put the words in Carmen's mouth.

Boky, besides being scheduled for Frasquita, was also one of the seemingly endless number of covers for Micaela. Although the young Jeannine Altmeyer, winner of the National Auditions in 1971, was official first cover for this role, Boky that day had to double up, a problem in Act Three when both characters are onstage at the same time. She nevertheless negotiated the hurdle well, quickly acting on Bernstein's suggestions—for example, that the scale she sings up to an A-flat when she tells José that his mother is dying be done without the customary crescendo. "I love it!" was Bernstein's grateful reaction.

The rehearsal continued with characteristic Bernsteinian insights, such as his singing "I'm so lucky to be me" to give Escamillo a clue to the extent of *amour-propre* to be projected when he is offstage still in Act Three, intoning his valedictory refrain of the Toreador Song, and his telling Morales (the young baritone Raymond Gibbs), when the very opening of the opera was looked at, that he must sing his initial phrases in one breath, lazily swatting flies, sexily, with "a little Marlene Dietrich effect."

"That's right, Ray," Reardon put in. "Go up and pose against the guardhouse."

Gibbs was not responding particularly well to the conductor's instrutions, his blue shirt mottled with the perspiration brought on by nerves rather than by the heat. "No, that isn't what I meant. I see I shouldn't have said Dietrich. And, Morales, it's 'drôle de gens,' a short 'o.'"

"No, maestro," an attentive Mme. Valin quickly inserted. "It's long. That's why the circumflex is there."

"Oh, really? Oh, well. Wrong again."

Bernstein, nevertheless, has an instinctive feel for French intonation (and for German and Italian as well, one is given to understand), even if an occasional detail may not be correct. His instructions for the quintet were very much based on word values, as is logical with a piece of sung music that moves at such a clip. "Be careful of initial 'a's,' as in 'nous *a*vons en tête.' Do not scant them. The words must be light, against the teeth. And please do not say 'con' for 'quand,' and make a difference between 'pars' and 'pas.' Right now 'Je ne pars pas, je ne pars pas' sounds like 'je ne papa, je ne papa.' That's 'fort aise' with a 't,' Jackie. And 'serais' is not as long as 'serai.'" Mme. Valin, obviously, had either an able assistant or a very knowing master.

The first assaying of the quintet went well, after Bernstein conveyed his basic notion that it must be done fast but without losing clarity. "It can be a miracle of a piece if we find the right weight. Phrases must be dovetailed. That will keep it off the ground."

The second time through showed up some confusion that had not at first been apparent, especially Boky's uncertainty about her "de vous" timing complicated by the question of which words were now for Frasquita that used to be for Mercédès. "I know it's murder, kids, but you have to go home and practice. That was beautiful, Jackie, but come in like a knife." Horne, on the repetition, had started to use gestures and gave a very provocative reading to "L'amour passe avant le devoir." "That's very nice, Jackie."

"But?"

"No, it's fine. Only give me a diminuendo on 'amoureuse.' Now, remember, everyone, on the reprise of the opening, when you get back to that tempo, to think in one and not in two—da da da dee da dee da dee."

The morning session drew to a close, and Bernstein was obviously pleased. *"Bravo, bravo, tutti quanti.* We're doing very well, you know. And do you realize the miles of Guiraud we're not doing?"

Bodo Igesz at the same time was conducting a blocking rehearsal of Act One, with, for music source, an upright piano riding the covered orchestra pit. This instrument stood surrounded by a jumble of stands, at one of which, on an elevated stool, perched chorus master Adler. On the stage milled chorus, soldier supers, civilian or *popolo* (as they were usually called) supers, and the children, some atop the guardhouse, others climbing the upstage courtyard gate. Basically the set had achieved finished form, although the lighting was being kept down to a work level and nothing more.

Igesz scooted around among this congregation, crying out orders, his gray-flecked hair flying in the breeze of his rushing. "OK, Morales. Inspect your men a little." Music was being played, although the children were clearly paying more attention to their histrionic deportment than to their tonal effect. Stivender had to keep reminding them to sing while Adler, in some slight exasperation at their inability to keep together, concluded that "they either climb or they sing. Which is it?"

Bernstein, with his retinue of Strasfogel and his personal assistant, John Mauceri, a twenty-seven-year-old conductor, then leader of the Yale Symphony, a former fellow at Tanglewood and the first conductor of his mentor's *Mass* outside the United States (the following June in Vienna), crossed the stage. The maestro sported a clean shirt and sipped at a container of milk. "Kiddies, you must yell out those numbers. 'Une! Deux!'"

Adler persisted in his pessimism: "I can see we're going to need six weeks' rehearsal, like Broadway. The rhythm on that trumpet call [to the pianist who was tripping heavily over the figure] is just like the word Amsterdam. Am-ster-dam."

Dutch-born Igesz, no stranger to Amsterdam himself, ended his chasing, took a long look at the stage, and sighed simply, "This we need to go over."

That new music for the Act Three Don José–Escamillio knife fight had been summoned from the house librarian, and Bernstein had a quavery Reardon and a tense McCracken read through it, making a few simplifying changes in the spoken dialogue. All through rehearsals, dialogue underwent as much pruning as possible, and smiles of satisfaction were always the reaction when the discovery was made that a line could be eliminated without doing violence to the logic of a scene. Sometimes the process got out of hand, and only at the eleventh hour was it decided that for story and movement reasons, a word or two simply had to be restored.

The clock now said two-thirty in the afternoon, a time marked down because it was the moment of this reporter's witnessing, live and up close for the first time, the famous Bernstein kiss. It was awarded to Reardon and Rosalind Elias (Horne's cover, scheduled for one performance in the spring) after the tiny close-harmony Escamillo-Carmen duet of Act Four. "Gorgeous! God, I wish I could sing," said the man who nevertheless often gives the impression of being able to do just about anything else. And then there it was, the fabled embrace.

Duets being in order, the one in Act One between Micaela and Don José was then a candidate for examination. Bernstein disclosed some of the thinking he and Gentele had done about the character of the soldier's hometown sweetheart. "We had a tremendous mutual desire to make a Micaela without basket and pigtail. We agreed on what she should not be, that is, a stock figure, but Gentele died before we could decide what she is. We know, however, that although she's shy, she's bright. She knows what she wants and she knows how to get Don José. She knows how to turn him on, when to say 'vous' and when 'tu.' She can turn him on by saying 'mère' a lot or by using a diminished seventh. So, Colette, sing it direct. Nothing fancy, no rubato."

Boky's voice sounded quite rich in the room. McCracken, however, was not singing full strength much of the time, claiming that his voice had not awakened yet, and nervousness about this perhaps caused him to come in at one point two bars early.

"That's a good cut," jibed Bernstein, lightening any tension this error might cause. McCracken wanted to know when in the duet he should kiss Micaela. "Not in the middle of a *portamento,*" replied the maestro. "I tell you what. On the second beat the entire orchestra will make a kissing noise."

Bernstein was also concerned about pacing, instructing Boky that her lines "Quel démon? quel péril?" referring to José's reflections on the Carmen who had just thrown him the flower, must be delivered quickly. "Otherwise it's endless. Also, the 'souvenir' section is gorgeous music, but the trick is not to sentimentalize it. I guess that's all for you today, Colette. You can go."

"No, I'm Frasquita now. You're stuck with me all day."

"True."

The card scene came up next, Bernstein expressing first his ideas on the tempo. "The problem is that Bizet tends to mark everything 'allegretto.' I want the first part with F and M [Frasquita and Mercédès] to be faster, almost a *scherzando,* a moment of lightness in this gloomy act. Then when Carmen comes in, it should be exactly at half that tempo, so that the two are related. There is a danger in this opera that you wind up with a series of set pieces."

Horne, however, when Bernstein first beat a pulse for her

section of the trio, found the tempo too slow. He prevailed to the extent of getting her to try it his way. He stopped Frasquita and Mercédès almost immediately after giving the signal to begin. "What are those words? ['Mêlons! Coupons!']. All I'm getting is melons and coupons." Other than a tendency for Boky, whose young daughter, as at many future rehearsals, was now patiently at her side, to hold on too long to final notes, this was his only complaint. Horne, leaning forward in concentration in her chair, was in splendid, creamy form, Bernstein punctuating her phrases with many an almost involuntary "Beautiful!"

Shirley Love, a mezzo covering Mercédès, was heard to mutter in awe, "Oh, that chest!" and Strasfogel could not subdue a smile as she got to an especially resonant C on "Toujours la mort!"

It was also clear that in actuality Bernstein and Horne did agree about the tempo, and he demonstrated the relationship by beating out the time of her music when Frasquita and Mercédès got to their reprise. Exactly half.

"Great, Jackie. We must keep that doomed tread and be careful to point up certain key words, like 'vingt fois' and 'impitoyable.' The 'impitoyable' was there. In fact you made a *tremendous* '-ble.'"

"Oh, you're so subtle, Lenny."

"Let's look at the Gypsy Song now. Jackie, at the beginning keep it very legato."

"Another conductor once told me that too."

"Your husband?"

Horne nodded. (Long before the Bernstein recording of the complete opera, the mezzo had made a single disk of *Carmen* highlights with Henry Lewis, her husband, conducting.)

The piano then began the sinuous introduction, Bernstein marking the grace notes with a little Hassidic dance step of his own invention. When Horne started singing, he bent to her like a frantic charade player. "Come on. Tell us more. Keep the narrative quality. Keep a forte inside that piano. Show that there's a lot more coming. Atta girl." He quickened the tempo, now beating with both hands and feet. "Tremendous! Tuhrrific! You see, there must be no place in this whole number where you actually hear a change in tempo. It is constantly *più mosso*."

Elias, watching all this, whispered, "He's going to make it very exciting."

Since Horne did not want anyone to be present at her first meeting with just McCracken and Bernstein ("We'll probably get into some private things," she smiled decisively), a peek in at the end of the Act One blocking battles on the main stage seemed a likely alternative. Hardly anyone was moving; just a few of the women, with cigarettes in hand, practicing their traditional *Carmen* slouch. Lethargy seemed to have set in on the chorus ranks. "You think so?" emended a knowing veteran of the administration. "Watch them when they're dismissed for the day. They'll be off that stage in fifteen seconds."

Act One dialogue and only dialogue, but as it fits into the music, brought some of the principals and Bernstein back to the second floor studio late that afternoon. Although ostensibly it was Igesz and his assistant, Fabrizio Melano, and Mme. Valin who were in charge, Bernstein dominated this "class" too. Word problems were not slow in revealing themselves. Donald Gramm stumbled relentlessly through his Act One exchange with José while Bernstein explained patiently the intent Zuniga must get and Valin corrected the pronunciation of McCracken's replies. The conductor could not resist singing a *soupçon* of the suppressed recitative—to everyones delight. "Ah, the good old days," he laughed.

McCracken, who never at any stage of the rehearsals let anything pass unless he had translated it into terms he could get on with—a very active and eager partner in all aspects of preparation—wanted to know how he could logically register that he was taken unawares at Micaela's entrance. "What's the big surprise? Everyone's been telling me about her for fifty pages?"

Horne's dialogue problem, on the other hand, was that she could not do a proper back-of-throat rolled "r." Her tip-of-tongue flutter is acceptable for sung French, but when applied to the spoken word, it made her sound like a Corsican. Actually, with a little preparation in setting her throat, she could do it correctly, but the idea was abandoned as too distracting for her even though McCracken was there to encourage her. "You see, you do everything you say you can't do."

Igesz remained unusually quiet through these discussions, perhaps still a little shy at his promotion to a full directorship. This was, after all, possibly the most exposed assignment at the Met in years. Valin took up the slack, even giving line readings on occasion, and Bernstein told Igesz where he would need to invent some business to fill a two-bar pause.

The post-catfight pre-"Séguidille" dialogue with Carmen, José, and Zuniga presented special problems because much of it has to be delivered over an orchestral melodrama. Timing, therefore, had to be very precise. Gramm as yet did not know what he was saying and was trying to get through the scene on the strength of his unquenchable good spirits and ability to find the humor in most difficulties. Pose or not, it suited him, especially considering his startling resemblance to television's Johnny Carson, but his decision to hold off mastering the dialogue until almost the last possible moment (and fully mastered it was) became a source of some irritation to his more serious-miened colleagues. McCracken also brought many a joke to a thorny problem, but one was always aware of his intense concentration. In a further dimension of humor, Horne's sense of it was of a more stagy kind. It always appeared to be serving a specific purpose. Bernstein's penchant for the witty remark was completely instinctive, and at the same time it often deftly unraveled many a psychic knot.

"Hey, hey. Décidément," Gramm fought on as Bernstein did another Jewish bit on the restored music of an accompanying melodrama. A wrong note sounded from Masiello's piano, at which Strasfogel bounded up, score in hand.

"Oh, for crying out loud. I know it's a G-sharp and not

a G-natural." The light in the room blinked and went out for a second or two.

"You see what happens when she gets upset," McCracken laughed.

"Donner und Blitzen," admired Bernstein.

In the dialogue just before the "Séguidille," McCracken wanted to add a word or two about Carmen's deception that she is a Navarraise and not a gypsy, "une Bohémienne." "You want to add!" exclaimed the startled Bernstein. "I'm trying to cut. Jackie, make sure your first words, you know, 'cette corde,' come before the plink-plink in the orchestra. I don't want any of those final plink-plinks to stop the action. Jim, how are you saying 'lieutenant'?"

"'Le lyu-te-nan.' It's just got to be right. I studied it all summer."

"Yes, that's right." Bernstein then launched into the day's farewell lecture, one concerning the linear nature of spoken French and its characteristic absence of up and down inflection. He was, of course, perfectly correct.

*

August 22

Tuesday, and it was still Act One on the main stage, principals and chorus in attendance, observers on folding chairs thickly planted on that covered pit. Osie Hawkins, the executive stage manager, stood in his customary spot on the stage side of the bridge that crosses the pit to the auditorium itself, where today all the chandeliers hung at ground level for crystal cleaning. Bernstein was trying to get Hawkins's consent to allow him to smoke. Hawkins would have none of it. Charles Riecker, the tactful and very popular artistic administrator (once described as a "Prussian hand in an Italian glove"), was on hand, chatting with Don Foster, the young rehearsal pianist. "Is the José-Micaela duet uncut?"

"Yes, but it's only two and a half hours now."

"Oh, good. It used to be three."

Bernstein, in a suit with an ascot tucked into his open-necked shirt, greeted Francis Robinson, who was also taking a look at this first day of rehearsals with leading singers working on the stage: "Francis, you're getting younger, prettier, and sexier all the time."

The children again raised the curtain, but Stivender, in front and far away from his charges, could not keep them under control. Bernstein tried to reassure him: "Look, if they rush, I'll rush. The main thing is to get rid of it. It's a bloody bore."

"They always rush at the point where it gets easy for them."

Igesz then dashed from the back of the house, heavy prompt book in hand, over the bridge and onstage to direct one of the boys to lead his cohorts down from the guardhouse roof. The youngster was also given a bit in which he was to discover himself alone and troopless, then rush out upstage in a panic at being left behind. The concept was not coming through to the lad, but Igesz persisted until at least the business could be timed.

Horne and McCracken now arrived, looked around them and mostly, to no one's surprise, at the carpet. The tenor granted at least that it would be fabulous on the feet, but he was reserving judgment as to how it might affect voices. Horne, however, had already made up her mind. "I'm going to raise a stink. I want to go on record." Costume man Caine described Don José's uniform to McCracken while Igesz sketched for Horne the blocking of her entrance and "Habañera."

"Cutaway in front?" the tenor questioned. "Oh boy, I guess I'll have to wear Mandate underwear. I'll never get this roll off in time."

Igesz and Horne had worked out her progress toward the initial confrontation with José up to the point where she is supposed to step off the large stage-right area down to stage level itself. It was a sizable jump, about one and a half times a normal step height. The mezzo got down awkwardly and with an exclamation too: "Traps!" Bernstein agreed with her, having also observed the chorus soldiers freezing at their marching approach to the platform, never being able to time their ascent or to know which foot to extend. A midway step was ordered from the carpenter.

Morales and Micaela (from now until Maliponte's arrival, Jeannine Altmeyer) were then shown their blocking, Gramm meanwhile plugging away at his dialogue with an assist from decisively non-Gallic pianist Foster. Since Bernstein was needed elsewhere, Adler took up his position on his high stool at the dark rim of the covered pit, and Act One began. The chorus, because of where Adler stationed himself, could not see him, and the requisite ensemble was definitely missing. Altmeyer, too, was having trouble finding the chorus master's cues. Hawkins persuaded him to come in out of the dark, and the music was resumed. The soldiers entered, and sure enough, one out of three tripped while negotiating the platform; the biggest hop-skip-and-jump was delivered by McCracken himself.

A discussion then ensued as to the sequence of maneuvers proper for soldiers at the command of "Halte! Repos!" McCracken had one version, a chorus member claimed his own as the authentic military one, but Igesz prevailed with his conception. He was establishing his authority.

Kuntner's lights played on the back wall, and the illumination in general was now bright enough so that some of the chorus people had taken to wearing sunglasses. The factory girls entered ("Back from lunch with crumbs and dirty blouses," quipped Gramm) and were drafted into conversation groups. Igesz on the run, the fingers of one hand habitually working away at a stray lock of hair above his ear while those of the other waggled at the girls, the "pimps," and "superpimps," made sure no one froze on the so-called new music that accompanies the "fumée" segment.

A half-hour break was called, time for the chorus to grab a quick sandwich, yogurt, apple, and coffee from a cart rolled into an offstage corridor (the ground-floor Opera Cafe was not as yet open for during-the-day patronage by the workers) and to exchange gossip and opinions ("Bodo's doing a great job, and he's not a faggot. There are plenty of those around").

The director, his sexuality thus established, at least to the satisfaction of some of his crew, next put them in position for Carmen's entrance. He wanted to station some of the men against the factory or guardhouse walls, a difficult position because these undecorated surfaces curved out sharply at the base as they flowed into the carpet.

Horne for some reason not appearing on her cue ("Stanley, call Miss Horne to A level," ordered Hawkins), the entrance business for chorus was redone. *"Voici la Carmencita,"* heralded Igesz in a rare instance of public lightness (he himself had met the mezzo for the first time the day before), and the singer, in red shirt and slacks, crossed the stage to take up her position at the upstage limit, from where she was to enter by climbing several steps into the courtyard. The chorus applauded her.

Horne's very first lines were to be delivered quite far upstage. ("How will she see the prompter?" "There is no prompter." "It won't work." "They'll improvise like Merrill." "You mean like Corena in *Fille.* Never the same dialogue twice.") Then she was to make her way through the crowd of suitors, all of them behind a goodly number of cigarette girls scattered along the edges of that platform. Horne practiced moving from hand to hand but rejected any hands that attempted to hold her ("We're not going to dance"). Not enough movement, she felt, had been given her for this important part of the act. "I have nothing to play against, Bodo, before I see José" (who appears cross-stage at the entrance of the guardhouse). Igesz gave the matter some thought while Horne looked about her, again at the carpet. "It's got to go," she said to Hawkins.

"Not with the lighting we have," he replied.

"Osie! Who's that taking pictures?" Indeed, a photographer was snapping from the wings but was immediately persuaded to desist. Horne hates to be photographed in slacks.

The entrance again, now with a different super the object of Carmen's attention on each phrase before she spies José. "It's not good policy to use supers for movement," commented stage manager Levine, but it seemed to work, with Horne feeling at ease enough to muss playfully the hair of one of her would-be conquests. At the same time, directing assistant Melano was preparing McCracken on his reactions.

Miss Masiello (termed "an orchestra in herself" by Hawkins, for she has the reputation of being able to play the score of *Pelléas et Mélisande* note perfect, not to mention a very convincing hot jazz repertory) had replaced Foster at the piano. When the first verse of the "Habañera" ended and a break was called, she head-snappingly startled everyone on that stage by quietly breaking into the strains of the Chopin Funeral March.

"An opinion or a prophecy?" someone inquired.

"An opinion" was her enigmatic reply.

This more than hint of pessimism was countered by the high-spirited Bernstein, who reappeared, talking about the excitement of the "douanier" chorus, and his pleasure at the response of everyone to his ideas (he had just been working in private sessions with some of the principals—"grabbing them as I can"). He then showed Strasfogel and Masiello how he planned to lead directly from the final G-flat Major of the "douanier" chorus to the five-seven chord of E-flat Major that now began Micaela's recitativeless aria. "It creates a tension—that new, ambiguous B-flat. Isn't that nice?" He also mentioned that McCracken might sing a falsetto B-flat at the end of the Flower Song. Masiello seemed shocked at this idea, believing that the audience would think that he had lost his voice. Bernstein rejected the notion. He went on. "Now, Alberta, I want you to pretend you're on the Opera Quiz. Answer this question. What is it about the Flower Song that really sets it apart?" and his fingers played the familiar music. "Do you give up? It's that it has no repeated phrases. Everything is new, new, new. This was a great invention of Bizet." Masiello smiled at this find of Bernstein's. "Alberta, I think it's shocking you have to sit here."

The chorus having returned from its obligatory break (ten minutes every hour), Carmen entered yet again, but Bernstein stopped the men almost immediately on their first "La voilà!" "Listen, kids, we can't have that kind of sloppiness."

Adler concurred. "The trouble is, the minute they get onstage the music goes."

Onwards. "Jackie, that's a quarter note, darling."

"Oh, and I have thirty years of eighths behind me."

Bernstein, very frolicsome today, took Horne in his arms and did a few tango steps between "Habañera" verses, at the same time getting the chorus to realize that its echoing of the verse had to be more rhythmic, staccato if necessary. Assistant Mauceri observed everything Bernstein did and said, usually making notes on his score either for the conductor himself or for later-to-be-conveyed notes for others. He leaned over to Masiello and asked her, "How much of this staging is Bodo and how much is Gentele?"

"I wonder," she answered. "It becomes more Bodo from day to day, especially as singers' needs present themselves."

The "Habañera." Osie clapped his hands. "Chorus, no talking. No whistling." Carmen's first encounter this time with a super did not go well. He reached for her, and one hand, quickly pushed away, landed on her stomach. Horne then made much of getting off the platform, as if to emphasize its nonfunctionalism.

"Alberta, no diminuendo on that accompaniment between the verses. It's marked double forte, even in Schirmer," Bernstein whispered. "Hey, I'm getting to like this tune." It finally ended, and that difficult, now twice-as-long cross to the playing of the fate motive was approached. Igesz's first suggestion for business here was for Miss Horne (he generally referred to Carmen this way) to take José's sword out of his scabbard and to draw, somewhat Prospero fashion, an imaginary circle around herself before the corporal grabs it from her, both of them then sort of tensing over it in close-range, eyeball-to-eyeball contact. This business was tried, and although its heaviness was laughingly obvious from the beginning, it was for the time being left in.

Riecker passed through. "How's it going, Alberta?" She kissed her fingertips, then smiled and shrugged her shoulders when the assistant moved on his way. Horne and McCracken left the stage, and in the time remaining, the even more difficult business of the factory riot was worked on.

Hawkins: "OK, girls. 'Au secours!'"

Masiello: "That's funny. You don't realize it."

The girls were separated into manageable divisions now being coached by Stivender while Igesz gave the soldier supers their instructions for controlling them. The director, recognizing the problems of this, by necessity, semichoreographed chaos, had obviously worked it out with some degree of finality in advance. The riot started with a shriek from chorister Stella Gentile ("She's our official screamer," said Levine), but the rush in from the factory was executed in silence, almost everyone missing the cue to sing. Again, still somewhat tentative, but altos and sopranos seemed to be enjoying pretending to menace one another.

It was now 4:15 P.M., just time enough for a glance at the last forty-five minutes of the ballet rehearsal, done this time not only with corps but with the Carmen, Frasquita, and Mercédès. Horne on her way there stopped for a conversation with George Cehanovsky, the former Metropolitan baritone who had now returned to the company to help with diction coaching for the first Russian-language production at the Met, a revival of *Pique-Dame.* Cehanovsky and his wife, the soprano Elisabeth Rethberg, have been faithful followers of the mezzo's career, always sending her flowers for an opening or a good-luck gift, such as the watch that the singer was presented with this day and subsequently proudly wore.

"Rethberg," she remarked, "had the greatest technique of any German singer. She and Ponselle were the tops."

The dancers were eating raisins for quick energy. They looked as though they needed a great supply of both. "You could write a book about how sore we are," said one ballerina, and some abused feet and lumpy knees, the result of Ailey's shoeless steps and on-the-floor knee turns, were exhibited. "I'm sure we'll drop like flies when we get on that rug." The word was getting around.

Horne, Boky, and Baldwin watched as the dancers, along with the stand-ins, went through their routine. It all seemed much more set now—more danced too—even perhaps a little more traditional than one had been led to expect from the reports of those first statements. Then it was done again with the singers taking their positions, the three in some confusion this first time, with Horne looking particularly apprehensive when the chair-swinging explosion was let loose. Igesz was also there, agreeing that Carmen should have a tambourine and advising, in his sometimes double idiomatic way, that the girls should "egg up one another."

Boky quite enjoyed herself. Although not a trained dancer (as her daughter wants to be), she stinted not at all on her hip-shaking routine. Baldwin, tall and stately, generally looked hung up. Horne, although it was hard to convince her that it was so, showed that she is basically a graceful woman, and had little difficulty in learning her steps. "Alvin, I can't do it without music," she stated as the choreographer called out some numbers.

"That's right. I forgot. You singers don't count the way we do."

A repeat, with Horne dancing and singing full voice, too, especially on the thrilling G-sharp of "tourbillon!" The room shook. "Alvin, I think I want to start it lazy"—exactly the right idea, of course, according to Ailey's original conception, which had Carmen moving among the semibare torsos of Lillas Pastia's male customers, patting them and sending them on their way home. Her final step was set, and it meant getting an assist from one of the boys to mount a chair on the ultimate trill. This business reminded Horne yet again of the Act One platform. "When I saw those models, I knew those platforms were a trap for me. Can somebody get me a No-Cal Cherry?"

Accompanist Irving had folded his book and left for the day, but one more run-through was asked for. Ailey put on the Callas recording. Said Horne: "We don't need it."

*

August 23

The next morning Horne was a half-hour late for her diction session with Mme. Valin. Her daughter, Angela, had come down with a staph infection, and the singer, this day, which was to be one of the most tense of the entire rehearsal period, was clearly worried. Nevertheless, she worked hard and steadily with the coach, starting with her lines before the "Séguidille." "Oh God, if my life depended on all those vowels, I'd die."

"But that's exactly what it needs—more vowels. Now remember, your openness contrasts with Don José's tightness. That 'sans doute' must be expansive."

Horne caught the inflection easily, but she had rather a hard time capturing the line she delivers coldly to Zuniga in Act Two: "Je ne vous conseille pas de revenir."

Valin, for her part, was being more and more the acting coach as well as the wordsmith. "Remember, you are ironic with José. Then you play the coquette, angry, then happy." This was said to give a clue for the longest unrelieved stretch of dialogue, that between Carmen and José in Act Two, which falls between his entrance and her dance. Horne, it was clear already, would be very effective, even lovable, in the scene's more playful sections, although one wondered how her lines to McCracken—"Mangeons de tout! de tout! de tout!"—would be received, considering the already well-fed look of these two. How bewitching would it be? Horne's business with the plate-breaking and castanets eventually came off quite well, but at this point she debated whether or not she might do the whole dance with plate alone.

Bernstein, she thought, would not go along with this. "And

'ça ne vas pas' always comes out 'son-of-a-bitch' when I say it."

While Act One's walls continued to receive their graying, as though getting ready for an air attack, on a side stage the crew was hoisting the latticework of Act Two into place, shoving the serpentine bar into its intended coil, carefully stacking a negligent-appearing pile of chairs stage left. ("It looks like my living room," Gramm informed us.) Dancers experimentally twirled their toes in the carpet, Igesz called for the tavern props —glasses and jug—and Bernstein remained quiet in a chair on the pit, studying his score. This session, too, was a half-hour late in starting.

The dance, this first time onstage, on the carpet, looked rather a shambles, but in part this was because some unexpected principals—Zuniga and Lillas Pastia himself—and chorus people were also now occupying space. Carmen, Frasquita, and Mercédès went through their paces in practice skirts which in their new uncertainty they violently swished back and forth, attempting to make this movement fill in for forgotten turns and steps. Boky with her imprecise enthusiasm ("Is that her Montreal nightclub act?" hissed one not very kind observer) and Baldwin with her rigid monumentality sandwiched Horne, who, when it was over, turned with a plea in her eyes to Ailey's confident-looking assistant. "We need more things to do." An echo of her "Habañera" entrance staging problems.

After several delays and another of those remorseless breaks, the dance was repeated, Ailey this time working to integrate the chorus into the hoped-for liveliness of the scene. The principals had already left for dialogue work.

"Unfortunately only two people in the audience will understand what we are saying, and certainly not the critics. They understand less than anyone." Horne was giving her opinion on the question of the spoken word—certainly, next to the carpet, everyone's favorite topic. One member of the cast had commented that ideally the opera should be sung in French with the dialogue in English, and another had stated that foreign-language dialogue in a house the size of the Metropolitan never worked unless it was delivered with almost excessive broadness, the way in fact it was handled in the previous year's successful revival of *La Fille du Régiment.*

Valin was feeding Gramm line-by-line readings for the Act Two scene just before Escamillo arrives. Horne playfully gave some of her replies in English and German, half as a joke, half to verify the sense of the lines. Paul Franke, the Pastia, after reading one of his three sentences (his entire part), announced that it would have to be very loud. "I hope we know that," replied a somewhat severe Valin.

Christopher was still finding physical difficulty in Dancaïre's words, while Velis had meanwhile unearthed enjoyment in the discovery that his "amoureux" was to be a kind of send-up mockery of Carmen's "amoureuse." And Horne had got the right tone for her short "oui" of admission to the accusation that she was "amoureuse." McCracken, intense even in this studio, into which the sound of the ballet music from the stage rehearsal was uncontrollably leaking over the intercom, finding that "certainement" did not trip lightly for him, changed it into "oui." This precedent set, Horne tried to eliminate "ça ne va pas," but *ça n'allait pas* with Valin. *"Merde!"* exclaimed the mezzo when her tongue caught around a particularly succulent bit of her eating scene with José.

"That's very good!" Boky encouraged.

"Ok, kids," announced the leading lady, as she closed her notebook, "I'm leaving for the Comédie Française."

That day's final session took place on side stage right, where all of Act Two had been moved. A soundproof metal curtain came down, dividing it from the main stage, which was now experiencing an adjustment of the lights for this act. Although the dimensions of the side stage equal those of the main one, there is no extra space around it. Therefore observers, covers, conductors, and directorial crew were all jammed into a row practically on top of the players.

Mme. Valin was not there. In fact, she was being discussed, Bernstein looking serious and expressing concern at her policy of giving line readings. "Lines come out of characterization." True, but one wondered how much emphasis that approach should be given at this point, with people who were basically not actors and who were speaking a language they in many cases knew rather sketchily. Igesz started off by conducting a dry dialogue–plus–blocking run-through, while Bernstein, somewhat grim, smoked illegally and heard for himself the latest status of the dialogue, helping out whenever a particularly messy bit came along. "Maybe by the time we finish, we'll know why Guiraud wrote recitatives," Christopher whispered.

The coordination of music with dialogue just before Escamillo's entrance was worked out, not without some amusing developments. Frasquita and Mercédès were to run to the upstage tavern entrance to see for themselves and announce that the toreador was on his way. Baldwin, forgetting to make the trip, stayed downstage and delivered her declaration. "She must have ESP," Horne laughed. When it was all finally clear, or so he thought, Bernstein stood up and cried, "Perfect!"

"Perfect?" Horne clutched her head.

Boky, still looking somewhat confused, came over to Horne and wanted to know who Zuniga was. "Is he one of us, one of the smugglers?"

"No, he's the lieutenant," came the answer, "but that's all right, honey. We know you sing Micaela most of the time." (Micaela and Zuniga are never onstage together.)

The matter of the pitfall-full quintet sneaked up, the first problem being, according to Bernstein's wishes, to get Frasquita to say her first lines of introductory dialogue before the final plink-plinks of Escamillo's exit music sound. And then a moment was spent to correct Velis's notion that "ville" was pronounced like "vie" and to marvel at the high F's he seemed to hit on the word "distingué."

By this time everybody was generally getting tired, and that same platform step—carried over from Act One—was not helping. Some of the logical positioning for the quintet had to be modified for musical reasons. The girls could not get too far from each other, nor could the men. A musical assault was begun. "Think of it in one," Bernstein instructed the rehearsal pianist as he set the tempo.

"Don't forget hilarity," Igesz cued the singers. "To get it, think of the tricks you, as smugglers, pulled in the past."

All proceeded well enough until Carmen's announcement, "Je suis amoureuse," at which point Horne lay on her back and kicked her feet in the air. "Well, actually, I would like to lie down and then get up on 'amoureuse à perdre l'esprit.'" This was tried, and it was a very unbecoming sequence of postures. It seemed odd that Horne would not realize this, but by the reverse side of the same token, a few minutes later she stated that she thought she was too short to stand against the bar.

"No, you're not. It looks like Jackie Horne at the bar," Bernstein reassured her. "How about giving us a chorus of 'Just Plain Bill'?"

"Love it!"

The quintet ended, and the five singers broke into stage laughter. "Oh please, no laughter." Bernstein squashed this holdover notion quickly. "No ha ha ha. That's so predictable. And, Jackie, I don't think the lying down works. This isn't *Thaïs,* after all, but you can stand up for 'perdre l'esprit.'"

Almost unnoticed at this rehearsal point, the Kolombatoviches, Oscar and son, had arrived. This pair, in Olympic blazers, specialize in arranging stage fights, especially in opera, and they had brought along the swords José and Zuniga were to use in their Act Two set-to. McCracken and Gramm retired with them far upstage to confer.

"Every time I turn around there's something else to make me nervous, like these swords," muttered McCracken, half seriously, one concluded.

A pause while the duel was basically set. Bernstein lay full out on the barroom carpet, Horne's head resting on his stomach, crooning and quoting LaRochefoucauld. Then, the clued-in combatants ready, the rehearsal continued from Zuniga's surprise entrance. "Jim, that 'Qui frappe?' will have to be sung. It simply won't carry *chuchoté,*" Bernstein insisted, at the same time drawing his protagonists' attention to a subtextual implication here that Carmen is protecting José. "Jim, you should freeze."

"But why am I afraid?"

The question was not answered, the duel went on clumsily enough, and the "Bel officer" section was immediately attacked.

"Jackie, remember the forte-piano business."

"I know, Lenny, but it's hard to remember everything when you're doing things like blocking for the *foist* time."

Then it came. Someone standing near Horne must have mentioned, quite *en passant,* something about the planned elimination of a prompter's box (actually, the Svoboda carpet was supposed to cover it at all times, and prompters were to be stationed in the wings instead). Fireworks! "Goddammit! They're changing too much. Now I hear there's to be no prompter in front. I need a prompter. For the dialogue especially." Tremendous silence and tight, tense lips everywhere.

"We had no prompter during the *Fille* dialogue, Marilyn," Velis offered.

"Look, I have as good a memory as anyone else and probably better, but sometimes there occurs that moment when something happens." Riecker, as if on cue, perhaps sensing it *was* his move, came through a door in the separating screen. "Charlie," Horne called to him. "Herr Svoboda—" she had picked up José's sword—"I'd like to have him here. I'm not kidding. Too many curves are being thrown. First this wall-to-wall carpet, and now no prompter."

Bernstein took his turn: "I agree with you about the prompter, but not about the carpet. I went out front and listened."

"Svoboda has used it many places," Riecker added.

"But not with me!" Horne wasn't going to submit that easily.

"Do you want to come to my office to talk about it?"

"Yes!"

"After rehearsal?"

"What about now?"

"OK."

End of day.

*

August 24

The previous day's mini-explosion had two direct results: (1) a prompter's box (dubbed, by the less reverent, the "Marilyn Horne Memorial Prompter's Box") was assured and the necessary scissors work was done on the carpet; (2) all observers were banned from attending rehearsals for the next three days. It was decided that since an outsider had been privy to a scene of relatively high tension, it would be wiser for him to keep a low profile. Also pushed into exile were all photographers and anyone else of a remotely journalistic stripe. Charles Riecker, however, assured those eyes, ears, and pens that their eager presence would be welcome come the following Monday. In the meantime he described the general mood as 100 percent better, a judgment seconded by several members of the cast when they could later be questioned. The only snag this first missed day, one was told, was that cover Andrij Dobriansky had to take over temporarily for Gramm, who had to fly back to Santa Fe for a final Golaud in *Pelléas et Mélisande.* No journalist could do very much with that.

(In a much later, strangely parallel development, no outsiders were allowed into the March 2 dress rehearsal for the Henry Lewis–led series of spring *Carmen*s. When this reporter nevertheless tried to get into the hall, diva Horne merely shook her head, muttered "Jesus Christ!" a few times, and retreated to her dressing room. Francis Robinson did the actual kicking out.)

*

August 25

If the mood had indeed not significantly improved the day before, and some sources close to Horne said that she was generally unnerved by the lack of direction in the production, it certainly must have been given a tremendous lift by an on-stage birthday party for Leonard Bernstein to which some of the press was invited. Horne brought the cake, Leonard kissed Marilyn (one of the veteran cast members who had also participated in the Bernstein *Falstaff* production was heard to quip that there had been so much kissing during the preparation for that work that the only way you could tell who was sleeping with whom was if they shook hands), and then the chorus sang "Happy Birthday." Bernstein, not totally satisfied with the performance, had them repeat it, his magic hand firmly and good-naturedly in control.

*

August 28

Monday. A fresh start in the C-level rehearsal room was somewhat clouded by Riecker's announcement that Teresa Stratas, because of a recurrence of aftereffects from a childhood bout with tuberculosis, had canceled her slated appearance as Micaela. He was trying to replace her with Adriana Maliponte, a soprano who had successfully sung Luisa Miller and Mimi the previous season, her first with the Metropolitan. For 1972–1973 she was already contracted for Juliette, Pamina, Marguerite, Violetta, Eurydice, and Mimi again, an unusually heavy load and one now apparently to be increased.

Attention today, however, was diverted from the blocking being done in the studio to the orchestra room on the same subterranean level where Bernstein, observed by Chapin, Riecker, and Robinson, was holding his first session with the instrumental ensemble. After a general shaking of hands, the conductor announced that because of the DGG recording sessions to start soon after opening night they would be "working twice as hard on a thrice-familiar score" made, however, a bit less familiar by the use of the *comique* version. "*Carmen,*" he continued in the cool confines of this packed room dominated by a Dufy hanging (for some reason the air-conditioning seemed to be working at less than full power everywhere else in the building), "is known so well that it makes it harder to play. The fortissimi, as a result, have to be done to the full. It has to be exciting."

He then began at the beginning, his left hand on hip, almost miming the pompous excitement of the Prelude. The eighth-beat rest that comes before the repeat of the opening was held just an instant longer than indicated to emphasize all the grandiosity of the statement. The timpani reached shatter level even though the mirrored wall behind the maestro was covered with thick black hangings. The conductor's left leg was twitching in syncopation to the rhythm, his sleeves getting a rolling-up, his glasses put on, then as quickly slipped off. The double dotting crispness of the Toreador Song refrain was insisted on from the first time it was played, yet the line of melody itself was to be molto legato. "And the tremolo of the fate motive has to be fortissimo, and this section is exactly half the tempo of the section before." (Another case of internal mathematical relationship to prevent the impression of the score breaking down into set pieces.)

Bernstein experimented with what he called strange dynamic markings in the "fate" section—harp and basses forte with the horns piano, a balance he rejected in favor of uniform forte. This willingness to experiment, correct, and change his mind always characterized Bernstein's approach during his orchestral sessions. The Prelude ended. "Great! Very good. I won't make you redo any of the tremolo section because that's too much manual labor."

The mood of the first scene—nonchalance, hot sun, and so on—was put before the orchestra personnel much as it had been for the singers. "It's not so *scherzando,* not dancing." It may not have been dancing, but singing was certainly in order for the conductor as he filled in for the missing voices when the door was closed on this meeting so that one could catch up on the cast's first encounter with a fully set-up Act Three on the main stage.

Much standing around, McCracken discussing José's divided nature—the accidental killing of a soldier referred to in the Act One dialogue and his crumbling every time anyone says "mère" to him. The tenor was also trying to reassure Horne, who, on first seeing and walking around Act Three's sharply angled carpeted funnel that very freely simulated a steep mountain pass, was close to speechless. "Jim, have you seen that carpet? Now it's not only wall-to-wall, but floor-to-ceiling. I think they should scrap the whole thing and start over. I don't trust anyone oriented toward the Central European theater."

Igesz was experimenting with a first notion for staging the card scene. He had placed Horne on the also steeply slanted carpet-covered forestage disk, which was, with the exception of the funnel, the only other solid element on view. It did not work. Horne said she was uncomfortable ("I feel like John the Baptist's head on a platter"), so she was stationed to the left of the disk, with Frasquita and Mercédès getting the circle instead to make into *their* nest. Altogether, this Third Act, at first meeting, struck all as more suited to gymnasts than to hefty practitioners of grand opera.

Everyone was onstage for the "Notre métier" sextet, Strasfogel conducting with Masiello at the keyboard, Valin and Elias keeping watchful lookouts. The dialogue between Carmen and José that follows emerged as surprisingly sharp, hinting for the first time that the spoken words would make the needed impact. Nevertheless, Carmen's line "Tu me tuerais peut-être" sat uneasily in Horne's mouth, she herself warning McCracken that "I'm going to spit it all over you."

The stage seemed alive with extraneous movement, Adler tending to the chorus, Valin discussing pronunciation with McCracken and motivation with Igesz, McCracken suggesting that time not be taken now to work out a piece of business, Igesz saying it was now or never, then McCracken himself giving Horne the reason for his turning from her and staring into the distance at the faraway village where his mother was supposed to live.

Then the card scene came up in context. Horne was uneasy with the size of the prop cards supplied and needed Igesz beside her to set with the music her pattern of laying them out. A break intervened, presenting a chance for a chat with a disappointed Miss Weidinger, who had hoped to move up in the Micaela ranks when the Stratas cancellation was announced. Altmeyer, a year older in the organization, sadly informed her that fairy tales don't happen anymore. And the relaxed Horne-Baldwin-Boky (today very perky in a paisley mini-dress) trio rapped about pot and who had smoked and when. None had.

Back in the orchestra room, Bernstein was just finishing the "Habañera," stating he was tempted to reorchestrate Carmen's exit music. It was two hours later, and the maestro's energy had not visibly flagged. He was working now for everything to be slightly bigger than indicated in the score—a piano diminuendo instead of a mezzo-piano one, for example. The players maintained absolute quiet while listening to him, surrounding him with almost palpable respect, attention, and affection. Stage manager Levine elaborated on this phenomenon by telling how during the *Falstaff* rehearsals the musicians made the unprecedented gesture of coming to Bernstein on their own time to discuss the way passages should be played. He readily compared this obvious liking for Bernstein with the idolization of Bruno Walter and Dmitri Mitropoulos. No joking here, although one orchestra member, during a pause in his score, took the opportunity to snap a photo.

Horne in a studio with Ailey working on her dancing, to the pen-and-pad-holding figure in the doorway: "This is the rough stuff. Out! I love you, dear, but you don't want to watch me clutz around." Everyone tried to manage a chuckle.

On the main stage Igesz was occupied with the entrance of the chorus at the opening of Act Three. The tendency, against which he worked, was for them to come down the funnel too slowly, creating a traffic jam at the top. "In a group. Stay together. No gestures, please. Look over your shoulders. It won't work unless you stick together as a group. It looks like a mess instead of something good." The painist banged out the music so no one could complain about not hearing a cue. "Don't observe the dynamics," seconded supervisor Osie Hawkins, always at attention.

Bernstein appeared on the stage, having changed into a Japanese saki shirt. He walked down the mountain pass with the rest of the brigands, liking the feeling inside the tube—at least more than one not-too-spry chorister who reacted to her required descent with an audible "Oi vay!" McCracken advised her to come next day in tennis shoes. She did.

Some other faces were also appearing around the edges—mezzo Shirley Love, coloratura Gail Robinson, and veteran soprano Lucine Amara, who took one look at the set and exclaimed, "I don't believe it." She also seemed to be in some confusion about just where she was supposed to fit in. "I thought I was first cover for Micaela, and now I understand Jeannine Altmeyer is first cover. Maybe I looked at the schedule wrong." It was not clear at this point whether she knew about Stratas's cancellation and how she might have expected this to affect her.

The act did not begin very promisingly. Boky got into the wrong spot, and most of the chorus was looking around them in that unconvincing "What is this place?" manner as in days of old. Horne lolled on the disk, which she now dubbed "Alberich's rock," an appellation that must also have been in the back of Igesz's mind when he took one glance at the three girls he had placed behind it. "You look like the three Rhinemaidens."

"On this set, what else?" laughed our Carmen.

One of the chorus girls, however, looked like no Rhinemaiden to executive stage manager Hawkins. On this hot day, a young, rather voluptuous mezzo had showed up in a backless halter-type blouse. "She shouldn't wear that to rehearsal. I must speak to her."

The chorus took another of their half-hour breaks—every other half-hour, it sometimes seemed—so Igesz went on with the card scene. "At least we won't have to show the chorus our terrible mistakes," he encouraged. It proceeded, with a prompter in attendance for the first time, Altmeyer and Weidinger mouthing along with Frasquita, but one of that lady's gold-digging lines caught Igesz quite by surprise ("Il meurt et j'hérite!). "Is that in it?" he laughed.

The moment came for Carmen's dramatic first note in this pivotal episode. All ears were bent. Silence. Expectation. A very superior Horne sneeze. "It's that darn carpet," she sniffled, to general hilarity. Clearly this phase of the crisis, that part which she could not win, had become a backstage standing joke.

"Why don't you offer a piece of the damn thing with each copy of your book?" a cast member suggested to the ever-present chronicler.

Horne was still having difficulty coordinating the card-turning with her lines ("Encore! Encore! Toujours la mort!" etc.), but no one doubted it was the sort of thing that would come with time, although for the superobservant spectator, "Carreau! Pique!" (diamonds and spades) rarely came up the right suits.

On to the "douanier" chorus, and the girls, Frasquita, Mercédès, and Carmen, now had the gaudy fripperies of a stolen basket ("We never travel without our box," giggled Horne) to work with. Actually, these highlights of color moved with great effectiveness, almost disembodied in the gloom of the stage. This scene created some difficulty because Igesz wanted first Frasquita, then Mercédès, and finally almost everyone onstage to mock José while it was going on, even to the point of making the horned cuckold sign at him, the corporal-deserter now isolated on the disk in a sea of inimical vibrations. Could McCracken easily negotiate the slope of the disk? Would it actually seem logical that absolutely everyone would be already on to his *coming* betrayal by Carmen? It seemed a weak, stagy inspiration, unmotivated to some and offensive to some tenors, at least. Placido Domingo, when he saw *Carmen* at the final dress rehearsal, stated flatly—and with empathy—that he did not like the way people were treating Don José.

Bernstein was now on his third shirt of the day, keeping up that reputation for superior perspiration established on nationwide television when, after the opening concert at Philharmonic Hall, he informed Jacqueline Kennedy how "sweaty" he was. McCracken, however, especially when he was baked under the Act One lights, offered him stiff, or rather limp, competition.

The conductor was trying to communicate to his men the

excitement of the little muted *fugato* section that follows the "Séguidille" as Zuniga consigns Carmen to José's care. It was already 3 P.M., and only Act One had been looked at. "That was fantastic. Only too loud. And I want to hear that descending scale better. And then right into the digga-digga-da, digga-digga-da."

A union-regulated orchestra break allowed Bernstein, towel around neck in the fashion of a boxer's second, and nursing a milk container, to look in on the Act Three rehearsal. Igesz was still experimenting with the placement of Carmen, Frasquita, and Mercédès around the disk for the card scene. Horne, seeing Bernstein, went to him, and in the process, slipped on the carpet. "It will kill me one way or another." Lennie kissed her.

He watched, ruminatively sucking on his straw, bouncing to the rhythm of the "douanier" chorus as Igesz directed traffic from stage center. The maelstrom was added to by Adler's coming onstage to get closer to the chorus, and assistant director Fabrizio Melano's summoning David Walker for a consultation on the content of the smugglers' basket. Confusion and crowds, with Christopher's intended cross completely blocked.

Hawkins, arms characteristically crossed on his chest, shouted at the chorus for quiet, and McCracken sneezed, commenting, "The acoustics aren't too bad. I heard that one come back." The tenor was now on the disk receiving the scorn of each and every passing smuggler, rejecting the direction to chase after the scoffers, instinctively judging that José would instead move away from them in anger. But that each girl was to exit looking over her shoulder at him with an identical sneer seemed more than a little contrived, especially when they then walked off in a line as if they were to have their hands stamped so they could later return to the smugglers' hop.

Again the dialogue after the card scene, and again much confusion, with McCracken worried about his movements in the tube. "I might make the mountain come down," he warned.

"I wish you would," chuckled Horne. Under her breath Boky, sauntering in her prop shawl and taunting à la Bardot, gave placement directions to McCracken, although she herself was finding it difficult to weave in and out of the chorus traffic.

But Adler stopped all movement of any kind by telling the chorus that it must sing *everything.* "This [the 'douanier' chorus] is a concert piece!"

"Bodo," Hawkins oracled, "you have ten minutes left with the chorus." (It was 3:45.) Igesz quickly decided to go back to the beginning of the act and the descent through the pass. Chorus members still tended to stop and block those behind them, so getting into their many downstage smaller groups in time to begin the first concerted section was not succeeding. "Where are you?" screamed Adler at a bunch that simply forgot to sing at all, the chorus master apparently unhappy that an ensemble was to be spatially fragmented, thus posing a greater challenge to their ability to keep together musically. The principals, however, except Horne, who seemed to be preoccupied with the reality of her first bitter but laconic dialogue with José, were beginning each in his way to look like their characters.

"That's it for today," called Hawkins just as Igesz opened his mouth to deliver an idea. To the second. Exit chorus.

Bernstein sang and acted the Micaela-José duet with orchestral accompaniment, pulling love and passion from the players. By this point he was no longer saying much to them, just an occasional "Too loud," "Light," "All lifting," each directed at the appropriate section of instruments. The fight music was not staccato enough for him, not light enough, not sufficiently crystalline. Again. And a repeat of the "new" music which goes with Carmen's embattled exit from the factory, including a repetition of the haunting, teasing love tune in A Major first heard after Carmen throws the flower at José. Bernstein really pulled out the stops for its arching sensuality. "That's great!" Act One, for orchestra at any rate, had been set.

On the C-level stage, a room with the outlines of Act One clearly marked on the floor, Strasfogel, Igesz, and prompter

Millard Altman led a rehearsal of the postfight scene with Carmen, José, and Zuniga. A report was made to Horne how brilliant the orchestra had been sounding—news calculated to balance some of her doubts. But her response was to ask if they planned to carpet the orchestra pit too. "It's only fair."

Gramm, just back from Santa Fe, still did not know the words of his dialogue portion and was still translating the text to himself as he went along. But whatever this subtracted from the reality of the scene was made up for by Igesz, who took the part of Carmen's antagonist, Horne playfully miming kicking him in one of his more sensitive areas. The singers were obviously all very fatigued at this end of the day, and McCracken was sure he was coming down with a sore throat. This was a cue for Horne, who immediately got out her portable medicine chest. "Jimmy, take ten thousand milligrams before you go to bed. In fact, I'm going to take some too," and chewable vitamin C was offered all around.

It was decided that throughout this scene Carmen should indicate her distaste for Zuniga, even in her cute "la-la" which the clarinet later imitates when she refuses to answer his questions. "What's a good dirty word I can think of for him? 'Salaud' sounds to me too much like salad." Someone suggested she try "sal con." "What does that mean?" The suggester gulped and translated.

Riecker looked in, and during a break in the action, announced that Maliponte would arrive Monday. He also invited Horne to look at a book of Svoboda designs. "You see, I've done some homework." McCracken, onset of sore throat or not, was brimming over with ideas, such as where the dialogue should start after the "Séguidille" or where he should stand—does he want her to shut up or not?—when Carmen throws her taunting reprise of the "Habañera" at Zuniga before she is led away.

Horne left for the day, and the first dialogue—that between José and Zuniga—was put under the microscope. McCracken was worried whether, in its now very pared-down form, the dialogue could establish his character. Igesz suggested at one point that Zuniga touch him, and McCracken immediately objected that a man threatened, as José is by Zuniga's new knowledge of his background, would never allow him to come that close. Igesz conceded the point. The bell that cues the entrance of the factory girls ends this exchange, and McCracken said it was like a signal letting him out of prison. "I know," Gramm threw in. "Why don't we just ring the bell at the beginning of the dialogue and cut the whole thing?"

The day was still not over for McCracken. The Kolombatovich team was there on the main stage to set the Act Three duel between José and Escamillo, baritone Robert Goodloe now standing in for the still missing Krause.

Igesz ran up and down the walls of the funnel, his possibly 135 pounds testing for support. McCracken did not look at all convinced by the maneuver, although he was very concerned that the fight should have enough realism not to look like a ballet. *Mirabile dictu,* he was also worried that too vigorous action would get the *baritone* out of breath, especially if he had to grapple with this particular José. Igesz suggested that José should hesitate before striking Escamillo when he has him down, explaining the logic of this as not so much stemming from his history of blind violence but as a counterpoise to Escamillo's decision to spare him when he has the advantage.

"Is my belly going to be bouncing around in that costume?" the tenor speculated. "And how will I be able to follow Bernstein's free tempi with my back to the audience?" Igesz accommodatingly placed him in a convenient position. Actually, the Kolombatoviches had not as yet worked out the details of the fight, but at least today they managed to determine where it would start and where the tenor and baritone would be when it ended, with the important idea of its climax established—José overcoming Escamillo—as a parallel to the overconfident bullfighter walking away from the bull that gores him.

*

August 29

A resumption on the main stage from where the Act Three action had stopped the day before—Horne, McCracken, Velis, Christopher present from the first cast, with Goodloe and Altmeyer covering, plus Igesz, Melano, prompter, and rehearsal pianist. Before starting—a good delay for unknown reasons after the 10 A.M. scheduled beginning—there was time for a conversation with the statuesque, maxi-skirted Miss Altmeyer, now perhaps for the first time finding herself the center of so much attention as Micaela-in-waiting. At twenty-three, the soprano had been with the Met for two years, but as yet had done only two roles onstage, one of them a Freia in *Das Rheingold* in Chicago, the other a Frasquita plus her debut role of the Celestial Voice in *Don Carlo.* She was happy about being scheduled for a Gutrune in Chicago, which was coming up in only three years. She readily admitted her lack of stage experience and stated her intention of leaving the Met at the end of her two-year contract. "Maybe I'll go to Zurich or some place like that."

It seemed amazing that someone with this much talent was not being put to better use or at least being trained. Evelyn Lear, an alumma of the European-experience route for American singers, later commented that having heard Altmeyer's promising final audition for the Met, she would have advised her not to accept the contract but to get herself off somewhere to gain experience. "Nothing good seems to happen to audition winners anymore—not since the war at any rate," added Thomas Stewart, Miss Lear's baritone husband. However, maybe this first cover assignment was at least a step in the right direction.

McCracken had an idea for his fight with Escamillo. He

thought it would be effective for the two of them to begin their final tussle—the fight being twice as long in this semirestored version—at the top of the tube and roll down its length to stage level. Bodo said that such a decision could wait, since the chorus blocking needed his immediate attention, an opinion that angered the usually good-humored if always high-voltage tenor. "I assure you this will be a weak spot if we don't work on it," he fairly shouted. "Screw the chorus! Let's work it out. Rehearsal is called for ten, and people are walking around!" (The singer, who lives in Connecticut and daily faced a long drive back and forth, had made an effort to be on time and definitely did not like standing around unused.)

He calmed down, and the incident passed. Bodo gave Horne the reaction he wanted her to register at recognizing the toreador, now pinned under José's weight. She accepted it but couldn't find her pitch for that entrance aside: "Escamillo!" "Would you give me those lovely notes," she requested of the pianist.

Goodloe exited up the tube and contributed his little joke to the no-longer-tense assemblage—a limp-wristed wave to the smugglers.

In the orchestra room, beige-turtlenecked Leonard Bernstein launched the opening of Act Two, the "Chanson Bohémienne." "Keep it light, everybody. Winds, as light and staccato as possible. When things work up a bit, I want to hear the strings *sul ponticello.* The secret of the dance," he repeated now for the orchestra's benefit, "is that at no point is there a feeling of increasing tempo. It is a gradual *più mosso,* and that is not easy to do. It will probably be different at each performance, but no one in the audience should be aware of these points of change."

One might not have thought it possible, but the conductor then devoted some time to dynamic gradations in the tambourine part, emphasizing a certain forte-piano effect he wanted. Triangles were coordinated with timpani and a trumpet crescendo set for the climax.

"I want the brass to play more in the French manner," he said, "a lighter, quicker forte. I don't want them to drown out the rest of the orchestra." The climax was repeated, and the orchestra got a Bernsteinian "Tuhrrific!" for its efforts.

For Escamillo's entrance music, Bernstein again asked for short, light, precise attacks. "Remember, this is French music." He also insisted on an immediate pounce on the fortissimo scale (after the "Vivat!" chorus) that begins the Toreador Song. The juxtaposition was electric now that no breathing space was left between the two numbers—another instance of Bernstein's not allowing the opera to break down into set pieces. He nearly jumped off the platform in his excitement. "That's a real kick, especially if all the little notes are played. Oh, by the way, is that a bad page-turning spot? If it is, we'll put the opening of the Toreador Song on an insert. We need everyone playing there." As he got to the refrain, he remarked to his men that he had no idea how the Escamillo, Tom Krause, intended to sing the music. (Where was Krause? How long would rehearsals have to go on without him?) "Up bows for the piano, down bows for the forte. Now, third horn, leave room for the crescendo. Start *piano espressivo.*"

Velis was curled up on the smuggler's disk as Igesz read a list of choristers, whom he still had with him, who would get to appear in the Lillas Pastia scene. There did not seem to be too much disappointment among those who would not quaff this particular drink on the house.

Then it was back to blocking the taunting and teasing exit of the "douanier" chorus, a José in anguish replacing the napping Velis on the disk. Igesz ran up and down its canted surface, indicating where and when he wanted his tenor. McCracken watched these acrobatics and cautioned: "Bodo, it takes me a little longer than you to get around." The act was repeated from the beginning, the principals marking, not singing, Horne intent on her card-turning synchronization, the disk wobbling worrisomely under McCracken, and all the members of the chorus giving him the *cornuto* sign, one even getting to kick him, this ostracized beast, isolated and surrounded on his pitched perch. The "Marchons en avant" at the end was even to be the prelude to derisive laughter.

Bernstein, on an orchestra break, arrived onstage and took over conducting the ensemble, getting an uncanny charge into a triple piano on the reprise of the "douainer" chorus. He then stood apart, watching Igesz make some adjustment in the chorus positions, noting some word mispronunciations and commenting that José had now become a Pagliaccio. Whether he considered this a legitimate light to throw on the unhappy hero was not altogether plain.

"I know it's hard, horns, but I would like it more legato and with a diminuendo." The orchestra had reached the Flower Song, which Bernstein told the musicians was a brilliant piece of composition, "one of the greatest pieces of music ever written," and he repeated to them his point about there being no repeats in the musical vocabulary of the aria until the orchestral coda. "This may be the only aria in a conventional opera that has this aspect. Not even Verdi was able to accomplish it. We must do it very carefully, because if it's a mess, it can sound like Schönberg."

He pointed out what he called bad traditions, phrases where a diminuendo had taken the place of a crescendo. He sang along in his tight, unmusical voice, his tempo strikingly slow at this first hearing. One diminuendo that he promised would stay was that on the B-flat scale ending in a high pianissimo on the words, just before the final phrase, "Et j'étais une chose à toi!" "McCracken is going to try to sing the high B-flat pianissimo," he announced (most tenors blast it). "He's marvelous. He's willing to risk everything to do it correctly." They repeated the aria, Bernstein noting a spot where the orchestra tended to rush: "That's also a tradition, because the tenor usually can't hold it, but I'm amazed it's so in tune. Or was it my singing that prevented me from hearing it? I may be losing my grip, but that is as in tune as I've ever heard it. Beautiful!"

The conductor, ever the discoverer, mentioned the similarity to a passage in Beethoven's Seventh Symphony of the repeated G's in the three-note figure that accompanies Carmen's response to the Flower Song. He had a hard time, however, getting them to accent these notes exactly as he wished, on the first instead of the third. Again and again he tried until finally: "That's it. At last. *Gott sei dank!*"

Jeannine Altmeyer and Colette Boky still did not know about the selection of Maliponte to sing Micaela. When it was finally mentioned to them by someone, their faces registered a studied neutrality. No one was moving up. Altmeyer was now doing her first Act Three singing—Micaela's entrance when Remendado (now, of course, Carmen; Velis did not get his lines back until Bernstein left and Henry Lewis took over) discovers her in hiding. The young soprano, reflecting the unwonted pressure on her, bore down heavily on her essentially attractive voice, but when it came to high notes she merely marked them, imitating perhaps her more experienced colleagues. Hawkins told her to sing out, a rather curious instruction with McCracken, after several rafter-shaking and diaphragm-jiggling fortes, substituting falsetto highs when he was so—and legitimately so—inclined.

The music here for Micaela is very emotionally charged and gives wonderful opportunities to the soprano to shine. Altmeyer was aware of this, as was everyone else listening to her (Igesz seemed particularly struck by her quality), but when Bernstein looked in, he conferred with Strasfogel and appeared not to be attending to her at all. The conductor, now pink-shirted, took over the podium for the end of the act, suggesting to Igesz what was the proper moment for José and Micaela to begin their exit up the tube. This occurs after José has flung Carmen to the ground and Escamillo's Toreador Song refrain is heard in the distance. "Look exultant, Jackie," advised Lenny. "It's your new trick."

"My ankles hurt from all that disk climbing." James McCracken stretched out on his dressing room couch. "This opening night, as everyone knows, was supposed, according to Bing's decision, to be *Tannhäuser,* so when Gentele changed these plans and picked *Carmen* I told him that if he didn't want me for José it was OK. I've sung José in St. Paul in a conventional production and in the parks with the Met, but never under first-class conditions. [*Tannhäuser,* of course, would have been a decisive McCracken debut as a Wagnerian.] But I had two meetings with Gentele, and we decided I should stay with it. It was such a refreshing experience to talk to him. With Bing I only talked about business, but Gentele was a man wrapped up in artistic matters. In those talks he stressed José's killing of the man in the fight, his streak of meanness. Of course, the Flower Song and the Act One duet with Micaela contradict this meanness, but it's there, especially in Act Three.

"I've gone back to Mérimée, so I know quite a bit about the guy. He's only eighteen and had studied for the priesthood. I'm sorry that the dialogue lines referring to that are now cut. He was a young hothead with both good and bad instincts, sort of a schizophrenic. At any rate, he killed this other man at a football game in a fit of uncontrollable rage. I understand this side of him very well, for my own father, a mechanic and a man of great strength, had to train himself to get the better of his temper and his physical power. I want to give José this dimension of temper, play him as more than a rural, passive mamma's boy.

"Yes, the dialogue bothered me when it was first decided to use it, but I realize that the recitatives just don't have the information. The dialogue will work if every line has an intention. I'm not going to make pictorial gestures to explain the dialogue. Some will get through if the intention is there. Of course, ideally, the dialogue should be in English and the opera in French, but the critics would kill us. I suppose the people who understand will get something out of it. Undoubtedly there will be complaints. With an opera as often seen as *Carmen,* traditions become commonplace, and everyone gets his own idea about what it should be like and remembers his favorite production. You can't please everyone." The big man paused, sighed, and wiggled his toes.

"Right now we're at the most difficult stage: making those

bridges between the dialogue and the music, and for me there is the added responsibility of being onstage many times when in other productions Don José would not be there."

Asked about the so-called Pagliaccio bit at the end of Act Three, McCracken admitted that he too was not totally convinced that everyone onstage at this point would be *au courant* concerning the deterioration of his affair with Carmen. "I really don't know about those looks on the exit, but you have to remember also that you are dealing here with the artifice of a chorus in the first place." McCracken paused to contemplate this not-yet-resolved matter. He then mentioned his small outburst at the beginning of the day's rehearsing. "Yes, I was angry this morning when my suggestions about the fight with Escamillo were passed over. Maybe rolling down the incline might work, maybe not, but we've got to find out. I've never seen a good stage fight. Have you? And what's the point of rehearsing with the wrong Escamillo? Oh, well, it's early yet, and I know Krause will work well."

A corridor comment—Bernstein to Velis: "Remendado is gay but not flighty. So he should never sing falsetto."

The end of Act Two in the orchestra room. Bernstein was working on the orchestral accompaniment to the "la liberté" chorus, especially the *rallentando* on the words "Comme c'est beau la liberté." "It will be the neatest trick of the week if I can get a hundred people onstage to do it." The conductor, still exploring, now decided to restore the first two bars of a cut he had made in the finale. But a spot in the orchestral *Nachspiel,* as he was prone to call the postlude of an aria or ensemble, disturbed him. "Dammit, this really should be rescored. Oh, but it won't matter. Everyone will be clapping. By the time we do the recording I'll make a new decision." The entr'acte to Act Three was played. The maestro required no repetitions. "Very pretty. Very nice. Bravo."

Two-thirty. A new first: Act Four set up onstage. With the urchins chasing around C-level stage and the adult chorus finding a shape for the first time, the picture could only have been described as muddy. Igesz: "Group C over here and the eight *popolo* supers over there. Now remember not to walk too fast. Pretend it's a hot day"—not difficult under the intense light.

New supers had shown up, including such favorites as a prosperous camera-store proprietor, a man whose clientele includes many Metropolitan stars as well as most of the Soviet delegation to the United Nations (he's fluent in Russian). He has been supering since 1935.

Igesz tried with this mob for an effect of controlled strolling—all to be moving in a vaguely circular formalized *paseo* pattern, just as people, especially Europeans, do who are accustomed to streetwalking as a respectable activity. Some choristers were placed atop the oblique stage left wall meant to represent a section of the arena's seating area. Their heads peeping over the top somehow looked like so many lined-up Kilroys.

The procession of banderilleros went through their paces and merchants proffered their wares, very much in a style that one would recognize from any *Carmen* in the last fifty years. A glimmering of props could already be discovered. One rather strange feature of the Svoboda set now attracted attention as people moved about it: An upstage wall made an acute angle with the wall parallel to stage front, so that from at least a third of the seats—on the left—in the house, all upstage exiting and entering figures would be either terminally or initially invisible. What was the reason for this?

"A *deux* cuartos!!" shouted Stivender, that same temptation to sing "dos" still persisting. The difficulty of dividing and reassigning the chorus into role groups, orange and cigarette sellers, fan sellers, water and wine sellers, program and lorgnette sellers, was attacked, a delicate matter with figures in constant motion and the necessity of making sure there was sufficient audibility from the target positions they had to get into and set firmly in their minds. In the recording one voice only was given the words of the orange seller, for example, but this was impossible acoustically in the house if any sound was to be heard.

The children waited in the wings for their rush-in cue. Each was sent to a different group of adults when the sounds of the corrida procession are first heard. This was a practical stage procedure, even if later, when costumes were put on, it did not seem entirely logical dramatically, for why would urchins in rags—seen as an autonomous crowd in Act One—link themselves separately to adults in bullfight-going livery, albeit of a markedly colorless sort, as if each was part of a family group? No self-respecting Sevillian would ever allow his little Paquito to make a public appearance in this sort of garb. It was a decision made for staging convenience, and with the chaos of running in, the need of keeping the groups fluid and findable, one could hardly blame Igesz for sticking with it.

Hawkins struggled valiantly to keep the talking level of the masses down. "Go, kids!" yelled Gildo diNunzio, an assistant conductor stationed in the wings. The idea was for the boys to run in and draw the attention of the less sensitive adults to where the parade was coming from. For this all the ranks were drawn downstage in a line and were to suggest their discovery of the direction by a concerted looking to the left, the children pointing, and then gradually moving their heads to the right as the procession advanced somewhere out over the orchestra. Not a terribly original device, and it can be effective only if everyone's eyes and pointing fingers are fixed pretty much on the same spot at any given instant. With a big chorus with everything to worry about, this rarely happened, and the illusion never quite came off.

A break was called for the chorus, but the parading supers remained—banderilleros, picadors, and so on—to work on integrating the Alcade and his family. "Terrible," muttered Igesz. "They're not together." And to them: "No swinging of arms! Ever! By anybody!"

But the most important labor of the day was coming up—Act Four from the entrance of Carmen and Escamillo, with all the principals except Krause (substituted for by Reardon, substituted for by Goodloe). The little duet between the bullfighter and his lady presented no blocking problems at this point, and Igesz went on to the exchange between Carmen and Frasquita and Mercédès, who warn her about the lurking Don José, a treacherous business ("It's the part of the opera that never gets done," remarked the director) because it is played at a shifting moment between two duets. Igesz decided to get the crowd movement going after the freeze during the previous duet, but this meant a difficult task for the three women (especially Frasquita and Mercédès): threading their way into place in time. Horne felt very crowded by the confining hordes, but Igesz said that was the effect he sought. The mezzo, however, seemed to be thrown by the confusion and missed her cue several times before the business was settled. Boky, against onrushing traffic, always seemed to make it into place for her first line just in the nick of time.

Bernstein wandered in, and an observing Rosalind Elias left for the day, having to go off to a rehearsal for a *Don Giovanni* Zerlina. The conductor inspected the stark set—really, and grimly, the rear entrance to the bull ring—and only remarked how abstract Act Three was in contrast. Igesz reminded him that with the planned projections, the tube's contours would make more concretely ocular suggestions. It was also pointed out that a new section of arena wall had just been added, Svoboda's original calculations having erred. "God, don't tell Jackie," remarked a sideliner. "It will only give her more ammunition."

The conductor threw himself into the rehearsal now, producing for the singers' benefit what were undoubtedly long-held convictions as to what Carmen's basic motivations are during Act Four. "Jackie," he interrupted the warning exchange, "you should not be surprised that José is there. It's just part of fate. It's like Carmen doesn't even have to look, maybe just the slightest look to confirm what you already know, that this is the day of your death. You're dressed to the nines, and you've come out with your new trick to die. You knew all about this in Act One when you threw the flower. You're always reading the cards, not just in Act Three. It's fate. You're like Dido, Jocasta."

The confrontation was repeated, and Horne stood rigid. "Tuhrrific atmosphere," approved Bernstein. This had been the sort of basic talk about characterization leading to a strong stylistic line of performance that one had not really heard before. Time and the complexity of numbers—chorus, ballet—were militating against Igesz's indulging in much more than movement manipulation. Added to these problems was Gentele's conception, an elusive quantity that inhibited him from striking out on his own if indeed he was so inclined.

"Now, Jackie," Bernstein went on, "say 'Donc!'" And he emphasized the nasality.

"But," laughed Carmen, stretching out on the carpet during this new pause and doing a few leg exercises, "I'm a bel canto singer." Igesz joined her there for a discussion of her movements while waiting for José to appear. Horne suggested that she describe an ever widening circle of agitation, reflecting the movements of the bull inside the ring. She called this "German thinking."

"Well," nodded Igesz, "this set calls for German thinking."

On their feet, and now joined by McCracken, they walked through the scene, speaking the lines, trying to decide at what point Carmen should interrupt her circles and face her nemesis. Bernstein looked on silently, puffing on a fugitive cigarette. Igesz warned that Carmen must have in mind someplace to retreat, perhaps inside the arena, while McCracken threw in the notion that she might wind up, at the end of her circles, stage right, where the little "conseil" scene with Frasquita and Mercédès had taken place, sitting on the railing (this appeared to be a sort of free-form hitching post of which some of the more limber girls in the chorus managed an ascent during the procession excitement).

"It's just a suggestion," explained the tenor. "We could start our scene close together on the small side of the stage, then build it out to the larger playing area on the left. I see we're in trouble with what we have, so I'm making a suggestion."

Igesz agreed to try this, but Bernstein ended his retreat and in a way, reiterating his lecture to Horne, told them that Carmen's action was to stand still, to remain inflexible in the biggest possible space where these two forces could face each other, to let José come closer and closer, and not to move until the first roar of the crowd was heard. Otherwise she should be dead cold. "I hope I haven't thrown in a monkey wrench," the maestro added.

"It's a good monkey wrench," the director acknowledged. Bernstein, now having accomplished the delivery of his thought, departed.

McCracken, adapting the conductor's ideas, was judging the speed at which he'd make his approach to Carmen. "I guess I'll just have to move very slowly."

"And we better sing very pretty too," laughed Horne. Igesz made an adjustment so that sidelines would be clear in this peculiarly angled set for José at the beginning of the duet. And now it began, the piano rattling on, McCracken thoroughly involved, for the most part singing full voice. He even found a place where Don José in his pleading could produce a hopeful little smile. So great was his conviction that when he finally touched Horne, her reaction was of an equally startling and convincing intensity—although all touching, Igesz decided, should be postponed until José's desperate "Ah! ne me quitte pas, Carmen!"

"You know, she's now using all sorts of new words here," commented Horne, "words like 'superflus.' Where did she learn that?"

Bernstein had apparently triggered something with her, a train of thought, and with McCracken, too, who sighed, "From here on in, this will take some real acting," not, however, without raising a few observers' eyebrows.

Igesz suggested that Carmen's reply to the José clutch—"Jamais Carmen ne cèdera! Libre elle est née et libre elle mourra!"—should be accompanied by a shove that would topple the kneeling tenor. "Bodo," Horne informed the director, who had put himself in José's position, "you must remember that you weigh eighty pounds. He's too big for me to make a push look convincing." Instead Carmen was to pull away and face him, turning upstage defiantly.

"Libre elle est née et libre elle mourra," repeated Igesz, making a rare witticism, "comme je vous disais au troisième acte [as I was telling you in the third act]."

Horne was brought a fan to work with (and joke with, putting it over the tenor's mouth with a big yawn on his "Tu ne m'aimes donc plus?"), and McCracken continued his experimenting with positions, attitudes, and business, but all in terms of the Bernstein concept. Both singers, in addition to considering possibly using the optional high notes for Carmen in the concerted section of the duet (McCracken wanted this because he found it difficult to sing softly enough in this passage), were also refining and simplifying their movements, with, most importantly, Carmen remaining the still point around which the agitated José revolved. It was beginning to look very good.

*

August 30

Bodo Igesz looked very tired this morning as he prepared to block the Toreador Song with cover Goodloe (all of course to be repeated as soon as Krause arrived) on the C-level stage. He was worried about the exit of the men at the end of the "Habañera," allowing that as of now he had no solution for the problem.

Goodloe, a tall, forthright baritone in the rather blustery typical descendants-of-Alfred Drake vein, tried to lighten the director's load by telling him about some of the Toreador Song's blocking that had been used in the last production. Igesz was not having any hand-me-downs, however, especially from the discredited Barrault staging, and worked out his own routine for Escamillo, one that ended with a mimed *coup de grâce* on the last note of the aria.

Bernstein's double-breasted cord jacket quickly came off in the close—and today un-air-conditioned—atmosphere of the orchestra room. He started the morning's rehearsal with a compliment on the work accomplished the previous day but added that he had got tired and now felt that he had scanted the end of Act Three, especially the José-Escamillo fight music, which he told them in any case was a weak spot in an otherwise "unbelievable" score. Some of the musicians' seating arrangement was switched around, and then the conductor lifted his baton at the notes to which Escamillo proclaims his own identification to José. Bernstein interrupted them almost immediately with a reminder about his insistence on strict observation of the forte-piano markings. "We did all that," he said by way of gentle reproval. He then skipped to the very end of the act, the music that accompanies the blackout and which he was determined to make fresh by telling the men to "do the opposite of what you usually do" in terms of diminuendo and accelerando.

But now came some real grist to be milled for a Bernstein interpretation—the fiery entr'acte to Act Four. The maestro did not stint in his detailed directions, even asking the tambourine to modulate its piano dynamic marking and the strings to "rip your skin off on those pizzicati. More flamenco nonsense!" He had devised a wild accelerando and crescendo in the middle, where the piece becomes most markedly Spanish in flavor. "I may kill all this, but that's what rehearsals are for." Nevertheless, he found the effect "sensational" and kept it.

For the beginning of Act Four itself Bernstein wanted his horns on their repeated note figuration to use what he called a "French" approach, a lightness that would keep the tempo from dragging. And yet he wanted the bass line, even though it consisted of only this repetition, to stand out. For this he lightened the other sections, blending this chorus into the march that follows without a break ("It should be like a cross-fade in a movie"). The march builds into the same material that appears in the Prelude, another instance where the conductor, by starting at a slightly slower tempo, worked for an imperceptible accelerando. "This introduction is a very spooky place, and remember, all we said about the Prelude at the first rehearsal applies here." As if to fortify the parallel, Bernstein was again doing his podium bouncing, becoming the embodiment of rhythmic pomposity. "I hope they carry this out onstage. Otherwise we'll be in the pit making idiots of ourselves. And bass drum, fortissimo on the upbeat, even more fortissimo on the downbeat."

When the music reached the Toreador Song climax of "C'est l'Espada," the players began to sing. "I love it," laughed the maestro. "Is that a tradition? [Many operas contain a spot where musicians jokingly sing along, at least in rehearsal, sometimes even at the dress rehearsal. In *Der Rosenkavalier,* for example, Annina's Act Three comic down-and-up scale gets vocal orchestral accompaniment.] Let's rehearse it. The singing was terrific, the pianissimi were not."

"It's a pleasure to watch a prepared director for a change. It's the best *Carmen* staging since 1948," remarked stage manager Levine as he watched Igesz on stage again attack Act Four, now from the point where the boys rush on. Still confused, the stage picture was nevertheless gaining some coordination, and the kids' faces were beginning to show real excitement. "Yes, keep pointing out things to one another," instructed the director, "but avoid waving and that 'Hi-there-how-was-your-vacation-in-Coney-Island' effect."

Igesz attempted to be everywhere at once, onstage, out front checking sidelines, getting group crosses set for the adults but keeping the children down front so that they could more easily get their cues (although Stivender stated that it had never been definitely decided what the children would or would not sing at this point). Chaos again as the run-in was repeated, one chorus member grabbing an urchin not assigned to him. "I'm not your kid," the tot scolded as he broke away.

The chorus and supers, all of whose names Igesz seemed to have at the tip of his tongue, and who were in an incongruous array of dress, including sweatshirts hailing "Stuyvesant Phys. Ed.," "Montana Grizzlies," or "Heinekins" and other favorite brands, gathered around Carmen and her escort to hail him on the final "Vive Escamillo! Bravo! Vive! bravo! bravo!" At which point the whole scene was begun again, Stivender automatically correcting any stray "A dos cuartos" that might have crept in—one from Igesz himself, as it turned out. Bernstein, jacket slung around his shoulders, looked in just in time to tell the rehearsal pianist what he wanted from that transition section between the "A deux cuartos" and the march, the "spooky place." Kids collided with advancing picadors, and the traffic jams in general proved that the patterns were not clear. Chorus master Adler simultaneously announced that he was concerned that musically the chorus appeared unsure of themselves. "There *was* some mighty confusion," sighed Igesz.

Another rare illogical bit of business, given the directness and naturalness of the crowd's behavior now being established, was Igesz's direction to them to turn away from Escamillo after all those vociferous bravos and freeze while he and Carmen performed the brief "Si tu m'aimes" section. It seemed like a very fickle, very unmotivated action for this holiday gathering.

After this duet some "new" music had been inserted dealing with the mayor's procession, measures that caused a frown on the face of the watching Lucine Amara, who expressed herself as against new music and dialogue in a house the size of the Met. She had something of a case, at least in the first matter, for the chorus dealt with its fresh material very weakly.

Petite blond ballet dancer on the Act Two choreography: "It's so sexy. I wish I could be in it, but I'm not the type."

Very few stops in the action as Bernstein went through Act Two in the orchestra room, the Beethoven Seventh triplets of the "là-bas" section after the Flower Song coming out with the accent properly on the first notes, the pizzicati of "La guerre, c'est la guerre," clean and precise. The act ended with a great accelerando and an approving "OK" from the maestro.

The Act Three card scene was picked for a run-through. "You're not together, basses and celi," Bernstein informed the strings. "It's a big moment for you, basses. You have the line above the celli." The Frasquita and Mercédès section of the scene was getting the *scherzando* treatment Bernstein had spoken about, the exact doubling in tempo of Carmen's lines. A quick look at the Act Four entr'acte again to wind things up ("We're ahead of the game") and to give Lenny a chance to do a Mick Jaggeresque routine on that flamenco ritard. He seemed carried away, but not enough to allow a mistake to get past him. He caught himself in mid-swivel and corrected.

Act Two had now made a move to the back stage, set up basically as it had been on the main stage in front of it, where Act Four was now in the process of yielding to Act One. This brief 1 P.M. rehearsal was called to integrate the Toreador Song blocking devised that morning into the overall picture. The miracle of the Met machinery made this possible, although the sound of dismantling and putting in place could never be masked sufficiently for any real musical work.

Gramm and Franke stumbled through their dialogue, but the chorus was registering genuine excitement about the bull-fighter's visit. Igesz plotted them around the fulcrum of Goodloe's Escamillo, giving them their mass reaction. "Pretend you see the bull he's singing about just as you see the parade in Act Four. Follow the imaginary bull. And most of all, forget all you ever knew about the Toreador Song. Make it really happen." Igesz cued their exclamations with his own "ee's, ah's, ooh's," running around, prodding members who were not sufficiently rapt, miming the bull itself so that they should know where their eyes were to be trained, demanding their rivited attention until he gave his final weaponless coup. Kurt Adler found his moment in all this drama to express his hope for some pianissimo-legato singing from his people, but the musical direction was lost in the mass histrionics.

With Act One's guardhouse and factory walls now in position and the carpet newly swept, Carmen could practice her post-"Habañera" teasing of José, filling up the new, longer statement of the fate motive, which ends with her throwing of the flower. "Now she's going to José," Igesz prompted the chorus. "Look at him. Keep the intensity on your faces. Wonder what Carmen is going to do." This was one of the most problematical moments in the production—an unreal, stylized change in the passing of stage time as the lights dimmed and the drama focused on Carmen's slow foot-in-front-of-foot zeroing in on her prey and doom-to-come. Could Horne hold the tension? Could anyone by sheer will, unaided by voice, and helped by very little movement gather thousands of eyes? They seemed good questions at the time, but ones that simply would have to wait for an answer. Certainly no one's concentration was being helped today by some really top-notch sweeping of non-Svoboda carpeting in the hall. Hawkins yelled, Levine commanded, and Horne continued her meaningful cross and persevered to her exit, which, at least, seemed to please Igesz.

The chorus men were let go, the women and supers remaining to block the fight among the factory workers. Bernstein, having been satisfied for this stage of preparation, had sent the orchestra home early (*The New York Times* later erroneously reported that this early dismissal of the musicians had caused considerable consternation in the Met management), and came onstage in yet another clean shirt to supervise. The girls' rush exodus from the factory was effected, but they were finding it hard to get their right cues from the backstage assistant, who in turn was finding it impossible to hear his cue from out front. They started their haranguing of Zuniga, but Bernstein soon stopped them. "Listen, you're all yelling. You're doing it all forte. Remember to tell the story of what happened between Carmen and Manuelita. And don't rush. The words will be missed. Make a crescendo. Right now it's a lot of yelling. Otherwise it's terrific." He then turned to Strasfogel to mourn that there was always a problem working against the music. "First they get onstage, and the music goes. Then, it's the costumes. Then the lights. Everything throws them. And I can't just sit back. I can't do opera that way. When I'm turned on, I'm onstage and involved."

McCracken gave his cue line—"J'épouse Micaela," etc.—("Good boy," chuckled Lenny) and the rush was on again.

Bernstein conducted from mid-pit cover while Igesz ran around the stage showing the supers how to link hands and divide the pro-Carmencita and pro-Manuelita groups into two separate factions. It all looked a bit ring-round-the-rosyish, especially when the girls stopped doing anything at the end of their initial lines. To keep a sense of continuity, Igesz, now again informed by Hawkins that his time before a break was limited, had their sung cries overlap into spoken demands for attention. "Monsieur! Monsieur!" they shouted at Zuniga.

Here again the restoration of usually cut music made for what could be a dangerous dead spot. When Carmen was led out of the factory for interrogation, it could be seen that about twice as much time as usual would have to be filled up. Right now everything came to a screeching (literally) halt. "Bodo, isn't there any movement?" queried the conductor as he continued to beat time for the piano. "This music is silly unless something is going on."

The scene continued, some girls actually exchanging hair pulls with sufficient vigor for one of them to lose her wig. At one point one was supposed to scream, "Oui, c'est elle!" from far upstage and run all the way down to attack Carmen, but she rarely, this day or any other, until almost the final rehearsals, got her cue early enough to make the trip. "That accelerando will be a disaster if you can't see me," implored Bernstein, but for the moment stage confusion reigned in the chorus ranks. Horne, very conscious of the timing difficulties here, tried to coordinate her fisticuffs with her almost simultaneous flirtation with José, adding a good laugh when she found McCracken unable to hold her back. "Jackie, remember not to start right away on those tra-la-la-la's. You're not that eager to comply with Zuniga's request. And we want that violin sting to have some time of its own." Bernstein had managed to combine a musical and a dramatic instruction in one.

The obligatory break came, providing a chance for Bernstein to work a bit with the parading urchins. He found their entrance awkward and suggested that some dialogue be included to cover their preparation to get in place. He conducted them like mad, but the guardhouse-roof contingent warred with those posted on the fence to see who could get ahead of the beat better and who could get behind best. Bernstein ran up to the fence, a prayer in his throat. "Kiddies, you're the backbone of this. I have to rely on you."

One coffee-drinking authoritative stagehand to another in a thick New York brogue: "Friday is a technical. We break our balls till two, then we have the whole weekend off. So don't call in sick."

"Bodo, congratulations. Over the speaker that sounded like the biggest catfight ever," Hawkins effused as the director took up the scene again from where Zuniga, via dialogue, commands

Carmen to reveal what she knows about the incident in the factory. Then on to the "Séguidille" without benefit of cord but with a mixup in cues (Bernstein: "What are you waiting for?" Horne: "You, to give me the cue." Bernstein: "I was waiting for you.")

While the "Séguidille" was getting Horne's and McCracken's attention, Igesz was already busy setting up the chorus in the positions for the end of the act, showing them how they would shut the gates on the soldiers after Carmen gives José the push that sends him up the Guadalquivir. When it came time to execute the closing, it did not quite work, the girls anticipating. Horne, reveling in her taunting reprise of the "Habañera" (Bernstein said she was making it as long as the aria itself), which ended in one of her most successful chest-tone excursions ("Prends garde à toi!"; "Don't forget to go to a forte and then diminuendo on that," warned Bernstein), informed her military escort of supers just where and when and at what pace she wanted to be hustled upstage. A rerun of the fight followed, with a few choral derrieres hitting the carpet and some jokes from Gramm, winding up this down-to-the-wire rehearsal for the chorus (whom no one would dare abuse at this particular time, for delicate union negotiations were now taking place) but not for the principals, who retreated to the back stage to continue with Act Two after Escamillo's exit.

Horne had donned a practice skirt, the first departure from her habitual slacks. However, this added touch of *vérisme* did not appear to help her colleagues, for they repeatedly blanked on the pre-quintet dialogue.

Bernstein insisted that Velis must get more lisping into his reading of Remendado. Oddly, even though the character tenor has played innumerable fops, and to the hilt, he cannot execute a proper lisp, which, admittedly is harder to do in French.

Musically, the quintet went, as Bernstein put it, in "that awful lazy way," Boky repeatedly off on those tricky "de vous, de nous" punctuations. "I thought we had that all straightened out," complained a clearly upset Bernstein, now conducting in the confined space in front of the lined-up singers. Igesz, also facing them, was on his knees and on the qui vive for a movement cue. When Boky did not come off a held high note in time, Bernstein stared at her hard and said quietly, "You always do that." The soprano looked quite frightened. The conductor was also concerned with the movement pattern for the five singers, fearing that they would trip over themselves if they had to keep looking at conductor or prompter and walking at the same time.

Matters of pronunciation still caused trouble: the difference between "en" and "on"; Velis was saying, ungrammatically, "des jolis gens"; and Horne forgot to make the elision in "fort aise." "Have you been taught to say 'for aise'?" queried the maestro.

"No, darling, I'm making a mistake," snappily chuckled the tired mezzo. She put three "t's" in it the next time the word came up.

Matters such as timing when to sit and stand for the five needed precise working out. As the group moved about, Bernstein went with them, commenting on the delivery: "Perfect!" for one achievement, a pucker and silent kiss thrown when something else went as he wished. The pace was breakneck, an impression heightened by playing the tiny coda even faster. "You see," crowed the maestro when it was over, "they don't even know they've done it."

Igesz then suggested to most everyone's horror that Dancaïre deliver his line of dialogue right on top of the final note of the quintet. "But there'll be applause," someone rightly argued.

"The house is so sold out, we can't even pad it," added Carmen as she looked in her bag for some vitamins.

McCracken now made his "Dragon d'Alcala" entrance, after which comes that extended dialogue with Carmen, the lengthiest talk patch in the production. Uncertainty reigned again, but the pace was improving, as well as spirits, enough for Horne to interpolate a few measures of "Dove sono" when she couldn't find her castanets. Bernstein for the moment became dialogue coach and, with Igesz quietly looking on, *met-*

teur-en-scène as well. "No, Jimmy, it's never *Car*-men. Accent on second syllable." When Carmen asks José if he would like her to dance for him, his line is "Si je le veux?" "I should hope to kiss a pig's ass!" cried Bernstein, revealing definitively the burden of the soldier's reaction. "This is *the* theater scene, kids," the conductor continued. "We stand or fall on this."

Starting from the top, Bernstein suggested that Horne turn her back to the audience for her first words with McCracken. "Oh, I don't know," warily intoned the mezzo in a marvelous imitation of Birgit Nilsson's speaking voice. "We ladies from Sweden don't do that." She was working very hard, playful and jokey but also taut, even a little manic in her feverish responses to the rehearsal situation.

Rosalind Elias, who had been watching, during a brief pause in the dialogue mentioned that many of the line readings differed noticeably from Mme. Valin's instructions (Valin was not present today), to which Bernstein replied that line readings were not her responsibility in the first place. "I don't like her giving that kind of instruction," he went on record once more.

And again, and again through the dialogue, Horne breaking plates, a shard in its exuberance grazing but not harming assistant director Melano. It was now 5:45 P.M. Were they done for the day? Well, almost. The Act One set was still set up on the main stage. The fire curtain rose reluctantly, and Igesz led McCracken and Altmeyer through the blocking of their duet. Done.

Photo: Burt Glinn-Magnum

ladies of the chorus rehearse their lines in praise of smoking.

reographer Alvin Ailey ponders his next step as his dancers, with
id of mirrors, observe positions.

Photo: Burt Glinn-Magnum

Photo: Burt Glinn-Magnum

Josef Svoboda and Rudolf Kuntner check the lights.

Ailey beats out the rhythm for Carmen, Marilyn Horne; Frasquita (Colette Boky in tam) and Mercédès (Marcia Baldwin in slacks) back her up.

Designer David Walker prescribes for the dancing gypsies.

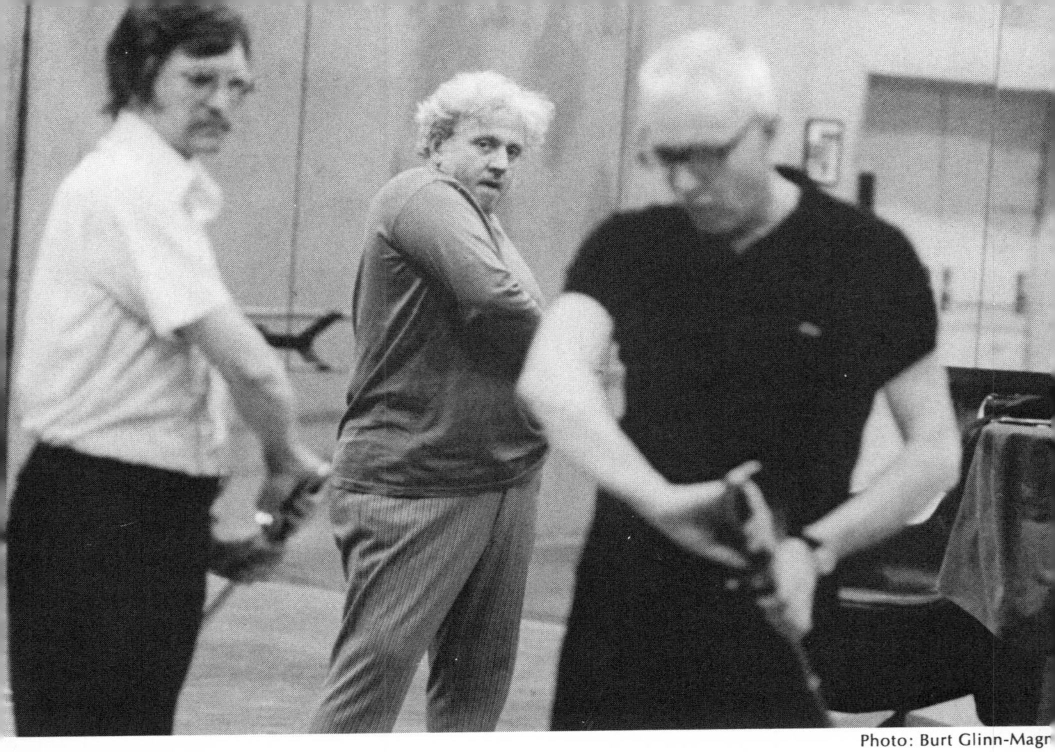

Photo: Burt Glinn-Magr

Tenor James McCracken learns how to draw his sword. *Left*, Don José cover William Lewis; *right*, dueling instructor Oscar Kolombatovich.

Conductor Leonard Bernstein and Horne discuss interpretation.

Photo: Burt Glinn-Magr

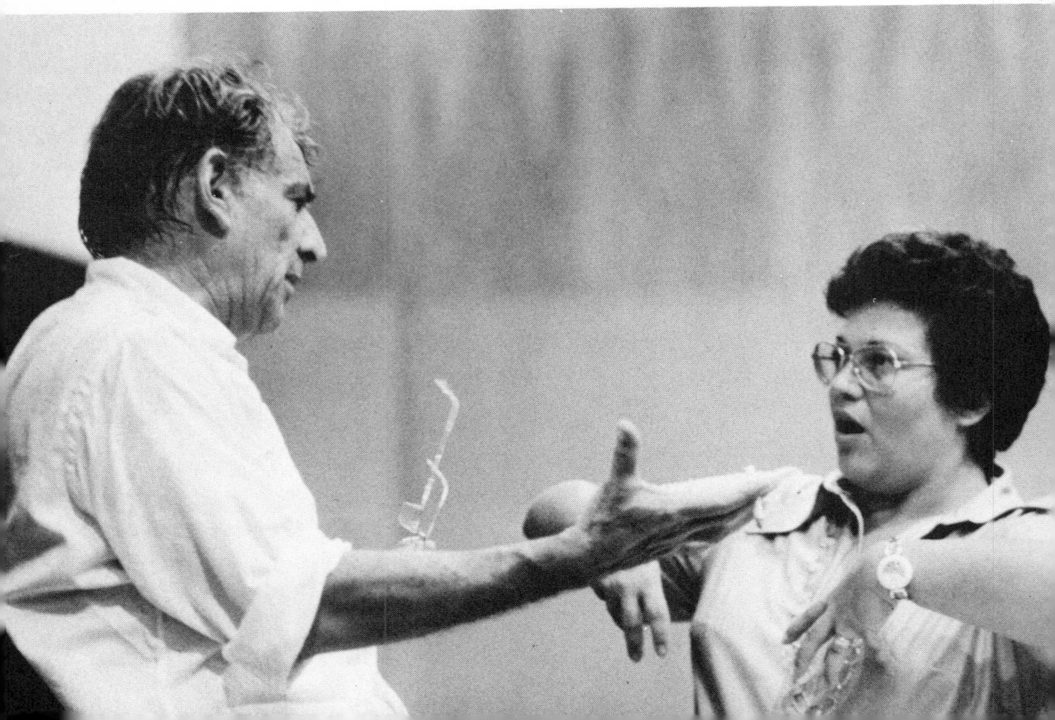

The maestro illustrates for the orchestra a moment of Toreador pomp.

hoto: Burt Glinn-Magnum

Photo: Burt Glinn-Magn

Director Bodo Igesz works with Micaela cover Jeannine Altmeyer and McCracken.

Photo: Burt Glinn-Magn

The *Sitzprobe* throng attends to Bernstein.

Photo: Burt Glinn-Magnum

Horne tries out the "Habañera" for her *Sitzprobe* colleagues.

Photo: Burt Glinn-Mag

McCracken executes the pianissimo final bars of the *Sitzprobe* Flower Song. To his left: Horne, Tom Krause, Andrea Velis.

Igesz arranges his smugglers around the Act Three disk.

Photo: Burt Glinn-Mag

Photo: Burt Glinn-Magnum

.e director demonstrates to McCracken how he wants Don José
react to a scornful Carmen (Act Three).

the pit assistant John Mauceri looks over the score with the maestro.

Photo: Beth Bergman

Photo: Burt Glinn-Magnum

Bernstein leads his soloists in a quick touch-up session before the curtain rises on a waiting set.

Photo: Beth Bergman

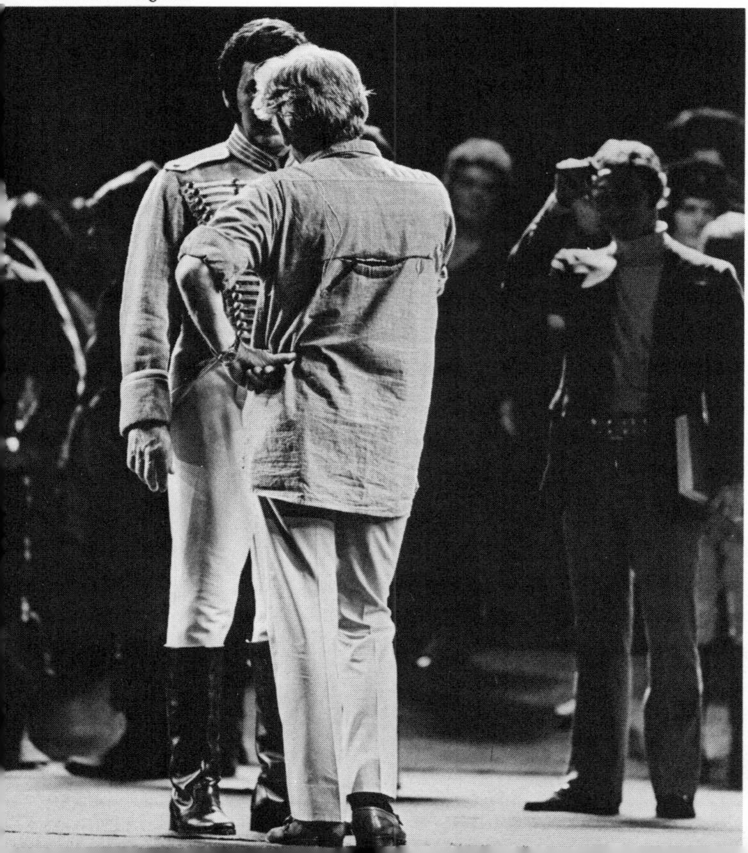

Bernstein, sporting his *Carmen* workshirt, comes onstage to make a point.

Igesz and Horne plot the Act Four Carmen-José duet while stage manager Stanley Levine uses a little body English on the crew.

Photo: Burt Glinn-Magnum

The silhouetted arms of Bernstein cue Don José's confession of murder.

Photo: Burt Glinn-Magnum

Photo: Burt Glinn-Magnum

The opening night conductor and audience sit for their portrait.

*

August 31

As though no night had intervened, Jeannine Altmeyer was still onstage as the Act One Micaela, this time being blocked in her exchange with Raymond Gibbs's Morales. Figures from every aspect of this production's life wandered about the stage, in the now open but still only piano-occupied pit and in the auditorium. Designer Walker took a few minutes to deplore the hideousness of the Metropolitan auditorium, admire the statuesque Altmeyer in what he called her "pre-Raphaelite" granny dress, and as a member of the older generation (he is thirty-eight), to lament the inability of young people to enjoy themselves. He seemed quite calm, even a little bored, pleased with the way the Met was carrying out his indications but not looking forward to the predictability of the weeks to come. He was happy finally (!) to meet Bernstein. Svoboda had returned to a hot New York from a hot Prague. Bernstein was keyed up about the orchestra *Sitzprobe* scheduled for the following day and concerned that preparations had gone this far without the opening night's Micaela and Escamillo: "I remember that glorious schedule—all principals to be here by August twenty-first."

The excitement of this day was manifest—the chorus in costume for the first time (principals still in mufti, however), and these clothes were to receive the full spectrum of the lighting plan. Svoboda admitted that the Act One set had had to be darkened because he was unfamiliar with the house's lighting facilities. He acknowledged that he was unhappy about the insertion of a prompter's box, which had, of course, been effected in his absence. He mentioned several German houses where he was accustomed to designing without having to cope with that obtrusive hole.

Louis Mélançon, taking a break from his photographic activities, looked on at the hubbub with all the bemusement of decades of experience and readily citable parallels. "In about ten minutes, when those stage lights go on, you'll have plenty to write about," he chuckled. "Wait till you hear those screams."

Meanwhile, in the "grabbed time" before starting at the top of Act One, Bernstein worked with McCracken and Altmeyer on their duet. Both seemed sluggish and excessively slippery in maneuvering their voices. Bernstein's purpose was to set the duet's tempi, which he had only worked on before with Boky and McCracken. He seemed not best pleased with Altmeyer, telling her she was holding the pace up and likening her vocal production to the "wa wa" effect of a trombone. Altmeyer accepted the criticism and on a repetition appeared well on the way to correcting these faults.

Igesz informed Bernstein that this mini-rehearsal, during which projections against the upstage wall nervously flashed in anticipation, would have to stop. Act One was to begin. The duet ended in mid-air, McCracken requesting a piano rehearsal sometime before the *Sitzprobe* to eliminate the remaining uncertainties. The house darkened, and the feeling that this was a new plateau in the pilgrimage to September 19 took over.

Hawkins called "Curtain!" and it began. But the launching had a limited reach. No one was in place to cue the chorus, and a halt immediately took place.

"Osie, don't bother to call curtain," instructed Igesz while Kurt Adler rushed forward to make sure the initial cue would arrive.

"Sing out," Adler pleaded.

"Bodo, do I have time to stop for musical things?" queried the conductor-in-chief.

"In a minor way," came the response.

"Gibbsypie," Bernstein later interrupted Morales, "you're getting faster. Remember the lazy atmosphere."

Bernstein may have wanted to stop for musical things, but he also worried, not surprisingly, about dramatic points. He questioned Igesz on the lack of a laugh from the observing soldiers on the exchange between Micaela and Morales ("Moi, je cherche un brigardier." "Je suis là. Voilà."). "They only laugh at *Tristan,*" comforted the saturnine Adler, who also expressed his dissatisfaction with Altmeyer's work. "Who coached this girl?" he announced more than questioned, loud enough at least for both Strasfogel and Masiello to hear.

Igesz's occasional instructions came over a loudspeaker from his mid-orchestra headquarters which he shared with lighting man Kuntner and other technical personnel. Bernstein for the first time was on the pit podium, though his entire orchestra consisted of young Don Foster and his amplified upright.

The inevitable children wended their slow way into position. Bernstein, purple tennis-shirted and nervously puffing on his cigarette, still commented on the dead dialogueless way in which this was done. In fact, everyone's entrance seemed executed at a snail's pace, completely without tension. And the dialogue, even from the first row, was barely audible, although Bernstein did maintain that his musicians in any accompanying melodrama such as the quasi-Hebraic one that underlines the Don José–Morales exchange would be more muted than was possible with an amplified piano. But where the dialogue was not low in volume, it was usually rushed or forgotten. As for cuing in general, Igesz broadcast a request for stage managers to be stationed in both wings.

The muted canary yellows of the soldiers was joined by the blacks, browns, and neutrals of the factory workers, some already walking with live cigarettes, and their male hangers-on. The drabness, the Germanic uniformity of the stage picture came through almost without relief. In fact, Marilyn Horne's red shirt worn outside her slacks provided the morning's first touch of color. The mezzo made her slow, upstage, stair-climbing entrance, obviously still concerned with the viability of her blocking. She walked through the measures of the "Habañera" introduction, but supers and chorus girls interfering with the sight lines had to be redeployed. Horne's positioning struck both Bernstein and Adler as too remote and hidden for comfort.

The lights, as Mélançon predicted, were getting a rise. Horne was making wide fanning arcs with her flower, while a sopping McCracken wanted to know who was going to pass out the salt pills. Even the carpet was reacting, some element in its fiber responding to the heat with a strange chemical odor that penetrated the empty auditorium.

The long "fate" cross of Carmen to José after the "Habañera" was still proving notably dead, and Altmeyer, followed by McCracken, flatted badly during their just-rehearsed duet. ("It's catching," groaned Adler. "This is impossible without musical rehearsals," Bernstein replied.) But for real confusion, they now had the fight on their hands. First, Bernstein forgot to give the initial cue, then, when it was given, the girls missed their entrance run, complaining that backstage noise interfered with audibility. Only Gramm seemed surer of himself in this sequence. Igesz wanted fewer soldiers on the guardhouse roof, but Bernstein and Adler feared that a smaller group would produce no sound at all (which was true). Girls, who in their rapid changes of position could not see the conductor, were told to watch the closed-circuit television monitors mounted in the wings.

"Sing it. Don't yell it," commanded assistant Stivender, who had jumped onto the stage.

Sighs emerged from the damp chorus as the overhead lights dimmed perceptibly, but the richest sigh came from Kurt Adler: "Labor has started."

Now that the girls got their entrance cue, they ran on with their "Au secours!" but could not find anything to do once they got there. A most unnatural stop, rivaled later in peculiarity by the sudden drop of movement when Carmen is led on by José. Was it a question of insufficient motivation, holes in the blocking, or the inability of attention to be strongly enough focused so that these moments of stylization could look intentional, even purposeful?

"They forgot the accelerando!" gasped Adler. "They knew it dead in the room, but with the action they forgot!" Carmen's tra-la-la's were overwhelmed by Igesz's instructions to the supers maintaining order among the girls. They did not escape the attention of Adler, however, who pronounced Horne "a cute little Rosina." A tired Stivender crossed the bridge into the auditorium. "What an opera," he muttered. The "Séguidille" skipped, the pushing finale was tried out, Horne and McCracken in place too soon, so that the shove came several bars ahead of time.

"It was either push or walk through the gates," Carmen defended her decision to act.

Act One costumes seen on a break's coffee line revealed themselves as remarkably detailed, appliqué effects on the gentlemen's jackets—black on black—and on the girls' bodices—off-white on off-white. Would any of this be seen from out front? Or was it necessary, in order to give a fabric some textural relief, merely to have it behave properly in the intense light?

One P.M. Tom Krause had arrived. Igesz now was compelled to repeat all he had done with Goodloe the day before so that at 1:30 the Finnish baritone could go on in the Act Two run-through. The director, waiting to begin, was in a dark frame of mind, stating frankly that he felt harried and pessimistic. "There just isn't time to tie up so many loose ends." He speculated, too, on what Gentele would have done at this pass in the preparations. Delayed the premiere? "He wasn't a fast worker, you know." Igesz had assisted Gentele during the 1962 Festival of Holland, so he knew more about the Swede's actual working pattern than probably anyone connected with the company.

"The trouble is," a rehearsal pianist offered, "the principals are not paid for rehearsals, so in a way it is up to them to decide when they should get here." The singers of smaller roles, the comprimarios, are on a weekly contract, so they are always and tightly on tap. "They're always overrehearsed."

Krause entered the C-level studio. Affable, blondish, somewhat resembling George London, and with a perfect command of mid-Atlantic English, he received Igesz's hurried Toreador Song plan with rapid-fire "Ah-hah's," as he grasped each point "But will people understand what these mimes of bullfight motions mean?" he queried, and was told about the chorus's planned reactions to his gestures. "Ah-hah! And where do I get the sword to kill the bull?"

"You conjure it up from space, from an imaginary assistant," Igesz told him.

"Ah-hah!"

Igesz then informed him of how he wanted the *coup de grâce* delivered right after the final "L'amour t'attend!" "You thrust," said the director.

Krause laughed, thinking it "a terrible Freudian symbol."

Then the two went through the whole business with music, Igesz and Melano taking turns as the imaginary bull. It was amazing how quickly Krause had the routine nailed down. His concentration was obviously of quite an acute order. His late arrival, it appeared, would cause minimal delay—very little once he learned his words of dialogue.

The little lights sprinkled across the undulating slats gleamed festively—"Like a pizza parlor," said one observer who was definitely not accepting them in the right spirit. They shone on the bare bodices of the ballet girls, jackets having been dispensed with. The girls' feet toyed with Lillas Pastia's carpet, Maureen Ting Klein, head costumer, adjusted a skirt here, Ailey brushed up a routine segment there. Act Two awaited. However, given the Krause situation, it was decided to begin with a quick run-through of the Toreador Song. Igesz stayed onstage for closer supervision. The preferatory dialogue, botched as usual, came and went, and then Krause and Bernstein spent a verse together hunting for a tempo, Stivender at the ready with instructions in case of any choral faltering.

For the end of the second verse Bernstein wanted the successive "L'amour" outbursts of Frasquita, Mercédès, and Carmen to be progressively slower. He called Krause over to him and repeated his notions about the aria's suavity, the double-dotted rhythmic emphasis of the verse. "It must be sexy, legato like a cello."

"Ah-hah!"

Act Two began properly now, the lights lowered to the right degree for Sevillean nightclub murk. There arose the question of whether or not Carmen would sing along with Frasquita and Mercédès on their tra-la-la's between the verses of the "Chanson Bohémienne." "Jackie, aren't you going to sing with them?" Bernstein asked.

"I don't know," admitted Horne (eventually she did not join in group tra-la-la's until the last time they come around).

The ballet looked quite messy, but certainly the unexpected darkness could at least partly account for this. Horne was particularly thrown during her rather intricate wandering during the explosive coda of the "Chanson."

Bernstein, ever alert to theatrical details, noted that a backstage work light was visible through the slats. He lost no time in drawing Svoboda's attention to it. Adler's attention, on the other hand, stayed on the chorus. When hearing their offstage cries of "Vivat!" before the Toreador Song, Zuniga inquires what the noise is all about. "Qu'est-ce que c'est que ça?" he says. "Nothing!" muttered the unsatisfied chorus master.

But Krause was already on his way to assimilating the Bernstein message. "Good!" cried the maestro when the baritone cautiously executed the double-dotting. "How about cutting the reprise of the introduction between the two verses?" Bernstein threw out, a suggestion which Krause declined, entering a plea that he needed these measures to get his breath back. "OK. You're the maestro." The conductor complied willingly as he undulated his hips in imitation of the fatuous pride he wanted the bullfighter to project. Upon conclusion of the aria (the Freudian plunge had not looked particularly meaningful—on any level) Miss Masiello received instructions from Bernstein about certain points she was to take up with Krause in a coaching session, and for the moment opera's best-known aria was left at that.

The first afternoon break came up very quickly, but it gave

Ailey a chance to pin down the "Chanson" steps for Horne, and for Igesz to take Krause yet again through the Toreador Song routine. Riecker and technical administrator Bronson made an appearance, admired the set, informed Bernstein that there was no chance, as had been hoped, of getting Maliponte for the *Sitzprobe,* and conferred with Igesz concerning what might be needed for a possible special Saturday rehearsal.

The break over, it was back to the Toreador Song, Krause oozing requisite suavity but losing the beat and being warned by Bernstein to watch for his cutoff signal. The conductor, however, missed a cue of his own when he failed to bring in the music for Escamillo's exit after the flirtation dialogue with Carmen. Boky *just* got her "de nous-de vous" business straightened out at the beginning of the quintet, which now had acquired a penumbral air from the dim lighting. Bernstein stopped them when the final accelerando windup went awry. Horne complained that they could not hear each other.

"You're too far away from each other," suggested the conductor.

"I suspect it's something else," rejoined Horne, her every word redolent of carpet reference—and Svoboda *was* in the house.

"Let's not go into that now," Bernstein quickly squashed the matter. Igesz requested a repeat of the quintet. *"O Dio,"* groaned the maestro, and the accelerando was still a mess. "I think there's too much movement, and they can't see me," Bernstein analyzed, again conferring with Masiello about her future work with the piece, especially pointing out the tempo relationships (again his point concerning the establishment of unity in the score) between the body of the quintet and the final faster reprise.

Now the dialogue devil raised his head again. Paul Franke, Lillas Pastia, did his bit of forgetting, closely followed by Horne, who read a line that had been cut. "Never mind," consoled Bernstein. "The spirit was there." McCracken worried that his offstage *a cappella* "Dragon d'Alcala" might be too loud, so Bernstein suggested that he turn his back to the stage for the first verse, then gradually turn forward to simulate his approach to the tavern. This the tenor did and entered, advancing on Carmen, but Horne this time forgot her opening line of this long spoken section, so that with nothing to stop him, the tenor comically marched right to the edge of the pit, and nearly into it. General laughter. McCracken and Horne ran a bit of the dialogue, the tenor suggesting that his line "Tu croques les bonbons comme un enfant de six ans" be restored to help them retain logical continuity. This was agreed to, but Carmen's dance and the Flower Song were skipped to the "Adieu pour jamais!" that precedes Zuniga's inopportune arrival. The stumbling block here was a literal one since no step had yet been put in to ease passage between the bar and the lower stage-left level.

"Oh that stupid step!" cried Horne as she awkwardly negotiated an ascent.

Finally, a musical question was considered, and it was that thorny one of Horne's high B and succeeding octave-and-a-half downward swoop on "La liberté! la liberté!" "If you're going to do that awful thing," reasoned Bernstein, "at least don't hold it."

"Can't *you* hold it?" Horne was not retreating.

"Yes," was the surprising reply. And she did it. Everybody's mouth fell open, half in admiration of the phenomenal vocal display and half in amazement that the conductor would permit such a trick, the kind that would do nothing but attract attention to itself as a piece of vocalism divorced from characterization.

"At this point we're going to insert an aria for soprano," the mezzo laughed, aware of the reaction she was getting and trying to minimize her victory.

*

September 1

Eighteen days to go. We were now in the same month as the first performance. A daunting realization! At 10 A.M. the big technical rehearsal got under way on the main stage, an hour before the important first meeting of voices and orchestra at the *Sitzprobe* in the orchestra room on C level.

A super stood in for Don José as the final light cues were being set for the spot on him during the "fate" section of the Prelude, the first note of this segment commanding the rise of the curtain. Kuntner, Svoboda, Igesz, and Melano were playing the big parts today, and the language was German. The Act One set itself was still being adjusted, with a pasty paint application going on the guardhouse to give it an effect of stucco. Projections on the *toldo* above the guardhouse and on the back wall flickered.

"*Prima,*" approved Svoboda.

"Attababy," Kuntner expressed to his crew leader.

The supers, stock still for long periods at a time or commanded into new trial positions, were melting in the heat. Kuntner at this hour was unusually calm, and Svoboda, as soon as a light cue was set, would go to his camera setup on a mid-auditorium tripod to record it for his own purposes. Much of the time he simply had to wait while Kuntner devised the technical means to achieve what was needed. This left him some moments for comments such as his desire not to create a "tourist picture" effect in this production and his dislike for the interior of the auditorium, especially for the gold proscenium which could not help but detract from the stage picture and always caused a light spill. "With all the beautiful theaters in America," he began, shook his head, walked away, and jumped onto the stage to supervise the guardhouse texturing. Too shiny, he decided.

Again the intense light evoked an odor response from the carpet. "That wasn't the only response," said Bill McCourt, the assistant stage manager. "When they were first turned on, it started to smoke."

"Hey, miss!" shouted Kuntner at a vigorously vacuuming cleaning woman giving the Dress Circle a once-over. "We have enough troubles without that."

Hardly another human being of any size could have squeezed into the orchestra room that morning. The orchestra itself took up most of the space, with soloists and choruses arranged on risers in back of them, covers and observers on a few commandeered chairs fitted in where possible; and those less fortunate or less official sat on riser steps, on the floor, or simply stood. The *Sitzprobe* (literally a "sit-down rehearsal," and the German word is always used at the Met), when all musical elements are assembled for the first time, is clearly a touchstone in the preparation, a synthesis without which a dangerous nothing.

For the occasion Bernstein wore his Japanese saki shirt and announced that he wanted to go through the entire opera without stopping. The Prelude began, the maestro strutting in time to the spirited allegro. For anyone in that room it was like being inside each instrument being played: immediate, electric, one's own body fusing with the intense sound. It was as close as an outsider could ever hope to get to being a part of a performance.

Gibbs's first Morales lines sounded very full here, his light baritone flattered by the limited space. Bernstein had a moment of difficulty in locating the exact spot where each solo voice would emerge, in their artificial arrangement, and his resolve to go through without stopping went out the window, if such there had been in this hermetic sound box, just before a visibly nervous Altmeyer's first line. One almost sighed with relief that he had not had to make the first stop for her, although he did caution her and Gibbs beforehand to stay in tempo during their mini-duet. The children looked excited, superattentive as time for their cue came, a cue which proved to be a trumpet stationed in the outside hall. The trumpet, however, really had no way of getting his sign until Stivender relayed it to him from the doorway. (Some singers, apparently less stimulated by the event of a *Sitzprobe,* passed the time reading newspapers: Gramm *The Daily News,* spread out on a covered drum, and cover Amara *The Armenian Reporter,* in her lap.)

The boys sounded assured but they slowed up, just as they had a tendency to do when they had to turn in their mock military maneuvers atop the guardhouse. "Kiddies, that's where it always happens," Bernstein stopped to tell them.

Only enough dialogue to cue an initial musical phrase was practiced, and while playing the introduction to the smokers' chorus, Bernstein looked up to beam a "Thank you, kiddies," at the departing urchins. The rushing ladies proved to be very un-*tutti,* and he went back so that at the conclusion of the *morceau* he could reward them with a "Perfect! That's it."

Amara, looking up on some new passage in the chorus, groaningly whispered, "It sounds so strange to hear all this different music." Clearly she was still unconvinced.

The Carmen arrival (in a white pants suit and aqua shirt today) did not get very far before Bernstein made some adjustments in the men's welcoming blandishments. "There is no change in tempo, men," he warned. The "Habañera" itself was nothing less than riveting, every eye in the room (and even an occasional camera popping up from under a trumpet case) on Horne, who today was in superlative form. Bernstein himself could not resist a "Sensational!" right in the middle of the first verse, his body shaking and his foot tapping *à l'espagnol* during the introduction to the second verse. Horne was giving it everything, thrillingly exaggering her chest tones in her second "Prends garde à toi!"—so much so that chuckles in the room welled up involuntarily. The very ending had to be repeated since Horne and Bernstein had not agreed on the cutoff which he told her she would have to take from him. It ended, and the room broke into fervent applause. "Tuhrrific!" judged the man on the podium, who had already complemented his saki shirt with a perspiration-absorbing red towel.

Altmeyer's big voice rose brilliantly if sometimes unsteadily in the José-Micaela duet, which was going much better than it had onstage the day before. Bernstein did not stop except to correct a triplet in the orchestra; Mme. Valin winced at some non-Gallic sounds from the California girl; and Amara patted her score, smiled up at the figure on the riser, and whispered, "I've always liked this part."

"We must try to avoid sentimentality here. We cannot slow down," Bernstein eventually interjected. McCracken ended the duet on a high pianissimo, but it was one which he could not hold. Bernstein said it happened because he ritarded too soon. "I may have to stand up or something," the tenor joked in his best falsetto.

The fight music broke over the room. Amara sang along, proudly acknowledging that she had sung these passages often in the chorus of the San Francisco Opera back in 1945. Krause smiled at the noise and Bernstein's obvious excitement, and Horne kicked up her heels as though they had been lifted by the will of sonic forces. But Gramm's first line of dialogue came out a jumble. The conductor looked at him quizzically. "Is that your Bar Mitzvah speech?" McCracken got all his words here, but they were hard to understand because of rushing and a tendency he had to give the consonants a very un-French, breathy, explosive pressure.

Bernstein indicated the beat for the "Séguidille," and its languourous spaciousness drew forth an audible "Oi!" from Horne. However, she managed the long phrases without any visible strain. The mezzo made a face of displeasure after the first verse, occasioned by reservations concerning what she had done. The second verse, if anything, was even slower. Again fervid applause upon conclusion. "We have to have two minutes at the piano for that" was Bernstein's only comment, and on Carmen's exciting "Habañera" reprise, which Horne did not at all seem to mind slowing down to an unexplored dimension, he looked at her and smiled. "Jackie, we may not make it by twelve-thirty." Act One did end, and moods seemed tremendously euphoric, with everyone congratulating everyone else and many comments on the order of "What a show this will be," etc. It was the first truly optimistic judgment on an important rehearsal in more than a week. McCracken, however, seemed to have a worrisome concern—not about himself, but about the gypsy: "Those slow tempi are great for Jackie," he commented, "but what will happen when somebody else has to sing it?"

People in the chorus not only were predicting that this would be the best *Carmen* ever but were talking about the general atmosphere in the house, the sharp increase in warmth that the brief brush with Gentele had brought about. One girl could not get over the fact that she, as part of a crowd, had been given detailed motivations in Act Four as opposed to the general attitudinizing of the Barrault production. Orchestra people expressed similar enthusiasm about Bernstein. "We're pros," said one, "and he's a pro too. You can't kid us. He makes hard things easy, like Karajan, and he makes old things new. I mean, who else would bother with tambourine dynamics?"

"He's learning," indulgently declared another player. "His *Cavalleria* was not good, but he's learning."

Just as Act Two was being set up in the technical on the main stage, Bernstein, now in a white shirt, prepared to begin its music in the orchestra room. "Now remember those imperceptible changes in tempo," he keynoted the attack on the "Chanson Bohémienne." It, too, on completion, got its quota of applause and a kazatsky "Hey!" from Bernstein, although Horne complained she still could not hear her colleagues. (No carpet here, folks.)

Nico Castel, covering Remendado, reacted to the upswing of the Toreador Song by sticking out his tongue, his excitement not leavened by the Boky-Baldwin mix-up on the "Vivat!" exchanges. Krause appeared to have completely assimilated all of Bernstein's wishes, and his voice came through rich and solid. "Marvelous! That's fantastic, Tom." The conductor handed out a gold star.

Franke, as usual, made everyone laugh with his exaggerated dialogue reading before the quintet, which, however, still showed its problems. "Sing! Sing!" prompted Bernstein, who insisted it all be repeated. "This is the hardest thing in the opera to do at a distance. And Andy: 'Dissssstingué.'" On the repeat the transition to the accelerando worked and got its Bernsteinian "Fantastic!" The next dialogue and McCracken's "Dragon d'Alcala" were passed over, Bernstein looking for his glasses to examine the score for Carmen's dance. "I'm so old," he grieved. "I never had to wear glasses before."

Horne's voice had taken on a miraculous lightness for the dance for José, on this occasion unencumbered by choreography or castanet playing, which today was done by one of the percussionists. This very difficult passage—on paper it looks so simple—was executed faultlessly by Horne, although Bernstein found the orchestra's strings in the measures that followed decidedly flat. McCracken's intonation, too, slipped at the beginning of the Flower Song, but he soon got hold of himself. The conductor stopped, however, for an orchestral correction. McCracken mistook the halt as caused by something he did. "Jim, that was terrific. I stopped the orchestra because they didn't remember that *'a temp.'* Why are you so full of self-hatred?"

They went on, Bernstein calling out over the orchestra to the tenor to keep the crescendo going and to the orchestra itself to make the line *"sostenutissimo."* McCracken ended the aria with the pianissimo high B-flat, actually not very well focused this time, but Bernstein wafted him an "I love you!" and the room rang with applause. "Keep that sinister beginning," the conductor instructed for the "làbas" section, and when it came to the end of the José-Zuniga duel, he threw a graceful, rather eighteenth-century gesture at Russell Christopher to key his "Mon cher monsieur" mockery.

Horne delivered her sixteen-octave leap on "La liberté, la liberté!" and Bernstein puckishly asked an astounded room, "How about that, fellas?" Actually this time Horne sang no words on the phrase, "la liberté" becoming "la-la-ah-ah." Associate conductor Jan Behr, who had dropped in for this bit of the *Sitzprobe,* shock on his face, turned to a colleague and wanted to know if Bernstein couldn't do anything about the interpolation.

A little confusion about whether a break should be taken between Acts Two and Three ensued, Bernstein becoming impatient and declaring that he did not want to waste a half-hour discussing whether there was or was not to be an interruption. The entr'acte to Act Three began, the French horns delivering many a wet fish. "I know that's hard," consoled the conductor, who did not stop. "We'll assume you've done it." The "Notre métier" ensemble, too, was off, each of the members having a separate notion about his double-dotted rhythm. "Chorus, watch the cutoff," warned Bernstein at the end. "Yours is different from the orchestra's."

For the card scene, Bernstein allowed no stops, calling out a *"sul ponticello"* to the violins but continuing so he and Horne could revel, most visibly, in the richness of the sounds they were making together. When it ended, a breathless Carmen told him that she did not know the last page of her aria would be so slow. Bernstein looked puzzled. "I was accommodating you," he said. "We'll talk about it later." The "douanier" chorus produced the usual effusive performance from the conductor, especially on his treasured "En avant, marchons! allons! en avant!" descending pattern.

Altmeyer stood for Micaela's aria, and an even finer grade of attention—mixed with some nervousness—permeated the room. The girl had a hard time finding the right beat, but Stivender, sitting near her, gave her supplementary cues. Amara pursed her lips in speculation. The always diplomatic conductor did not stop and pronounced at the end that Altmeyer was a "great girl" and that they had never worked on it together. The applause was warm.

Krause, on the other hand, now gave the impression of having rehearsed for at least three months with the conductor when it came to his intricate and somewhat (because of restorations) unfamiliar fight scene with José. "Tom, you remembered everything. You're fantastic," Bernstein beamed.

The succeeding ensemble turned up some difficulties: a too-fast Christopher, a late Horne on her discovery of Escamillo, and trouble in the cello section on the Toreador Song reprise. But Altmeyer came in like gangbusters when she, Micaela, is brought out of hiding. McCracken was relaxed enough to do a sort of sit-down pantomime of this highly dramatic end-of-act scene, his voice full and sure. Bernstein performed a veritable leap on the fortissimo triplet that closes the act and asked everyone, "Have you ever heard an orchestra play *Carmen* like that?"

"Never! Never!" came the response from all in the room.

The entr'acte to Act Four, if anything, increased the admiration everyone was feeling for the orchestra's work. Every soloist's, every chorus member's face (including those of the boys, who had now returned) was transfixed by what they heard being done to this possibly most colorful spot in the score.

Some adjustments were needed in the chorus for the opening of the act. Adler recommended that all tenors now sing both "Le programme" and "des évantails" and not just the first tenors, as indicated in the score. The intensity of the children as the combined choruses built was remarkable. The pressure at the fortissimo climax, "C'est l'Espada," was so overwhelming, that involuntary tears began to course down many an observer's cheek. Bernstein was perspiring profusely, but he was not so carried away that he did not stop Horne and Krause at the beginning of their duet to relate more precisely its tempo to what had preceded. He also requested, without missing a beat when the duet got under way, that the mezzo not sing any alternate notes here. "The others are so pretty."

"OK," agreed Horne.

Boky began the warning scene: "Carmen, un bon conseil"—and then forgot what it was she was going to counsel against ("ne reste pas ici"), but Bernstein cued her and built up to a furious accelerando (during which he nevertheless was able to dismiss the children) that culminates in the appearance of José. The duet went mostly well. Horne missed a "jamais," but she was also showing her sensitivity to words—smiling at her new one, "superflus." The effect of José's first "Tu ne m'aimes donc plus?" begun in near silence, electrified. Neither singer appeared in the least thrown or impatient when Bernstein would stop to give a direction to the orchestra, a sure sign that they were very much on top of their music. The hallway trumpets hashed, and the "new" measures at Carmen's stabbing had to be repeated, but Bernstein, in a tearful sweat, laid down his baton to many ovations. Exhilaration, exhaustion, but a very "up" day.

At 4:15, when the *Sitzprobe* ended, there was still time to look in on the technical rehearsal, or what was left of it. The supers were now moving about the Act Three tube, being either quietly respectful or, more likely, succumbing to fatigue. It was late and the last cue, number five, was set, giving both the dappled hung carpet and the floor one an even more mystical Bayreuth quality than before. "Give me work lights and house lights," Kuntner called out. "That's it for today."

Mme. Valin, who had sat through the entire *Sitzprobe,* came onstage to see Igesz. She was in a turmoil. True, that portion of the dialogue which had been heard that day did not exactly "detract" from the music. "Yes, the music is wonderful," she brooded, "but the dialogue doesn't exist. They think it's funny. They don't work." Igesz listened to her complaints while everyone else left the stage, Svoboda heading back to his hotel after these technical exertions. Nevertheless, he was not averse to taking some moments in a corridor corner to discuss the production. It seems that his first discussions with Gentele had taken place the previous fall in London. By the following spring he had made the set models in Prague and devised the light plan. He had also discussed with Gentele other projects—a *Katia Kabanova* and a *Boris Godunov*—for the future, but no specific contract was made for them. Instead he now had many commitments with the new Liebermann-Solti regime in Paris and with the Théâtre de l'Est there for which he was also acting as architect. (In the spring of 1973 it was announced that Svoboda would design and light the following season's Metropolitan revival of *I Vespri Siciliani.*)

The broad-cheeked Czech emphasized that his activities were far-flung geographically and in nature, being about 50 percent in opera and 50 percent in the legitimate theater. Of course he had done *Carmen* before, even in a production that had been mired in encrusted tradition, and to illustrate the point, he rose and performed a very unexpected mini-flamenco. He wanted to eliminate all operetta elements from his Metropolitan version and cited, like Walker, the influence of the Doré illustrations. He had nothing but praise for the Metropolitan's technical staff under the supervision of David Reppa, who generally has the task of translating design into reality. He was not surprised at the small changes that had been made, his long experience in opera having prepared him for this. He was definitely less thrilled with the house's built-in physical limitations, however. He particularly mentioned what he called the "antique" (!) lighting system which did not include reflectors and which did not allow for the satisfactory lighting of certain parts of the stage. Svoboda said he had known of some of these limitations while he was creating designs, but that the inadequacy of the lighting to achieve the illusion of depth through a "contra" system (sources high and to the rear) had surprised him. He was doing the best with what he had.

"And gold curtains are impossible, as is a gold proscenium," Svoboda continued. "A proscenium is bad enough, but a gold one! It should be painted black." At least he had succeeded in having the great outer swag curtains removed as long as his *Carmen* was the show of the day.

Svoboda was finding the *Carmen* experience rather special, to say the least. Compared with Europe, where he generally worked closely with the production's director, his contact with Igesz had developed into a fleeting thing. His exchange of ideas with Gentele had been quite general; basically it established that this was to be a production based on a stylized concept rather than a realistic one. "Fate has made handicaps for us all," he muttered, "but I know that the stage picture cannot be good unless the direction is as well." What the ultimate judgment would be he was not to witness, for in eight days he was to leave for another European assignment (*Boris* in Hamburg) and miss the premiere.

Asked about the great carpet controversy (someone had made a joking equation between the Svoboda carpet and the Richard Tucker rug—his toupee—that had caused Joseph Mankiewicz so much anguish when he had attempted directing that tenor years before in *La Bohème*), Svoboda seemed a bit startled. He admitted that he never mixed with singers, so he perhaps had not been aware of the undercurrent of antagonism to his floor coverings. "The carpet doesn't affect sound. I've used it before, and I always think of the acoustics. First of all, the carpet even helps a singer because it deadens the noise of moving feet, and in *Carmen* there are usually a lot of those onstage at any given moment. Secondly, singers are forward most of the time and I know the arcs sound makes. The carpet does not have a chance to absorb it."

Mr. Kolombatovich, the fight choreographer, passed by in discussion with Leonard Bernstein, the latter relaxed and unwound, joking with Kolombatovich on the appropriateness of his noble Yugoslavian name to his profession and the former stating his philosophy that stage sword fights should never look like duels.

Svoboda left, Kolombatovich retreated to the inner recesses of the dressing room area and Bernstein, with entourage, found his way to a waiting open car. Someone congratulated him on the success of the *Sitzprobe*. "Yes," smiled the maestro, "even I enjoyed it."

*

September 5

Perfidious Labor Day had deprived the schedule of a day of labor. It was Tuesday, Act Three was still set up onstage, and the omnipresent cleaning ladies were still doing their thing, over which racket Kuntner, from mid-auditorium, shouted such mysterious instructions as "Front blue two on center" or, looking at a light-absorbing super, "he's too far forward. We can't hit him with the tormentor."

And Svoboda was there to adjust: "Rudi, Rudi! *Etwas stärker.*"

Kuntner was in fine form for any 10 A.M. crisis: "What the hell's the matter with you? Kill the blue!"

But a voice of considerably more mellifluousness came into the middle of this quickie posttechnical technical. Adriana Meliponte had arrived. Exactly two weeks to go, and *Carmen* finally had its Micaela. Riecker kissed her warmly, and he and Igesz took her over the Act Three carpetings, the director almost immediately showing her the blocking for her big aria. Maliponte nodded agreeably at each point made, her version of Krause's "Ah-hah!" coming out "Si, si, va bene!" (Another language was added to the demands on Igesz—actually two, because Maliponte was able to switch from Italian to her fluent French but not to communicate too well in English.) Igesz, however, was tense today, and in an unusual burst of annoyance, turned to the various milling chorus members and technical crew who were casually occupying the set: "People, please clear the stage. This is not a kaffeeklatsch. I'm rehearsing!"

Bernstein, blazered, arrived and climbed up the tube to shake hands (no kiss?) with Maliponte. She then continued marking the aria while Bernstein discussed with Riecker the logistics of rehearsals: scheduling, switching, and all the breaks that would accompany them. Bernstein also mentioned his involvement with the upcoming Norton lectures at Harvard, another distraction for his energies. The conductor admitted that throughout his life he had had a hard time liking *Carmen*. "The only production I've ever enjoyed," he averred "is *Carmen Jones*." Which brought up another recent new *Carmen* staging, that devised by Regina Resnik, a great Carmen in former years, in Hamburg.

Riecker, certainly not by way of reassuring, told Bernstein that she had had a rough time, but that "she did her homework."

It was already 11 A.M. and the rehearsal had not started. Horne had not arrived, the milling on the stage continued, the quintessential crosser being a red-hatted and green-shirted porter who, someone said, in his thirty-five years with the Met had never put in an entirely sober day. Boky arrived wearing one of her jaunty tams, a new item in her carefully put-together and rarely repeated ensembles. Fortunately, Elias was present, so when it was decided to begin the act she became the morning's Carmen.

Again this was a costumeless, piano-in-pit rehearsal. The orchestra was not scheduled until the following day. Don Foster played the entr'acte, including a wonderful dissonance that had Bernstein laughing in approval. Entr'acte completed, the two men stopped to wait for the lantern signal light of the smugglers that was supposed to be simultaneous with the opening horn call. It did not come. Kuntner defended the no-show light by claiming that he had not been told about the cue relationship. The chorus, working its way down the tube, still needed considerable encouragement, especially in the almost unrelieved darkness, which today also had McCracken concerned. One chorus member spoke up: "Bodo, we need light on that stairwell [leading at the back to the top of the tube]. It's murder." Hawkins reported that the chorus refused to come up the stairs without lights. Everything stopped.

The break gave Mme. Valin a chance to comment on McCracken's machine-gun approach to his dialogue. "They all have to slow down. The problem with singers is that singing and speaking involve two different kinds of voice production. I wish I had more time with the principals." The *Carmen* leitmotiv again—time.

Adler shadow-conducted behind Bernstein when Act Three set off again, sitting near enough to Valin to query her about some pronunciation. "Plaît" does not rhyme with "play," he discovered.

The card trio was interrupted several times by Bernstein (more staccato for Frasquita and Mercédès, "like a snake" for Elias). Elias did not attempt to deal the cards, but she did sing at full voice. Igesz rearranged some observing chorus people around the disk and warned the others then onstage to be sure to stay behind the staircase far upstage where they could not be seen from the auditorium. No walls, no flat surfaces here behind which to conceal oneself.

Mme. Valin now got her chance to interrupt when Christopher missed a line of dialogue. "Take your time, Monsieur Christopher. If you push it, we can't understand it." Both Igesz and Adler took great exception to the work the chorus was turning in, the former over his midway mike telling them to do anything but stand in line, the latter popping up from his front-row seat, leaning forward, and shouting "Tenors!" when he could not hear them. They also appeared to have forgotten all about their taunting of José on the mass exit at the end of the "douanier" chorus. And Boky missed a cutoff again.

"Good morning, Jackie," Bernstein welcomed Horne.

"The tunnel was backed up to Kalamazoo, Michigan," offered the mezzo from mid-stage as Elias handed over the death-dealing pack of cards.

Igesz directed the group to begin at the top of Act Three but to skip all dialogue because this set had to be struck by 12:30 if they hoped to get to Act Four after lunch.

"Pianissimo!" Adler loudly cried to the chorus on their opening, but Bernstein was more concerned about their rushing. McCracken seemed to be having a good time with his prop rifle, this object and interest in its handling carrying him through so much of the action where he played a very passive part. Maliponte merely marked her aria, but Bernstein was concerned if her first words, uttered, as they were, at the top of the tube, would be heard. Adler seemed to think it would be no problem.

Krause was next to appear tubetop, but Igesz halted the action to make sure that both José and Escamillo get onstage together and at the same time after Micaela's exit. *"Bonjour,* Krause," called out the very well-tempered conductor. "You were terrific the other day. You learned so much overnight." The baritone and tenor *did* do their dialogue, because most of it occurs over an accompanying orchestral melodrama. McCracken was still having difficulty with his words, Krause not, the equation being reversed when it came to the expanded fight music. It was as though all security went up that ramp and hid at the bottom of the staircase. A hole indeed. Mme. Valin put in a pronunciation correction on José's "Tu m'épargnes, maudit," but an impatient Igesz broadcast a request not to stop for such things now. Bernstein, however, did get a chance to get off one of his very personal lines of interpretation to Krause: "I'm not in the man-slaughtering business. I'm in the beef-slaughtering business." With such a mnemonic device installed, who could ever forget his words? He was equally good on motivations a few minutes later when Escamillo kisses Carmen after his generous bullfight invitation is issued: "Meet you at the hotdog stand near gate three."

The fight itself had only been sketched, but the two men tried a very tentative roll down the incline, a difficult business, with McCracken having to make sure his weight did not rest directly on the baritone every time he came up on top. Bernstein looked on anxiously, mostly concerned about Krause's breath supply during this. After a repeat of round one, where a charging José is temporarily put out of action by Escamillo, McCracken hit the deck with such energy that he bounced down the side of the parabola for several feet.

"Bodo, only ten minutes to break," called out Hawkins, as ever stationed at the proscenium stage right, guarding the bridge into the auditorium.

The chorus, *walking* in to break up the fracas, certainly had not caught McCracken's sense of truth, and Horne, probably still put off by her harrowing commuting problem of the morning, flubbed her Micaela discovery line. Maliponte was led through her stage movements by Igesz for the rest of the scene as it proceeded without break until the chorus's sullen exit. This too was a rather strange bit of collective business set to take place during Escamillo's offstage "big tune" reprise. Just as the tension between Carmen and José built to an unbearable pitch, for some reason this group of onlooking smugglers was to lose interest in the conflict and walk off to leave the heroine alone clutching her cards, perfectly framed for the blackout and curtain. It *was* a nice picture, but again one which could not withstand the application of too much logic.

Krause's voice came over loud and clear, so his placement in the wings had to be changed. Hawkins called the break, and Maliponte, in French, addressed herself to the man on the podium: "Please excuse me, maestro. I'm tired today, so I do not sing. Now I will have a sandwich." Act Three was rolled away.

Don Foster sat at his piano pit post, reflecting that to him it seemed that the recent and brilliantly successful new production of *Tristan und Isolde* had been easier to put together than this *Carmen*. For one thing, there now seemed less time available to take care of the complications.

Igesz addressed the chorus, already in their curtain-up Act Four positions: "I did not like Act Three this morning. We have little time, so we must not waste a second. Keep in character at all times, and when you are not onstage, assemble in the back.

"We are not just doing another production," he continued this strategic pep talk. "Please forget that you have been doing operas season after season after season. I think we can agree that we owe that at least to Goeran Gentele." He then once again outlined the blocking for the opening.

Adler conducted the piano, Bernstein now being closeted with Maliponte. The downstage pointing-out of the parade was going in all directions. Igesz wanted everyone to get where he was going much faster, at least once the excitement of the arrival of the bullfight participants was supposed to become an influence, and Adler held out for more voice. Stivender ran from children to the on-high, in-the-bleachers choristers to tell them for Adler ("personally") not to joke and laugh.

The children forgot to crowd around the Alguacil, another very mysterious bit of staging because it was almost impossible to suggest why the urchins disliked this official. The problem was not aided subsequently when this character, who stops for a minute, proclamation in hand, before being "A bas"-ed off the stage, was not given a costume that could lend him even a marginally offensive air of authority. Igesz just had the time to get the banderilleros in formation before Hawkins announced the imminence of a five-minute break and that wedges were needed to prevent some of the platforms from "moving out." Svoboda rushed to the stage to inspect the problem, and Igesz got in one last "Move!!!" for the climactic "C'est l'Espada," with here some girls, now balanced on the hitching post, craning for a look at the splendid Escamillo with his equally splendid date.

Igesz, however, had no break. Gibbs happened to wander across the stage, and the director grabbed him to tell him how to do Morales's Act One commands to the troops; then Igesz himself received some instructions on the correct way of carrying banderillos.

With the chorus watered and refreshed, the action picked up again from the beginning of the Carmen-Escamillo duet, the one on which everyone turned his back. Very unpredictable in their interest, these chorus people. Igesz explained their exit into the bull ring, which, along with the appearance of the Alcade, was marked with some restored music. "Once in the stands, people," he called out, "give the impression that you are watching the bullfight by singing upstage, and lean forward so we can see your heads."

"And another Micaela just bit the dust." Bernstein had returned.

"What?" gasped an alarmed Horne.

"No, I mean I just went through everything with her."

Now that Bernstein was back on the podium, Act Four began anew. The conductor found that the promenading chorus was getting behind, and he told them to cheat looks at him or to watch him on the monitors. The subdivided sellers sounded most tentative, the maestro himself confused as to where each one was located so he could cue them. A line had to be changed: "Merci, mon officier" to the plural because there were now several participating in the buying and selling of oranges, lorgnettes, and so on.

The hot lights had not slowed the chorus down enough for Igesz's taste. He still wanted a more leisurely pacing before the advancing parade, whose announcement by the children came after the rather dead-spot run they executed to get into position. Horne and Krause, sitting in the orchestra, were caught by surprise by their upcoming cue and raced across the bridge to reach offstage battle stations, but unsurprisingly, it was time for another mandated ten-minute chorus break. The pleasure of their repose was somewhat undercut by Igesz's announcement that he wanted to continue today until 4 P.M. General groaning.

Rosalind Elias was not set to do a *Carmen* until the second half of the season, and then only one, the last of the season. (The death of her father deprived her of this performance.) She looked on at these rehearsals with no apparent bitterness, always availing herself of any opportunity to declare how fabulous she thought Horne was. She could not quite muster such a confident look, however, when she mentioned that Michael Tilson Thomas, the young wizard from Boston and Buffalo, who at that time was still scheduled to lead the spring *Carmen*s, had never before conducted an opera. (After Thomas's cancellation, Frenchman Roberto Benzi, at the house for *Faust,* was approached. He declined, and the assignment fell to Henry Lewis, Horne's husband. Benzi, incidentally, is the husband of Jane Rhodes, the only other Carmen Bernstein ever worked with. See the later description of the *Carmen* television program.)

Horne still sang the alternate roles in the duet with the bullfighter, but Bernstein did not stop her, finding much more meat for improvement in the chorus's subsequent *a cappella* greeting of the Alcade. Frasquita and Mercédès still encountered mighty difficulties in weaving their way through the crowd to warn Carmen about her ex-lover, and Horne forgot that her checking on this information was to be effected with a single look. Her circling seemed orderly, but she undercut whatever impression it was supposed to make by an unfocused smile. The lights were producing real perspiration from the mezzo as well as from the always damp tenor, whose French today seemed also dampened by the temperature. Horne's pitch fled her on "Jamais [G-sharp] je n'ai menti," and McCracken was plagued by an oversupply of spittle. And just to keep itself an active issue, the carpet tripped up Carmen on the turn, ending her immobility, of "Libre elle est née." The prop man ran in with a fan, which was put to good use.

"Nothing!" cried Adler when the offstage chorus could not be heard on its first interruption. Bernstein wondered what could be done about making them more audible. Igesz suggested that the chorus people placed on stage level be moved into better positions, but Adler thought that only a jump to their feet by those in the stands would help. Igesz wanted to save this visible excitement for later. "They just weren't singing at full capacity," he decided. "Standing won't help. They're just insecure." On a repeat the "Vivat!" exclamations *were* better, but the important "Victoire!" (marked triple forte), before Don José resumes his chase, was barely perceptible. They went on, Bernstein apparently more concerned about trying to build a sense of continuity.

Carmen has a high A-flat with a *fermata* ("Je répèterai que je l'aime!") just before the chorus's next distant outburst. In fact, her final mute "e" comes right on their first "Vivat!" Horne reached the note and enjoyed it mightily, but Bernstein went right on, cutting her off. "Eeeek!" she screamed, half comic, half panicky. "You wouldn't do that!" He nodded and went on conducting. When it came time for the chorus to sing the Toreador Song reprise when Carmen is stabbed, they were no more audible. Bernstein announced, "Now that tune they know," thus putting an end to the "security" theory as a rationale for inaudibility.

McCracken's "Vous pouvez m'arrêter" was addressed to only that one row of outside figures who, as one, turned heads from the killing in the ring to the murder outside. It seemed only a barely more motivated line than when José is forced, as in some productions (that of the New York City Opera, for example) to address no one at all. Certainly the crowd could stream out through those upstage gates and do some proper looking on. As if to make up for this lack of *verismo,* McCracken cut himself on his knife (he was quickly brought a prop substitute) and Horne practiced her fall. The heat from the lights crept out over the pit and into the auditorium.

Back to the first cries of "Vivat!" When that A-flat came up again, Horne held up her arm and like a traffic policeman tried to delay the cutoff. No dice. "I'm trying to keep this thing going," the conductor said without missing a note. Something went wrong on the cuing of the chorus at the moment of stabbing, however, producing a humorous effect as if her reaction to the knife was a three-part choral exclamation. McCracken, confused, asked Bernstein about his blocking here. "I know nothing about the staging," he said, for the nonce resigning responsibility.

Horne was smiling as she stood up from corpse position, but her plea for her high-note extension was deadly serious. "I'll give you a beautiful *portamento* and signal when I'm through," she bargained, to which Bernstein replied that he had already given her a full bar extension on it. They tried the phrase, and again he came in with the "Vivat!" before she was through. Horne drew herself up and filtered through what was targeted as a laugh: "If you cut me off, they'll think I can't sing, or they'll think you can't conduct!" And offstage she walked.

Kolombatovich was rhapsodizing over McCracken's idea for the roll down the tube in the Act Three fight. "That kind of willingness to try things, that inventiveness, is so extraordinary in a tenor. Be sure to mention it."

It was now after 4 P.M., and a sopping Marilyn Horne but considerably drier Colette Boky and Marcia Baldwin descended to the C-level ballet room for another go at the "Chanson Bohémienne."

"Snap, turn, snap," called out Ailey as the three went through the routine.

"You know, Horne is really very graceful," remarked one of the minuscule-waisted dancers.

As if to contradict her on the spot, the mezzo mimicked the bumping and grinding Ailey was showing her. "Oh come on, Alvin. I can't do that," she guffawed, as she rapped him in the tummy with the back of her hand.

Frasquita and Mercédès were having mostly a traffic problem, as seemed to be always the case with them, the cross-stage exchange with the dancers not yet cleared up.

One time through. Ailey looked at Horne, and as if reading her mind, questioned, "And what was that all about?"

"Alvin, I'm worried about ending up in the dark" (her end-of-dance-on-chair stage-left position).

"Then we need light over there."

"There's either too much or too little," the mezzo sang to the tune of a song with a similar message, which signaled a time-out for the two to serenade each other with excerpts from *Carmen Jones*. Horne, of course, had done the sound track for Dorothy Dandridge back in 1954, and Ailey reminded her that he too had been in a production in the earlier days of his career.

Ailey wanted Horne to throw her arms straight up into the air at the end of the dance. "Alvin, my arms are too short for that gesture," she demurred. Ailey went about altering some of the corps patterns ("He keeps changing it," groused a chorine), and Horne caught her breath on the sidelines. "I've never rehearsed so much on things that don't count," the mezzo remarked. "And now we've got to rehearse evenings. [That night a very private session on Act Two between Horne and McCracken; union clearance came through in the nick of time.] The chorus and ballet are rehearsed thoroughly, but the individual scenes are not. They're going to think I'm the bitch of the world. Every day I've got a new gripe. The lights? The lights are impossible and the costumes heavy, heavy."

Accompanist Irving Owen helped Horne straighten out her syncopated tambourine slaps, and Ailey got a not-unwilling Boky to shake her hips. Horne looked exhausted, but the high notes kept coming and the room shivered with their beauty.

Costume man Charles Caine raced down a corridor. "McCracken has twenty minutes for an Act Four costume fitting," he gulped. "What a gruesome time."

Charlie Riecker sighed. "The cast is all here, but we need more time."

*

September 6

An orchestra in the pit! And that was not all. The big asbestos curtain, in place, separated this new gathering, plus most Act One soloists on folding chairs, from what was going on on the stage itself—a piano rehearsal with chorus, supers, and children plus Morales and Micaela. Horne's husband, conductor Henry Lewis, was among the onlookers as the mezzo and McCracken went through some light warming up.

Bernstein, looking glum, removed his jacket in the hot auditorium and proceeded to adjust some of the orchestral seating arrangement. "Is everybody reasonably comfortable?" he inquired. "I find it hard to concentrate after that beautiful news this morning. [The kidnapping and murder of the members of the Israeli Olympic team had occurred the day before.] Bastards!" His voice was tight, infinitely bitter. "Want to do a little dialogue to pick us up?" he asked Horne and McCracken.

They began with the pre-"Séguidille" segment, the rehearsal on the other side of the curtain a detectable background. When the orchestra finally came in on the "Séguidille" introduction, a smile crossed Horne's face and she could not resist beaming. "It's heaven!" It did not get very far, however, before Bernstein called a halt and asked for the beginning to be done at about one-third the sound level at which both Horne and the orchestra were pitched. Horne looked concerned, tucked her shirt down around her hips and ran her hands through her short coiffure, and then launched into the aria again. Bernstein liked it, especially the end, but the mezzo was worried there about a French horn crescendo. "It can do me in."

"No, no. Let me be the judge of that," the conductor dismissed her concern. Maliponte, her dark hair cascading around her shoulders, emerged from behind the asbestos to run through the José-Micaela duet. She was on to Bernstein's insistence that the first lines of dialogue get out before the last plunk-plunk of the previous segment's windup, but her voice fluttered unattractively whenever it went much above an F. She phrased very attentively. Not so the strings this time, for the maestro cautioned them not to make rough *sforzandi:* "Make them lyrical, beautiful left-handed ones." He approved of Maliponte. "Perfect! *Una piccolina cosa:* a little crescendo. *C'était très bien.*"

"Thank you, maestro."

McCracken did receive some attention too. Bernstein wanted to know if a certain diminuendo in the duet was hard for him to make without going falsetto. It seemed it was, and McCracken said he would throw his voice into the wings to get the right dynamic effect and at the same time watch the conductor via monitor. The duet ended with both Maliponte and McCracken apparently in nicely sensitive agreement with each other and with Bernstein, who rewarded them with an enthusiastic "Lovely!"

Associate Strasfogel: "The orchestra always complains about the size of the orchestra pit. Even though this one in the new house is much larger than the old one, the first thing the orchestra said about it was that it was too small."

Observing Carmen cover Rosalind Elias: "I can't get the stage action by just sitting out front and watching. I need a stage run-through."

"Maestro, we're ready." Hawkins came forward after a half-hour to announce the imminence of the Act One curtain. Chairs were whisked away, the asbestos raised. The house was in darkness. The swagless curtain rose on the fate motive.

"Where's the special effect?" called out Bernstein. No light had fallen on the immobile José. "I thought that was the light cue. Bodo, isn't that the cue?"

"No," came the answer from mid-hall. "It's now a fade-in

on the next music. We can't get the chorus on fast enough to bring lights up on that chord" (the A Major one just before the fate motive begins).

"Oh, Jesus, let's go on," muttered a somewhat perturbed Bernstein as he took up his baton and simultaneously indicated to his assistant, Mauceri, that the matter merited further discussion.

Gibbs quickly got behind, as did the chorus on the first sung measures. Bernstein wondered if it was an acoustic problem and cautioned that all had better *watch* for their cues and the beat rather than *listen*. "The distances are too immense for that," he summarized. The "look rather than listen" admonition was one Bernstein kept renewing until the final recording session.

The eyes of forty people saw Igesz now run onstage to modify the Micaela-Morales blocking. Bernstein wondered again about the absence of laughter from the soldiers when Morales offers himself to Micaela as a substitute "brigadier" for José, but Igesz held on for the elimination, and the maestro was strongly distracted by the strings' difficulty with what they have to play just before the laugh or no-laugh bit comes. It took many repeats to iron out that descending triplet figure. The orchestra was definitely sounding less impressive now than it had at the *Sitzprobe*.

The chorus and orchestra found it difficult to stay together. The children were now rushing where previously they had dragged. Bernstein stopped. "I don't know what to tell you, kiddies, except to watch." Soldiers were late to pick up their marching cues. Igesz therefore drafted himself and strode with them. Gibbs's dialogue was inaudible, and he was allowing plunk-plunks, or at least the trumpet equivalent of them, to end before beginning it.

"So far," announced the conductor, "everything has gone wrong—not an entrance, a light cue, or a tempo. Only the recitatives, and they don't exist," he added as a sort of gesture toward gallows humor. Miss Masiello added her note of bad news by telling him that the trumpets were making a terrible echo in the hall, much worse than usual. This was not growing into an altogether happy day.

Morales spoke up, and the balance with orchestra was better, but as if to counter this improvement, the children went sufficiently haywire for Bernstein to dub their participation a disaster. McCracken suggested to him that it might help if the children picked up their feet and put them down again in rhythm. "Tell Bodo that," advised the conductor, now in addition worried about an onstage trumpet that, pointed upstage, was not coming through. He too, positioned behind the guardhouse, would have to get his cue from a monitor, but Igesz said that there was an assistant conductor stationed there to give it to him. The problem, when it was finally analyzed, proved to be that the man charged with this music simply did not as yet know it very well.

The repeat of the urchins' chorus was better, but when atop the guardhouse they were supposed to turn and do their military maneuvers in another direction, they and the orchestra parted company. Adler stated that you just could not move children around that way without asking for trouble. Bernstein went on, Stivender asking him if he wanted the children to remain. "Ask Bodo," was his answer.

Valin called out to Gramm and McCracken not to rush their Zuniga-José dialogue. Bernstein noticed the cigarette girls lurking upstage waiting all too visibly for their entrances, but the "fumée" chorus, when it came, went well, uninterruptedly continuing, except for blocking adjustments, right into la Carmencita's arrival.

"Bodo!" It was Horne's voice. "I don't think we can have these gates." (Svoboda was in the house.) "I can't see." But Bernstein here was more anxious about the chorus's visibility problem, again sounding the "gotta watch" theme.

Horne really did appear to be buried behind supers and chorus for this pre-"Habañera" segment (and even for the first part of the aria), and she tried to adjust the blocking around her to make it more comfortable for herself. She quickly lost touch with what was going on in the pit. "I just can't hear back there," she informed Bernstein between verses, but he was also busy reminding the strings about a rest they had been ignoring.

The lighting during the "Habañera," with its sudden switch-over from flooding sunlight to spots to pick out Carmen and José, gave one the odd feeling that an eclipse had suddenly struck Seville, but obviously this tactic was necessary if any focus was to be kept on the long, fateful flower-throwing cross which follows the aria. The eclipse only lifts when José receives the bloom on the chin or, as on this day, when he sees it sailing past him stage left. Horne would have to put in some target practice.

A little real-life drama not scripted by Mérimée was meanwhile unrolling backstage. Jeannine Altmeyer, the girl Bernstein had praised for her courage, was taken off first cover for Micaela. Amara, who said Gentele had not wanted her in the part because her voice was "too mature," was replacing her, although, unlike Elias, she was not scheduled to sing in any performance. (One of Amara's colleagues said she could never do this Micaela because there were three things different from the past production in her blocking. This turned out not to be correct: when Stratas again canceled the spring Micaelas, Amara did them all.) It was a cruel disappointment for the beautiful young Altmeyer, who, when encountered backstage, could not succeed in concealing her tears at this latest denial of advancement in her career.

Maliponte's Micaela, it could be seen from her work so far, would not be very different from the traditional pallid pigtail-and-basket interpretation. At this stage in the game it would be very difficult to make it otherwise. Her dialogue voice now in the Act One meeting with José seemed very small, but musically the scene went smoothly enough. Like the other latecomer, Krause, Maliponte was a quick learner. Her aplomb only disappeared when at the end of the duet she forgot where she was to exit.

And then the catfight. The girls started slow, bringing from Bernstein yet another admonition to watch him. "Eyes, not ears!" That ring-'round-the-rosy effect of soldiers encircling the two groups of partisans still disturbed and stopped all movement. Bernstein looked at the stage and shouted a desperate "Activity!" and, turning to Mauceri, judged that perhaps six months with Walter Felsenstein (the notoriously slow-working, meticulous director of the East Berlin Komische Oper) might fix things up.

Stivender was getting excited, but Adler for once defended his crew. "David, it's no use. It's not their fault," to which his assistant replied that the mess had to be fixed just the same.

Bernstein said he wanted to go back, to the beginning of the act preferably, but time pressed, and if they were to get to Act Two that day, they would have to continue. Horne's mid-brouhaha entrance from the factory still resembled King Philip's stately advance in the Auto-da-fé scene of *Don Carlo* more than the arrest of a tigerish gypsy, but today Gramm's Zuniga had begun to take shape and his jokes no longer seemed needed to divert attention from lack of preparation.

The scene continued until Carmen's upstage enemy was supposed to screm "Oui, c'est elle!" and run and attack her. Horne cupped her hand to her ear. No "Oui, c'est elle!" Her concentration seemed off as she cut into some of José's lines during the dialogue, and Bernstein and she were not in harmony concerning the "Séguidille" tempo. A little dancing, however, now made its debut during that aria, about which Amara wondered whether or not it would be heard at all, so quiet did it seem to her.

Bernstein cut into Horne's languorous, teasing "Prends garde à toi!" with its chest trumpetings that Fernando Corena mimics so devastatingly when the two singers apply themselves to the horseplay in Act Three of *Il Barbiere di Siviglia.* And his baton swept the act to a close. The curtain fell slowly, reaching the stage floor long after the baton had come down. "Late curtain," Bernstein pronounced.

"That's the fastest it can go, maestro," Hawkins informed him.

"Then it has to start earlier."

Tom Krause's mother to her son while snacking in the Opera Cafe, at last open to the artists during the day: "Now what is the name of the girl singing Carmen?"

Bernstein had to begin the entr'acte to Act Two twice because he discovered that the players had a tendency to anticipate his beat. The bassoon and clarinet echo in the virtually empty theater was ferocious. The conductor, without stopping, looked at the set and pronounced it "sensational." Thus encouraged, the act produced an opening dance which, if not entirely solid in its routine for the singers as yet, at least was beginning to look like something. (It was accompanied by a mid-theater discussion, quite energetic, between Svoboda and Kuntner.) Bernstein did not stop even when Krause fell below tempo and pitch during the Toreador Song. "No ritard!" called out the conductor as he continued. The quintet, too, tended to drag at the beginning, but he got the group back on the track. The number was stopped midway, however, so Bernstein could tell them to move their chairs into place (the quintet had something of a lined-up "reading" look to it) before getting into the more complex part of the ensemble during which they should watch him. On the repeat their togetherness proved of stronger stuff, the singers reacting well to each other and perhaps even a little more at attention now that photographer Mélançon was behind his tripod in the auditorium, snapping away at these scenes of preparation. Velis at least was certainly deeper into his swishy characterization, having inadvertently described himself as being "amoureuse."

The succeeding dialogue between José and Carmen (McCracken skipped his high G at the end of "Dragon d'Alcala") did not go so well, although Horne's frenetic (on purpose) search for her castanets and her use of a plate (today mistakenly pre-broken) to replace them got a good round of giggles from everyone watching. Her dance here looked quite convincing, Bernstein cheering from the podium and throwing out some mock-sexy encouragements which she could not hear but which amused everyone else no end. The dance left the mezzo out of breath, but the scene was moving along well, climaxing with the near-strangulation that occurs before the Flower Song. This bit of action, while quite in character for the excited and violent José, could not help but recall the end of Act Three of *Otello,* as recently staged by Franco Zeffirelli, when Iago bends over the fit-stricken Moor and barely restrains himself from choking him. It was a highly controversial moment of direction for the Verdi work, one which was omitted in the production's second season by one baritone, although Sherrill Milnes, the first Iago, restored it when he returned to the role. At this not very distant remove it would seem that the gesture, when repeated in *Carmen,* just might stand out for all the wrong reasons. Undeniably valid, but risky.

McCracken sang his aria sensitively, but fatigue was taking its toll and many attacks emerged as excessively slippery. Pitch slipped too, and then the tempo's essential pulse began to elude him. Still, the end was gloriously real, tremendously affecting, quite a testimony to this tenor's ability to concentrate his energies and create illusion, especially when one realized that one was no longer noticing his physical amplitude. ("Why do you think McCracken is so fat?" Amara had rhetorically inquired a few days earlier. "It's all the potatoes and spaghetti he ate while he was a poor singer in Europe.")

Horne responded to McCracken's passionate application of his powers with her own brand of concentration, which today now appeared a little frenzied. It worked, even though little things easily got her out of character, yet not so much that one was prevented from imagining that with her glasses off and a wig on we would begin to see her. The scene ended with Zuniga's knocking and McCracken's judgment that one could easily see where it had been rehearsed and where not. Bernstein wanted to redo the entire Carmen-José business, a seemingly impossible demand on the singers, but they agreed.

Horne did ask Bernstein, however, why there had been laughter during her dance. "I made a funny," he told this world-famous artist who apparently could rarely be talked out of her self-consciousness. More seriously, the singers complained that they had a hard time hearing each other. McCracken even suggested that the again very open set be separated by a cyclorama from the offstage areas where so much noise, necessary and not, was originating. This, of course, was out of the question.

Another problem that was eventually not settled until the eleventh hour was how the castanet playing was to be handled. For the moment, because Horne could not physically make the rolling hand motion which produces that extended clackety-clack, Bernstein suggested that she just do the initial rhythmic clacks of punctuation and that then the percussion man in the orchestra could take over. "Don't worry, Jackie. It's working." Ailey turned to his assistant and told her to take notes on Horne's arm positions during the dance. Surprisingly, the dance was causing McCracken worries too. He found it difficult to time his interruptions with the slow tempo Bernstein had fixed on.

"Don't forget the ritard on 'amuser,' Jackie," cautioned the maestro now that they were into the tense scene after the dance. Horne began simply to mark high notes, and Bernstein spared McCracken a repeat of the Flower Song. The orchestra's break came up, during which Mélançon took some pictures of an unpopulated Act Two. ("Get off the set, Alvin, and you, too, Carmen.") Someone congratulated Horne on the scene's coming to life.

"It may be coming to life, but I'm dying," she replied. "Do you realize we blocked this for the first time last night?"

"Let's take it from the endless embrace," Bernstein called out when the orchestra reassembled. "It will be boring, strings, unless you use no bow. All left hand. Jackie, Jim, try and feel it." The endless embrace ended, and in the heat of the following acrimonious exchange McCracken left the "t" off "soit," a point Bernstein immediately entrusted to Mauceri, nothing being beneath his concern. However, he missed the illogic of Carmen's response to Zuniga's knocks when she delivered her first "Tais-toi" to José in a whisper, then read the second louder. This was not to be completely straightened out until the recording sessions, whose organizer, Thomas Mowrey, was making his first rehearsal appearance this day.

Like high notes, the Zuniga-José duel was only marked, Igesz leaving it for the time being to alter Carmen's and José's positions in the final ensemble. Horne must have been really tired, for she left out her cherished full-voice high B on "La liberté!" Bernstein smiled. The curtain again fell slowly.

"All right. What do we do with our last twenty minutes? We need Act One, but obviously we can't set it up again." Hawkins was curious too about this time dividend. A run-through of the quintet was called for. It drew an emphatic "Very good!" from Bernstein. "Orchestra sensational!" (The only sticky point was the pronunciation by the men of some of their mute "e's," Valin being called back to the front after the relatively light chores she had with the really multilingual Maliponte and Krause.) And then the finale from "là-bas, là-bas," whose tempo this time pleased Horne, an approbation she showed by giving the finger-circle sign to the maestro. Igesz adjusted some Zuniga-José interrelatings, and Bernstein signaled that Horne should make more of her "Ah! le mot n'est pas galant! Mais qu'importe," her reply to José's "Il le faut bien," a line he sighs when asked if he has finally decided to join the smugglers. The conductor later underscored this moment's significance because it foreshadows the full-blown disdain which Carmen shows her lover in Act Three and which the audience never sees develop—except in this fleeting exchange.

This time the mezzo did sing her high B, but as at the *Sitzprobe,* no words accompanied the notes. Nothing was said. One wondered when the matter would be settled. It was hard to believe in the passage's eventual survival as Horne was now doing it.

Four o'clock signaled the end of the day for the orchestra and for Bernstein, although Igesz was taking another, requested hour with Act Two blocking. (Horne and McCracken were hustled up to the costume rooms for fittings.) Work lights came up, and a piano rolled out onstage. Strasfogel took over whatever conducting was needed. Tom Krause killed the bull once again, Igesz stepping in for the absent Carmen. The finale also was subjected to his and Ailey's scrutiny. Peripheral matters like light leaks were attended to, and some equally peripheral gripes were aired, such as "Why does the chorus have so little pride in their work? And why do they always put the fattest girl in the center?" and Igesz relieved some of his own tension by telling Melano, who now dropped in after an afternoon of whipping *Un Ballo in Maschera* (scheduled for the season's fourth night) into shape, that he had nearly blown up at Lennie. It was that kind of end of day.

Actually choreographer Ailey took over the stage for the very final fifteen minutes to integrate chorus and supers into what happens during the ballet of the "Chanson Bohémienne." "Dancers, stretch!" and he mimed a huge and pantherish extension which he wanted in order to help establish the late-hour lassitude pervading this nightclub. "Yawn! Use the chairs. Make the chairs move with you. Make bigger moves. Soldiers, keep moving. Never static. Even though you're sitting, keep moving. Change your positions. Nine-two-three-four-five-six. Ten-two-three-four-five-six. That was better, but fellas, you have to exaggerate the moves more in this big space. Whenever you don't know what to do, yawn."

*

September 7

It was almost impossible to recognize them. Krause in makeup and costume no longer the fair Finn but now indeed a dead ringer for George London, Baldwin and Boky pancaked so that their features coalesced into a kind of gypsy unanimity. McCracken, too, was in costume on this day of yet further steps toward completion, but without any greasepaint on his face. Behind the asbestos the two men practiced their roll down the tube. In front of the curtain seven tripods could be counted, waiting like border guards for shots at the player-smugglers in their Act Three mountain retreat. A piano accompanied this first short phase of the rehearsal. Then, in front of the asbestos, Bernstein selected some Act Three spots for work, the soloists again on folding chairs. The card scene was about all there was time for, the conductor, looking somber, telling Boky that she was dragging. "You're not used to keeping going. You're used to making a cadenza." Horne, still in slacks and shirt, was keeping her voice down, saliva troubling her, and Baldwin had a coughing spell.

"Osie, how much time do we have?" queried Bernstein.

"You're finished," was the uncompromising reply.

The Act Three entr'acte finished, the curtain rose, actually rather too soon to suit Bernstein, who nevertheless—after a brief negotiation with the solo flute so important in this segment—gave the orchestra a "bravo!" Svobody immediately announced that the lighting was *"zu hell,"* and the chorus member in charge of lighting his signal lantern on the second (answering) horn call forgot to do so. Tried again, it was managed. However, the opening chorus was hardly to be heard at all. Adler groaned. "We're losing half the chorus. David, tell them to give more voice." He conferred with Igesz, who said the problem was that they stalled at the back (top) of the tube and did not get on in time for their first lines. But Adler thought that Igesz was getting them off the stage too quickly, not letting them stand onstage facing front for the bulk of their number. "Let them stay for a minute before they go off. God!"

Horne had done a quick change act and now was able to begin the "Notre métier" ensemble in costume but without wig and with glasses. Bernstein warned that they were losing the crisp double-dotting they had worked so hard on. It was back to the beginning. "Once more into the breach, my friends."

At last some headway was made, with only a few bobbles marring the flow—some jumped lines in the dialogue, choristers interfering with clear views of the principals and Boky forgetting to sing her last "Fortune!" at the end of the card scene. More disturbingly, Bernstein was most unhappy with his beloved "douanier" ensemble. "What happened to the *piano* dynamics? What happened to this great performance? I would like to repeat this."

From his point of view, Igesz saw the chief trouble here as the congestion of chorus around the big stage-center chest containing some samples of smuggled goods, most notably some brilliantly and deeply colored shawls for Carmen, Frasquita, and Mercédès, which in the half-light seemed to move independently, disembodied, like three graceful, gaudy tropical fish. Igesz pushed, pulled, and prodded people into place so that Boky, especially, could have space to put her saucy ways on show. But Bernstein was impatient with the delay. "Can we go on, please? We have to keep moving."

Maliponte, also looking dark, unblond, with basically the same skin tones as Frasquita and Mercédès, could not be heard from the tube top on her aria opening, the trombones completely covering her. Igesz walked the soprano to a spot farther forward. She was in trouble today, fighting Bernstein's slow tempo every inch of the way. The breath this required took its toll in uncertain voice production. She exited coughing. "That'll have to be worked on," Bernstein nodded to Mauceri.

Marilyn Horne to her waiter in the Opera Cafe: "You have no Diet Pepsi? Honey, this is an opera house!"

The entr'acte to Act Four refracted all the requisite bounce Bernstein had beamed onto it. Mauceri smiled and watched his mentor, and although seated, tried some pelvic rattling of his own. But the color of this orchestral set-piece was fiercely undercut, when the curtain went up, by the drabness of the set and the crowd's earth-tone costumes. "The chorus is behind as usual," announced Bernstein. "You have to look."

"You have to cheat," Adler added. "And the first 'A deux cuertos' is inaudible." Adler suggested that all the men and not just the baritones be put on it.

The curtain fell. Again from the post-entr'acte top. Silence. "Are you ready back there, Osila?" called Bernstein. Nothing. "Let's begin and see what happens," he suggested to the orchestra. They did, and the curtain obeyed this prompting. Now it was noticed that much of the chorus was still working without props (lorgnettes and so on), that the children's running entrance was another dead spot and that the "A bas" rejection of the Alguacil still made no sense. Once the picadors started parading in, color entered the stage picture, but the real kicker of the morning was the appearance of Carmen herself. She was in gleaming white! Bernstein lay down his baton, and the photographers, including some with movie cameras, went wild. "You look gorrrgeous!" Bernstein cheered.

"Here comes the bride," Horne camped back. One's first reaction to the decision for white was incredulity. The set was white, the chorus was dark neutral, Escamillo was in a dirty gray *traje de luces*. It was most peculiar and hardly a flattering tonal decision for a woman of Horne's proportions, although now with makeup she had become a convincing figure of eroticism, even if, as Walker had said, it was in the well-upholstered Victorian mold.

Since the costume had stopped everything, Bernstein went back to the kids' entrance. He wanted to know if they couldn't sneak in a little more convincingly, to which inquiry Igesz replied that it was a musical problem because they had to get on fast and be in place so they could watch the conductor for their first lines. The children rushed out and rushed in yet again. They too were in makeup for the first time, their hair darkened and their faces identically sullied to go with their uniforms of rags. It all rather looked as if Escamillo, in 1960s John Lindsay fashion, was making a tour of the slums.

Krause was warned about holding onto the last note of his duet, a note that would cover the choral announcement that the Alcade was arriving. He found it difficult to watch Bernstein and his woman at the same time. "Watch the monitors!" Adler shouted to his forces, who now had that new *a cappella* section to sing. They were getting very flat. Again it was a dead spot that the spirit of restoration had drawn in its wake, Carmen and Escamillo frozen and the chorus barely with a movement to call their own. However, the new motionlessness made it easier for Frasquita to get to Carmen for her warning, although not everyone, after this, could get off in time or with sufficient motivation (especially Frasquita and Mercédès) for Carmen to start her anxious circular pacing.

Bernstein was dissatisfied with the entire Alcade sequence. He wanted to change it so that the mayor would appear earlier, but Igesz rejected the suggestion, saying that it would only create a hole somewhere else. They continued. McCracken came on and looked a very convincing figure of desperation, albeit a quickly drenched-in-perspiration one. Horne stopped things next because she was concerned about the cutoff after the concerted section of the duet, and Bernstein reminded McCracken to keep his next line, "Tu ne m'aimes donc plus?" quite soft and its repeat wildly frantic. This he did, managing simultaneously to uproot a section of everyone's old friend, the carpet.

An even greater fabric tragedy then took place. José is supposed to kneel in supplication before the merciless gypsy on "Ah! ne me quitte pas, Carmen!" McCracken bent his knee and therewith split his trousers from Mandates to boot tops. "I got a problem," he informed musicians and photographers with matchless equanimity. Times and unions being what they are, this did not stop the rehearsal for more than an instant.

Horne, when corrected by Bernstein on some point, soon thereafter remarked in palpable exasperation that "it's hard to know what's most important today—the music, the staging, or the *Pictures!*" And she threw some not very warm kisses in the direction of the brigade of tripods.

"I think we can safely say," Bernstein calmly answered her, "it's not the pictures." This time when it came to the high A-flat that had caused something of a flap a few days earlier, conductor and mezzo were almost—at least passably—in agreement. The offstage chorus barely came through.

A ten-minute break was called. Leonard Probst of NBC descended on Bernstein, begging for an interview. The tired conductor could not have been less enthusiastic at this disposal of his remaining energy, but he agreed grayly and turned in a performance for the quickly flashed-on television light and camera that would not cause him any harm. He paid homage to Gentele, Mérimée, Greek tragedy, decried the operetta tradition of *Carmen,* and emphasized that this would be a production that centered more on Don José's point of view than on Carmen's. Probst did his job, the cameraman smoked his cigar. They then packed up and left, and the house lights lowered for a repeat of Act Four.

The chorus problem looked not much nearer solution, and the "C'est l'Espada," which in its corny way had been so overwhelming in the *Sitzprobe,* Bernstein dubbed a "letdown." Krause continued to find looking at Horne and Bernstein simultaneously a quandary he would have to solve by using a superior brand of cheating. McCracken, now out of costume, and Horne began to mark high notes, both fatigued and suffering under the lights. Igesz got on stage to coax their acting field more toward the center, but the conductor stopped them only when the offstage chorus and band could not be heard on their calls of "Victoire!" McCracken, as once before, thought he had caused the halt. "No, Jim, you were right, but whatever the chorus does, I'll keep the tempo. This is a dangerous place." Horne, stabbed, did a triple roll across the carpet, stood, and hid from the lights under the overhang of the set, fanning herself while McCracken sang his confession. The curtain fell.

*

September 8

Bernstein was ill, and it was said there was little chance he would come to rehearsal today. He was suffering from exhaustion and a sort throat. Nevertheless, a rehearsal would take place on the C-level stage with piano. It would be a day to repair, patch, and fill in where dramatic and blocking holes still existed.

Horne arrived early, refreshed after nine hours' sleep. She said she didn't mind waiting for her entrance while other matters were discussed, since it was all "for the cause." McCracken, however, and many others were tired from yesterday's ordeal. The tenor also had some extra costume worries occasioned by yesterday's slapstick pants accident. He couldn't understand why in this day and age stretch or knit fabrics were not being used, fabrics that would react better to his size and his large-scale perspiration problem. Nevertheless, he announced himself as full of ideas for motivations, especially for Act One, which was first on the agenda today. First of all, he wanted to run his dialogue scene with Zuniga in English to get "the reality," as he put it. This he and Gramm did, but the experiment broke up when the two men improvised a discussion of Micaela's age and decided she was twenty-nine. "Twenty-nine!"

"If there's a lousier scene in the opera I don't know where it is," the tenor concluded, and he and Igesz decided that it would be improved if certain lines could be thrown away and *all* references to Micaela cut. No one could figure out why she should enter the Zuniga-José conversation, although to one observer it seemed that the appearance, fresh from the country, of a soldier's comely sweetheart was reason enough to mention her. The cut was made, thereby reducing the number of opportunities for McCracken's French to make a rat-a-tat-tat in space.

Such a point as Carmen's throwing of the flower, it might seem, would not cause any special difficulties, but Horne reported that Bernstein thought she was throwing it at José like Elektra—that is, not with the playfulness that conceals her fateful purpose. Several other things bothered Horne: her turn away from the audience to José at the end of the "Habañera" (solved by McCracken himself coming further downstage) and all the business that the end of the "Séguidille" entailed (Igesz wanted to wait to deal with this until they arrived at it in the sequence of the act's rehearsal).

The fight, of course, was difficult for everyone. Igesz suggested that Horne should try to be a bit more playful with José when she is led from the factory. That lengthy entrance McCracken described as taking enough time "to end the whole opera." Horne, of all things, had to get her spitting synchronized. "But why does she spit at me?" Gramm wanted to know. "We never even met before." He was told it was his uniform of authority that did it, and Horne informed that she would have to do a lot more struggling and spitting at choral adversaries and flirting with José while being held by him to use up time. Gramm also inquired why he was angry with Carmen. Igesz said it was because she had made him cut a bad figure.

This portion was run, Mauceri bouncing around and snapping his fingers à la Bernstein, checking up from time to time by telephone on his mentor's health. There was some blocking confusion, with Gramm getting in front of Horne and blocking her view of the conductor (now Strasfogel). "You're heaven!" she told him. The coordination of melodrama music and words was still to be worked out. McCracken suggested he take more time tying Carmen up, thereby expending more of the music. Evidently, he was feeling particularly marooned by the gaps in action. Action, business, motivations. They were all hungry to fill up meaningfully their time onstage. For instance, Horne asked why Zuniga "has it in for Don José when he consigns Carmen to the corporal's protection." McCracken took the initiative: "There are things in these personalities that cannot be fathomed. Listen, I'll explain it to you. Zuniga can't get anywhere with you, so he gives you over to the fat tenor."

"Besides," added Gramm, "I have a thing for fat tenors."

"Now it makes sense," concluded McCracken. They went on to the complicated matter of José tying and untying Carmen. Horne was given an ear-biting bit, and the tenor and mezzo both seemed more at ease with the flow of their dialogue, although Mme. Valin said she thought they both needed more work with her on diction.

Masiello began the teasing introduction of the "Séguidille." Horne murmured as she got herself set, "And now mad tapping is heard on the carpet." She sang one verse, but then Ailey came in and worked with her on her dance steps to be executed while singing. Igesz said he thought that what he had seen last time around was too heavy, and Horne objected when Ailey raised her arms. "No, Alvin, I can't do that. First of all I'm being obliterated by a French horn and I'm having one hell of a time with the tempo. We've got to get him [Bernstein] to go faster." A turn was also rejcted because Horne did not want to turn her back on the conductor at that particular bar.

The second verse was to involve a certain amount of ensnaring byplay with the rope between Carmen and José. Horne warned that they would have to take care not to make it look comical, like a tug-of-war. McCracken suggested that she pull on the beat to minimize the possibility that it would seem she was hauling him around. Horne decided that she would end her final tra-la-la by throwing the rope at José's feet. Igesz rejected this. "José has to come to you.

"Bodo, I can't give the last note in his face. Jesus, this is still opera. Everything goes to him. There are still set pieces. A move at the end will kill my applause."

On that note of atypical operatic concern, the party was adjourned to the Opera Cafe for purposes of eating. Horne, asked by this chronicler to lunch, scotched the invitation. "I don't want to lunch with any darn newspaper people," she laughed. By way of a kind of consolation prize, Igesz extended an invitation to join him, Francis Robinson, and Tom Buckley of *The New York Times,* who was there to do a piece on the production in progress.

Buckley asked Igesz to discuss himself as well as *Carmen,* but the talk over sandwiches centered, as was to be expected, on the Gentele inheritance. "There was some blocking in his copy of the score," Igesz acknowledged. "Not very much, but in the carrying out of any preconceived staging you do not stick to details. Otherwise you run the danger of making a museum out of the opera house." The irony of Gentele's death, Igesz continued, was that the morning of the tragic day he arose and told his wife that he now had definite ideas about *Carmen,* which he wanted to discuss that evening, an evening, of course, that never came. What was left were fractured concepts whose pieces were shared by Svoboda, Ailey, and Bernstein. "Gentele himself was not a great talker," he added, but, of course, there had been a Gentele *Carmen* in Stockholm, one in which Ragnar Ulfung, who was to sing later that year at the Metropolitan, had played Don José. Igesz had, naturally, consulted with Ulfung to see if anything of that last *Carmen* could be applied to this one.

"It is my duty to pick up the threads," he stated with some resignation. But this was no novel situation for him to be in, having been before this season an assistant Met stage director since 1963, the man in charge of stitching up the worn spots in productions after the original director had departed for other fresher, prestigious assignments. Now, at the age of thirty-seven, he was facing the biggest challenge of his career, one he said later he could not win, for if the production succeeded Gentele would get the credit, and if it flopped Igesz would be blamed for letting down his side. He was right, of course, but his promotion was still a fact, and later in the season he was entrusted with an elaborate repair project, the almost complete restaging of Günther Rennert's 1959 *Macbeth.*

Interestingly, Igesz, unlike just about everyone else, had

grown up with the dialogue version of *Carmen.* At least one person, then, did not find it a problem. He too mentioned Mérimée and said that he had read him to understand the weight of the dialogue and to put José in the proper perspective. Don José was a killer, a point not only brought out by the Zuniga-José dialogue added by Gentele for Stockholm (and commented on not altogether very positively by McCracken barely an hour before) in Act One but by his violent quasi-strangling of Carmen, an Igesz touch, in Act Two. "José is no puppet."

When the question of integrating such an unlikely-looking pair of lovers into a production's framework was more than hinted at, Igesz said that in opera you cannot come to singers with preconceived notions. "A production is a team effort. You cannot create an external effect and then impose it on the singers." A specific question came up: What about that awkward matter of the ending, José's "Vous pouvez m'arrêter," sung to a row of inclined faces far above him? The explanation was quite simple: The gates to the arena were hinged to open upstage—very good for people exiting from the *stage,* but an impossible barrier for their sudden emergence from the *arena.* The peering heads, he admitted, were a compromise. To the more general question of stylization, Igesz answered that there never had been an idea of approaching the direction as a matter for stylization. The sets, yes, the direction, no. (Bernstein, however, had remarked the day before to Riecker on the dropping of any attempt of staging stylization, specifically in the case of duets that he said Gentele had envisioned as soliloquies which had come together.) He quickly glided over the question—with the aid of a quick-acting Robinson—of why Strehler had turned down Gentele's offer to direct *Carmen.* "He just didn't want to. That's all." Obviously, he was not going to comment on the story that Strehler had rejected the job because of Horne's and McCracken's appearances.

David Walker to Marilyn Horne: "I like the way you look in those advertisements for your London excerpts from *Carmen.*"

"Thank you. I was twenty pounds heavier then."

An edgy Marilyn Horne to the chronicler: "Putting together a new production is the most difficult task imaginable. As to my ideas about Carmen, what I do now is a composite. It's hard for me to remember what ideas come from which production I've done in the past."

John Mauceri: "Lenny is definitely not coming in today. He says he can't think straight."

"I can't sing it at that tempo. It's got to be slower. I do all the slow tempi he wants, but here it's impossible! It's unsingable. And if I can't do it, I guarantee you there isn't another singer in this register who can." Lunch was over and the Act One cast had reassembled on the C-level stage. Horne, starting the afternoon session with the "Séguidille," had just stopped after her first few lines and thrown down her prop rope in a firm declaration of opinion.

"I know," agreed McCracken. "I break into a sweat. I may make it, I think, and I may not, and then you have egg on your face." (In the spring *Carmen*s, after Bernstein's departure, McCracken lost no time in jettisoning one possible egg-on-face spot, the pianissimo high B-flat at the end of the Flower Song. He sang it forte, just like every other Don José in every other production of the opera.) Masiello, who had again been the one-woman band, said quietly and evenly that she thought Bernstein would accommodate any necessary changes in tempo.

"God knows," said Horne in a sort of mock-Mildred Dunnock *Death of a Salesman* voice, "I've tried."

Ailey, too, was back for the dancelike blocking of the "Séguidille's" second verse. The rope-tugging was tired, a movement that McCracken, contrary to what others had expressed on the subject, seemed to think was appropriate—"In this story what am I but a lamb being led to the slaughter?" He also had something to say about everyone else's self-consciousness concerning the protagonists' size: "Why all this worry about looking clutzy just because we have a few extra pounds?"

"That's silly," responded a most diplomatic Igesz, although a few minutes later, when McCracken and Horne were told to sway back and forth to the aria's seductive rhythm, he told Ailey that it all now looked too much like a Viennese waltz.

And what about that final tra-la-la gesture? Horne joked that she could hold the applause and any position they devised "for eternity."

"Six beats before eternity," McCracken smiled, "I'll cut it with my line."

Horne's giggling riposte to this was that she would then do the same thing with her "Non," the first word she utters after the Flower Song.

McCracken, once seriousness (?) was restored, complained that he still felt at a loss in terms of motivation during the "Séguidille." Working out the end had now become a real block for everyone. It was decided to leave the question for fresh examination on Monday. They short-circuited to the end of the act itself. Horne put in a very effective, well-timed, and provocative curtsy to Zuniga for Carmen to execute while being led out to her prison, her hands supposedly bound behind her. As usual, she had no trouble whatsoever singing the incredibly drawn-out and caressed "Prends garde à toi!" her last lines of the act.

Referring to the previous two days' work, Charlie Riecker commented that he had seen general rehearsals that were worse.

On the main stage a *Roméo et Juliette* setting dominated all. Already, of course, the house was more than thinking about what came after *Carmen,* and the supers, those soliders and pimps of Seville, had become the quarrelsome citizens of Verona. In the orchestra room, too, the echoes of *Carmen* were being erased by Peter Maag preparing for his debut leading *Don Giovanni.*

Act Two—little problems: Horne practiced throwing the sword at Don José's feet when she cries "Adieu pour jamais!"

Krause polished Toreador Song flourishes with Igesz, and Valin corrected some McCracken dialogue.

Horne dug into her oversized purse and came up with some chewable vitamin C. She gazed at Valin and McCracken: "I feel sorry for her, because no one wants to see her at this point. The last French coach left after two weeks of trying to teach French to Corelli."

Horne: "Henry says if the rough edges are fixed, we'll have something."

From the Act Two entrance of Escamillo, with Valin, continually throwing out pronunciation corrections to Gramm and Paul Franke, almost taking over for prompter Millard Altman.

Krause, when it came time for the Toreador Song, said he wanted to be farther downstage. Horne agreed: "Yup, get down as far as you can."

"Just don't fall into the orchestra pit," cautioned Strasfogel.

After the Toreador Song there comes a flirtatious dialogue between Escamillo and Carmen, at the end of which he asks her how she would respond to a declaration of love. Carmen whispers her answer in the bullfighter's ear. Whatever Horne whispered that Friday sent Krause into gales of laughter. "Wild!" He could hardly get his breath, but when he did he asked Igesz what indeed Carmen would whisper to him. Igesz thought for a moment and suggested that probably it was only that she had another lover. No one ever found out what Horne had invented for the occasion, but she certainly was in good verbal form that day. She listened attentively to Krause repeat the Toreador Song and asked him when he had finished what led him to think he was going to get to sing it so fast.

Altman energetically prompted the quintet, one would think a nightmare for the man in the little mole's hole. No, it really wasn't, he informed, primarily because it has to be so well rehearsed that no participant in it really needs reminding. The real killers for a prompter, he enumerated, were the riot in

Die Meistersinger or all of *Salome* "because it swims so." The only difficult parts of *Carmen* for him occurred when there were rhythmic changes or when he could not hear the orchestra, such as the cue for the children on "Les voici!" in Act Four.

At this stage the rehearsal became a bit diffused. Someone from the costume department came down with a pair of boots for Horne to try on, while McCracken went upstairs to see about some stretch slacks. Baldwin and Boky started worrying about their assignments in *Roméo et Juliette* (Boky had just found out that she was now first cover for Anna Moffo) and how they would work out overlapping rehearsal schedules. Even questions from other acts came up, such as how Carmen should sing "L'on m'avait même dit de craindre pour ma vie," which comes at the beginning of the last act.

"Oh, the poor shnook," suggested Horne for her sublinear text.

"That's the idea," encouraged Igesz.

When McCracken arrived back on the scene, they launched into the long Act Two exchange between Carmen and José. "Now, Carmen, be sure you take some fake bonbons I've provided." Props in this scene—food, trays, sword, shako, plates, castanets—had become little prickly monsters which had to be tamed if it were ever to run smoothly.

Horne said that she would really like to do the dance for José with pieces of a broken plate, rather than with castanets. She pointed out that this was Bizet's original idea, but that Célestine Galli-Marié, the first Carmen, like Bernstein, wouldn't buy it. "Galli-Marié thought it was vulgar. Well, everyone knows I'm a vulgar singer." Ouch! Something was pinching somewhere. Horne even suggested, much to Igesz's surprise, that she might use the plate onstage while castanets were played in the orchestra. That was not the way to simplification.

The mezzo was perched on the bar bending all around her in search of her castanets, movements that were presenting observers with not very flattering views. Igesz interrupted: "Can you avoid that one?"

Horne immediately realized the problem. "Why? Does it look awful?"

"Yes," admitted Igesz fearlessly.

"Well, just tell me."

They continued the scene, still tripped up by the intricacies of text and action. "When I saw that dialogue back in August, I knew it was the bitch of all time," sighed our Carmen before gamely throwing herself yet again into the struggle.

"But it's a good scene," reasoned Igesz, and indeed, even now, with all its maddening pitfalls, it came across as a potential winner. For one, the predominant tone was light, the words were simple, and an audience, even one that did not understand the language, would have a chance to enjoy itself. Horne, especially, would come off very well here, her eating, flirting, plate-breaking, and castanet-hunting being, if nothing else, really entertaining. It was a welcome bit of play interrupting the progress of relentless fate.

Horne dominated these moments and dug out all their amusement value. She said that she wanted to camp up the dance, so that even the invitation that precedes it—"Mettez-vous là, Don José; je commence!"—would be delivered with satirical pompousness. "I would like to do this whole dance as a put-on," she announced to Igesz.

He replied, perhaps more quickly than he should have, "Well, you won't have to change it much, if you'll forgive me."

"That's what you call leading with your chin," observed a cheery McCracken. Horne let the remark pass and went on to do battle with the castanets, the putting on and taking off of which always bothered her.

The section that follows with Carmen, in her scorn, repeating note for note José's declaration of love, a wonderful bit of restoration that helps build to the soldier's fury before the Flower Song, fit Horne with ease. She was good at getting angry at the interruption of her preplanned seduction ("If I get a good head of steam up, it'll work"), although as yet she had not devised any way to make that repetition ("Il souffre de partir," etc.) clear as mockery. The quasi-strangling business was set for the climax. Horne asked Igesz if he wanted her to gasp "like I can't get my breath. Well, I can't," and she did a trial collapse onto a quickly rolled-out pad.

No "Air de fleur" today, just the "là-las" section to the entrapping embrace (the endless kiss) that José almost succumbs to. Like all stage kisses, it had to be carefully plotted. It was a little difficult to get Horne and McCracken arranged because she, so much shorter than the tenor, still had to appear to dominate the clutch.

Unbelievable as it seemed—it was now 5:30 P.M.—the "Chanson Bohémienne" came up to bat. "We always get to this at the end of a perfect day," mused Horne, but the good work done on the difficult scene with José had buoyed her spirits, and she and Ailey regaled Igesz, who had never heard it, with "Beat out dat rhythm on a drum," the counterpart of the "Chanson." "All I need now is to do it in blackface," the mezzo laughed. All, indeed, since her husband was weeks from becoming the first black man to conduct at the Metropolitan. Igesz had his bit of fun with the singer, too, as, looking back to European, less spotlit days, they gathered round the piano and sang the now suppressed recitatives to each other—in German.

The finger-snapping and skirt-waving she and Boky and Baldwin put in that day was sufficiently successful for reporter Buckley, who was still on the premises, to ask Horne if she had any Spanish blood. A faraway look came into her eyes as she denied this but confessed that she had always been fond of Spanish things.

"Weight on the left foot," commanded Ailey.

"Be sure and sing, Colette," commanded Horne. Fiercely twirling, her hair plastered to her forehead by perspiration, she hit a magnificent, rich, skin-puckering G-sharp. A fitting end to a grueling day. "Well, there goes another pound," she announced with sizable satisfaction.

*

September 9

It was Saturday afternoon, a homestretch Saturday afternoon at that, and therefore a working one, again on C-level stage, again without the ailing conductor. McCracken too canceled this rehearsal. Someone said he was either bored or sick. It was hard to believe that at this stage of the struggle the tenor found the going tiresome. In any case, he was not there, and William Lewis, his cover, an amiable, youngish tenor who this season was to fill in for Corelli on his several canceled Romeos and was to sing the spring season's next-to-last José, took up the challenge.

After a half-hour wait for Horne and Krause, who were having costume fittings (actually the delay gave Lewis a chance to run lines with Valin), Alberta Masiello began with the Act Three "Notre ḿetier" ensemble.

The Don José of the day was understandably shaky, and when it came time for him to deliver his bitter question, "Tu es le diable, Carmen?" it sounded like a request for factual information. Since no one had any cards for fortune-telling, the rehearsal moved along to the "douanier" section, today made more authentic by the presence of a full basket of contraband. The package was so heavy that Velis speculated (fancifully) that the stage crew might charge an extra fee to carry it on and off.

There was a certain amount of lightness in the air, Velis purposely mispronouncing words for their comic effect, Horne kicking up her heels (although in her just-run brief exchange with José she seemed angry enough; sometimes, actually it was difficult to distinguish between the angry mood of Carmen the character and the annoyance Horne the singer might be feeling). But Masiello brooded about the tempos she had been instructed to hold to. She particularly wondered why Bernstein insisted on making the two sections of the card scenes so polar.

One improvement for sure: Russell Christopher's pronunciation had come along splendidly. He was now in the ranks of the easier to understand. The "douanier" blocking did not yield to clarity, however, and Boky and Baldwin were still getting in each other's way (this happened today, too, in their Act Four scene with Carmen) as they traced their paths around the casket, reached into it, snatched shawls, and tried on jewels.

When Igesz asked to repeat this ensemble, he asked everyone to place the objects back in the basket. "May I have some of the earrings back?"

"No!" was the thunderous, unanimous reply.

Krause, in this room, appeared in very good voice today. He was also being rather inventive, altering the blocking after his altercation with José is broken up and also that for his invitation to the bullfight and farewell. His suggestions were solid ones, however, and accepted, making his presence impressive enough, at least in the studio, for Horne to utter a wonderful Hispanic-Yiddish "Oich!" as if to indicate how pleased she was with the new man she had attracted.

A short rehearsal, as it turned out, and one that ended with a few scatological references to "positions" in Act Four and the intelligence that the Act Three set had been unofficially dubbed "the hairy hole."

*

September 11

This was Monday, the first of only three rehearsals before the full dress rehearsal that Saturday (full dress rehearsals at the Met, in front of Opera Guild members, company members, and interested people from the music world, are actually more performances than working run-throughs: stops to correct are rare). It was the last real rehearsal with orchestra.

All lights! All costumes! All makeup!

Eleven A.M. The house lights went down and Bernstein, recovered, gave some general directions to the orchestra, the most important of which concerned his restoration of the G-Major plunk-plunk in Act Four before the urchins' entrance. "Any questions?" he asked. None. He made a tight, pursed-lip mouth movement to clue the pomp of the Prelude, lifted his baton, and we were off.

Only one halt was necessary in the Prelude, and that came when the brass failed to wait for the conductor's downbeat in the Toreador Song section. The pulse-beat hesitation before the crash into the reprise of the opening was properly devastating.

The Don José "fate" light came up correctly, as did the full light on the fortissimo diminished seventh that ends the Prelude. Crossed fingers were exercising their powers right up to the first sung words of the men's chorus, which were late. Again, Gibbs as Morales came on, his mopping of brow too small-scale to read as a significant protestation of the day's heat. While this scene continued, members of the stage crew and scenery department inspected the overhead fly curtains for light spills and the walls of the set for visible seams. (The lack of decoration in this *Carmen* meant that extra attention had to be paid to the exactness with which flat surfaces were matched; and today, for some reason, many of the previously worked-out projections were not being used, making the plain, almost drab walls that much more vulnerable.)

Micaela entered, Bernstein strongly signaling his men to keep their volume down. Maliponte made it and got off. The onstage trumpeter that replaced her as a fleeting center of attention was considerably less in character, being in street clothes except for his soldier's hat. He blew his fanfare, answered by a somewhat too rushed trumpet in the orchestra, into the motes of dust glistening everywhere in the hothouse light. Evidently the sweepers also could not get the better of this carpet. The kids today were absolutely in time until their very last phrases. A great source of worry had been eliminated by Maestro Stivender.

Gibbs's speaking voice, light and conversational, was not coming across with enough carrying power, and the dialogue between José (McCracken was already drenched in perspiration) and Zuniga seemed less logical than ever.

The smokers' chorus needed several repetitions, Bernstein declaring that he preferred working on problems as they came up rather than repeating the entire act. Igesz communicated with the women over the music from his mid-orchestra microphone, Bernstein spoke to the men ("Tenors, don't forget your crescendi-diminuendi") from the podium, and Adler screamed at them all from his front-row seat.

With the absence of projections, it was surprising how the chorus ladies' smoke puffs helped relieve the tedium of those blank walls. But was that a spit-curl Miss Brewer was wearing? Fabrizio Melano, an onstage emissary from Igesz, moved the girls about some, as Bernstein reminded the men yet again about a point of dynamics they were neglecting.

The entrance of Carmen brought all forces to a halt, supers being in the way. This corrected, Horne repeated her untraditional, slow approach as she mounted the steps to stage level, her balance somewhat precarious in those new shoes. The beginning of the "Habañera," from so far back, was inaudible, and Bernstein told her she was behind the beat.

Horne explained that she could not hear the orchestra because of noise from the wings. "Well," reacted the conductor, "that should be automatic. I can't believe. . . ."

So they started again and got through the whole aria without interruption except that Horne spotted a photographer in the wings. "No pictures, I have no makeup on, dammit!" she hissed at him between verses. It seems that Maliponte had arrived late and the painting procedure got behind schedule; so with Micaela appearing first, Horne had to do without makeup in Act One. Nevertheless, this did not prevent her from digging in luxuriously into her chesty "Prends garde à toi!" She was not holding the tension, however, for that long, dim-lit cross to José, an episode further diminished in effect by the failure of several chorus members to fix their gazes with the needed intensity on these protagonists.

Vengeful fabric again played its hand. McCracken's uniform trousers decided they did not like his way of bending down to pick up the just-thrown flower and split a nice long seam. The tenor blinked, sighed, and welcomed Micaela, whose first line of dialogue, like so many others' first lines, could not be heard. She screamed it on a new attempt. *"Oui, comme ça,"* approved Bernstein.

The duet itself also received his approbation, as well it should have, for it was the first time that day that the elements involved—at this spot, few—were able to coalesce into something reasonably like a performance. "Beautiful, both of you. But at one spot—'de ma part'—we were not together." Those words are the signal for the tender, chaste kiss José bestows on his sweetheart.

"I missed it," admitted McCracken. "I have to get in position."

They decided to go back, although Bernstein expressed concern at the stress quotient of repetition. "I don't want to tire your voices. You have a whole opera to sing." Maliponte did not seem quite so worried about fatigue, for when she made a mistake on the eventual repeat, she just winked in acknowledgment at the prompt prompter and went right ahead.

During McCracken's spoken soliloquy that follows Micaela's entrance, the first oboe gave the orchestra its tuning A. The sound startled the tenor, but he reflected, with some edge in his voice, "I like that. Keep tuning. That's what this dialogue needs. I mean it."

The girls in their deshabille poured out of the factory door. For once Bernstein did not have to stop for them. The orchestra, holding back too much, provided the halt. The melee was all very tame and dead, the men on the guardhouse roof to all intents and purposes mute, so much so that Kurt Adler, because there were only seven of them to begin with, decided to forget about them. Horne seemed to break down her movements into component parts—a spit, then a dash at an adversary—rather than making them naturally connected. She was full of chuckles.

Hawkins reminded Bernstein of the intricacies of the choral break regulations. Bernstein waved aside the technicalities. "I can't follow that, but whatever has to be will be." Indeed. He also soon changed back to a previous way of executing a bit of Zuniga's dialogue. Gramm was now talking over a clarinet (melodrama style), and it was impossible to pick out his words. Bernstein separated the two elements, but this left Gramm with the problem of getting out his line before that woodwind had to come in. The result was that he rushed the words, and one still could not understand what he was saying.

Concentration was not the strongest commodity in supply by now. Carmen for some reason reacted with anger to Zuniga's command that *José* would take her to prison, rather than to the previous information that she was going to prison in the first place. And the rope-handling during the "Séguidille" (rather faster today, although Elias still found it abnormally slow), remained rough, and to cap the act, McCracken's other pants leg went into "operation rip." The final push and group laughter worked better than they ever had in the past, but the curtain still crept down, leaving everyone with too much of a good thing. Bernstein, dripping with perspiration, wanted to repeat from the "Séguidille" to the end, but a mandated half-hour break (the time needed to change the set) overruled him.

After lunch, or whatever anyone could consume from the Opera Cafe, hallway vending machine, or yogurt-cellophane sandwich-orange drink-or-coffee cart in a half-hour, Bernstein, a clean shirt on his back, brought his baton down on the Act Two entr'acte. He was not too happy with the orchestra here, having to remind them about upbeats, phrasing, tempo, and the fortissimo before the diminuendo to the reprise, but when the curtain rose on Act Two, the warmth and the depth of the stage picture impressed as a soothing relief from the hard bareness of Act One. Svoboda, if nothing else, certainly knew a thing or two about contrast.

Horne had her makeup on now, and she looked good, the choice of wig, the choice of makeup tonality, and her own features complementing one another. Lillas Pastia's café was mellow as were all its clients, especially some of its soldier-drinkers who, in their tipsy enthusiasm, had decided to remove their upper garments. One well-built super found his way into the light, just like a soprano of the very best old school, and flexed and preened throughout the "Chanson Bohémienne." One wondered if Horne, Boky, and Baldwin appreciated this dab of pectoral upstaging. But the girls had their hands and feet full with choreography, probably too much so to notice or care. Boky forgot to sing at one point and got lost in her steps at another, while Horne was tripped up by her syncopated hand and tambourine claps. The ballet people, conversely, had never succeeded so well as today. Even Skiles's scratching of her posterior read loud and clear. No stops.

The living ghost of living George London, in the person of Tom Krause, strode on and caught a bravo from Bernstein for his suave reprise of the Toreador Song. His postaria cross to Carmen, however, looked tentative, and now his French proved not all that clear on his query as to how Carmen would reply to a declaration of love. But no stops! In fact, one of these did not come until after a rather tardy offstage "Dragon d'Alcala" from McCracken and his subsequent entrance. Horne had noticed that a chair which needed to be set exactly against the bar to facilitate her climb to its top was not in place. "Great, no chair!"

Bernstein put down his baton. "You should say, 'Sacrebleu, pas de chaise!'"

Horne appeared somewhat thrown by this interruption for that long dialogue scene, and she was not getting the quick changes in tone that this sequence calls for. But once she got her hands on the plate and broke it, she was in delightful, funny form, especially when her head and arms suddenly popped up from behind the bar and, having found those elusive castanets, she announced triumphantly, "Tiens, les voici!" Dancing, though, she forgot the forte-piano alteration (later dropped entirely under Lewis) in her seductive song. Bernstein, without stopping, shouted a reminder, but she threw back an uncomprehending "What?", one of two words she set among those la-la-la's, the other being "Shit!" when she tripped over the carpet.

Bernstein stopped. "It's too fast and you didn't ritard," and again, when they moved on, he had to correct a change of tempo she was putting in. The mocking repetition of José's declaration also did not come over as anything but straight statement. A non-French audience would not have a clue to the passage's intent other than from the exaggerated string accompaniment.

But José's choking looked terribly real, much more comfortable for these two than previously. Unfortunately, McCracken was now too tired to follow Bernstein's tempo indications on the Flower Song and he struggled with pace, pitch, the awkward (for this big man) sinking to knees, and an unlovely falsetto B-flat. One questioned the effect this would have on an audience unless he managed to bring it off in every respect. As McCracken said, he could end up with egg on his face. Nevertheless, Bernstein rewarded the streaming tenor with a bravo, undoubtedly aware of the stress the rehearsal was producing. Horne found herself in an awkward prone position, and inching forward commando-style for her "Non! tu ne m'aimes pas!" corrected matters, so that by the time of the climactic moments of the duet, with McCracken now vengefully awaiting his "Eh bien! soil . . . adieu!" the two principals were working at top efficiency.

The finale had its troubles, however, with Gramm's timing off on Zuniga's entrance, a messy, messy duel, Horne's wordless "La liberté!" leap, and again, a very slow curtain. To any one who entertained a notion that some repeating might be appropriate, Hawkins quickly announced that they had to go on immediately to Act Three, that there was no time, that they would not finish by 4 P.M. as it was, etc., etc. A break was called.

Putting up the tube turned out to be not quite so easy as anticipated, and getting it down was even harder, so that the idea of doing Acts Three and Four without a break had long been abandoned. At peak efficiency, it would have taken the crew at least eight minutes to change the set, three minutes if the slight rake to the Act Four floor had been eliminated. Igesz had opposed running Three and Four together because of the implied time lapse in the action. He expressed gratitude that in any case it was technically not feasible.

Act Three was difficult to strike because the huge section of carpet had to be lowered before being raised and flown out. And that the steel supports for the disk proved particularly move-resistant added to these bothers. The wooden truss of the tube itself had cracked and had to be rebuilt. As for Acts One and Four, those thick-based walls also did not lend themselves to easy manipulation.

A violist worked on his difficult passage for the card scene, his lovely sound filling the deserted auditorium. Bernstein conferred with Ailey, Adler, and Igesz, the last then going behind the lowered curtain for some quick restaging touches.

"Everybody is pulling apart today," said one veteran participant in many a Met preparation. "They're discouraged. And these breaks are the hardest things to cope with. I'm afraid the sets have proved impractical. I ask you, a prima donna who has to step *up* on her entrance?"

Starting positively, although Bernstein forgot to cue the important flute solo on the first attempt, the entr'acte to Act

Three moved smoothly to the simultaneous light and horn signal. "Thank you, Bodo," acknowledged the conductor. He wondered, however, a few seconds later if the opening chorus was sufficiently audible. This inquiry, posed to that day's observers, received a chorus of no's except from Igesz. "They're absorbed in that carpet. Give more," Bernstein instructed. Stivender supplemented with a suggestion that the chorus make more of a crescendo, especially on their repeated "Ecoute, compagnon." "Make an accent," Bernstein chimed in, also erasing a *sforzando* he had previously put in for the violins.

The darkness of the set continued without break until Carmen began her section of the card scene, at which point a spot was focused on her. Although José stood nearby, he could barely be discerned, and the juxtaposition failed to make a point. Today, however, Horne finished the card scene and then made a subtle transition into her first words of dialogue, establishing a carrying-over of mood. This realism evidently impressed some others among the smugglers. For instance, Velis tried a new reading of "Bartolomé," the name of one of the guards he mentions as being easily persuaded to let the brigands pass. The implication, difficult to project, space and time being what they are, was that Remendado had his own kind of nonkosher influence with this certain Bartolomé. Velis still said that he found it difficult, given the text and stage opportunities, to find any rationale for Remendado's homosexuality. Lisping and mincing, therefore, had to fill in the blanks. Now, however, he found he could insinuate something into that one "Bartolomé," which would also help Horne, who had to repeat the name. This she now did with a fleeting acknowledgment to Remendado's predilection.

In contrast to her work at the general rehearsal, Maliponte showed herself completely in tune with Bernstein's tempo and direction for her aria. The only problem for her was still that flutter which marred her intonation in notes much above G. It struck one as a pity that this fresh, well-used voice should have that drawback. One supposed it would just have to be accepted, and it certainly was that day, for the observers applauded her enthusiastically.

Krause also seemed on top of his material, Bernstein helping somewhat by stopping to facilitate one of Escamillo's spoken lines by moving a chord from its interrupting position to the end of his sentence. Although the knife fight lacked a few passes, the roll down the tube began to assume conviction. Bernstein asked McCracken and the baritone if they wanted to do it again. "Not really," replied the tenor, but Krause was worried as to whether he could still sing a rather long phrase at the conclusion of the wrestling. Bernstein was equally solicitous of his comfort. He corrected a ritard Krause was putting in—this would help his breathing—and he wanted to know if the orchestra itself was encountering any difficulties here. "Naaa!" volunteered one and all. Bernstein even jumped into the staging for an instant, something he had tried to restrict in deference to Igesz during the last few rehearsals: He suggested that Don José must make a threatening, *readably* threatening, gesture when, in the course of Escamillo's invitation to the smugglers to his bullfight, the baritone sings, insinuatingly, "Et qui m'aime y viendra."

The finale, true to the pattern today, weakened, the chorus falling behind, Horne missing her cue to discover the hiding Micaela, the whole tugging-and-pushing bit between José and Carmen very unclear. Maliponte even hunted for a note (which Bernstein immediately supplied) when she had to come in on "Hélas! José, ta mìre se meurt." Bernstein also worried about the offstage Toreador Song, the last singing heard in the act. Could it indeed be heard? Strasfogel said there was no trouble, not the case with the blackout and curtain, which, both slow, left Horne high and dry on her disk.

Altmeyer, encountered in a corridor, commented on being bumped from first cover for Micaela (she was now second cover). She allowed frankly that it was all very discouraging, and as a result she was determined now more than ever to go to Europe.

It was already 4 P.M., and Act Four had not even begun. Bernstein suggested that to save time they skip the entr'acte.

This brought cries of disappointment from the orchestra, for they enjoyed revving up to Bernstein's flamenco motor rhythm. However, there was a delay in the curtain—Igesz explained that it took Hawkins longer to organize all forces for this scene than for any other—so they played it anyway. Many of the same trouble spots were still plaguing the chorus—weak hawking of "évantails" and "lorgnettes," the rather directionless pointing of the children, and the mysterious, unmotivated "A bas" cried at the Alguacil, although today a *different* extra had the *same* costume on, instead of the other way around, which might have been more to the point. ("He should be a policeman, not a town crier," Bernstein had said.) But more importantly, the sound was full and the climax at the appearance of Carmen (her white dress now rinsed to an unbleached muslin tone, a dirty white different from Escamillo's) and Escamillo made more impact than it had since the *Sitzprobe.* Although the Alcade had lost the acolytes in his retinue, for the first time Frasquita and Mercédès promptly found Carmen for the "conseil" exchange.

The final duet also looked more coordinated, even if Horne was sufficiently bothered by offstage noise to cry "Quiet!" into the wings while, hands twitching in a convincing miming of apprehension, she awaited McCracken. The light continued to play experimentally on the antagonists as they prepared to fulfill the prophecy of the cards. Megaphones had been given to the chorus, so the "vivat!" cries came through clearly. Really no mishaps except for one word mix-up by Horne and a dropped cue from McCracken, and the mezzo executed a very real backward death fall. The previously immobile heads on the balustrade made their automaton-like left-hand turn to gaze on her as the curtain fell—on time.

"Four-thirty on the dot!" announced Bernstein.

Gildo DiNunzio, an assistant conductor: "I wonder how many people realize that it was Svoboda who was responsible for the brilliant Czech Pavillion at the New York World's Fair."

A cast member: "I'm sure that Kuntner is purposely dropping the projections from Act One. It's a kind of lazy sabotage," an opinion contradicted by stage manager Levine, who speculated that the films for the projections in Act One were fading. "Either they are trying to save them or they're making new ones or they have decided not to use any."

*

September 12

One week to go: three rehearsals, only two onstage, only one a really working rehearsal.

It was in this down-to-the-wire atmosphere that at 1 P.M. the cast assembled in the C-level orchestra room for what developed into a "correction" session. Bernstein was in blazer and tie (for the first time); he had a date later to play squash at the Yale Club. What equanimity, what energy, said one and all.

McCracken brought up the confused crossing to and pushing of Carmen at the end of Act Three, while Maliponte, looking in a compact mirror at her décoiffée, wig-disturbed hair, mused that it was hard to be a woman and a singer too.

Note number one from Bernstein: "All dialogue to be louder!"

"But not faster," an alert Mme. Valin slipped in.

Note number two, also from Bernstein: "In the second part of the Act One Micaela–Don José duet, they must never touch. If they do, it then becomes 'Ah, Sweet Mystery of Life.' Instead, it should be a double soliloquy."

A rather rare visitor to the rehearsals—he had been at part of the *Sitzprobe,* and that was about it—Acting General Manager Schuyler Chapin, dropped by. Bernstein (his former employer at Amberson Productions, the composer-conductor's own company organized to handle his enormous range of artistic and commercial interests) and Chapin kissed as though years had intervened since their last encounter and posed for a few pictures, for even here, in the basic bones of the house, one photographer from each interested party—the company, *The New York Times, Opera News, Fortune,* Deutsche Grammophon—was present.

"Everything's going swimmingly," Bernstein assured the

man he was, at least for the term of his engagement, now working for.

"Swimmingly is the word," ambiguously commented McCracken, but Chapin smiled and joked about their good fortune that there had not been any additional cancellations (since Stratas) among the cast.

Gibbs, the first solo voice in the opera, found that he had a problem of sitting on a diminuendo. Bernstein said that if it hindered, he should not sit but in general make more of his crescendos and diminuendos. Bernstein was in a directing mood, still persisting with his point that Morales's fellow soldiers must laugh when he suggests himself as the "brigadier" Micaela is looking for. And for her reply, he got Maliponte to make a gesture of rejection while singing "Mon brigadier à moi s'appelle Don José." A tiny moment, but a question of coordination that had never worked. The soprano had never been able to synchronize a convincing negative gesture with the words of the text, and no one apparently had had the time to clear up this mini-block.

Bernstein found too that Gibbs was slighting the double-dotting needed on his "il y sera" and was slipping back into a quasi-triplet figure. It was very important to him because he said that this part of the opera must contain enough vitality, rhythmic and otherwise, to hold attention until Carmen's first entrance. In much the same echelon of concerns he warned Maliponte to stay in tempo on her exit here ("Au revoir, messieurs les soldats!") or otherwise "it dies." And, too, Morales must, on the next line ("L'oiseau s'envole," etc.), go back to the lazy tempo of the beginning. "And this involves a diminuendo."

"Walk slowly," prompted Igesz with a weapon from his own arsenal.

On the whole, Bernstein seemed calmer, more confident, more cheerful today. Of course he was being helped by the fact that no elements other than the solo singers were being treated. That surely might have cut into his positive mien if he had allowed himself to think about it.

A skip was taken to the José-Zuniga dialogue. Now McCracken said something that rather startled Bernstein. He reasoned that José could be a "joyous boy" at this point because he had still not met Carmen. "Oh, never joyous," the conductor cried. Was this a slip? Hadn't McCracken been beaten sufficiently with the theory, talked about from the first day of rehearsals, of Don José's doom-heavy violent life, a life whose culmination could only be as negative as that of Carmen's?

Horne felt she was still hidden for her entrance, but the conductor convinced her that blocking around her was now far superior to what it had first been. Nevertheless, he told Bodo that she needed more "Lebensraum." They would check it tomorrow. They agreed that the silence of offstage hands had to be complete, certainly of primary importance in an opera with dialogue. Horne also declared that she needed more reactions from the supers on her first line ("Quand je vous aimerai?") and someone posted nearby with a pitch pipe.

"Your pitch isn't the problem here. That comes in the second-act dance," contradicted Bernstein.

"Well, I'm bothered there by the dancing," she replied. "And every time I watch you, I forget what I'm doing."

"You gotta do both. Oh, and Jackie, don't forget the grace note on 'je t'aimé in the 'Habañera.' "

"I know. I've been doing it wrong for years."

As for the long cross of the fate motive, Igesz suggested it would be helped if Carmen paused a bit before she actually began it. "How was the flower-throwing?" Horne wanted to know.

"Better," Bernstein assured her.

McCracken mentioned one matter that still bothered him: the unnaturalness of his standing still after he and everyone else hears the first screams from the girls inside the factory. "I feel I should move forward," he reasoned. This basic reach for a natural impetus to movement also prompted them to decide that when José leads Carmen out of the factory to confront Zuniga, he should do so quickly, disregarding the rather placid rhythm of the restored music here.

What follows in Act One was given careful examination.

First of all, Bernstein suggested Horne begin those defiant tra-la-las lightly and build on them. He reminded Gramm that he must keep in a look that travels between José and Carmen to establish the idea that Zuniga suspects there is something between them.

"And, Jackie," said the conductor, now in full cry as a director, "there should be a response from Carmen on the clarinet imitation of your tra-la-la's. Defiance and infinite desirability. Toss your head. We need smiling from you. Otherwise it's too *Semiramide.*"

They set once again the cues for Carmen's fighting. Horne, pulling her blouse outside her slacks ("Is *The New York Times* photographer gone? Can't I let it all hang out?"), relaxed into her work and with the right spirit began flirting with Zuniga (still a little confused now about where, in relation to the music, his melodrama lines should be said) as if she thought this might get her out of her prison sentence, although she still did not produce any additional reaction on Zuniga's announcement that he would write out the order for her arrest. Nothing was said about this.

Bernstein did say that he had lost all hope of coordinating rope-tying with music. "If we had weeks . . ." and his voice trailed off. Oddly, when they then tried it, it worked out perfectly. "Now, Jackie, give Jimmy more reason to straighten up when Donald works himself out of the crowd. Be a little more seductive. Kiss him. Now smile. Right. That's the Carmen. Sudden changes establish the character. She is both childlike and experienced, fun and severe." This crucial point about the volatility of Carmen's nature came up again immediately afterward, when the "Séguidille" was begun. "There are obvious points of change," continued Bernstein, "for instance when she sings about her officer, 'Il n'est que brigadier,' that should be one such place, not regret exactly, because then she says, 'mais c'est assez pour une Bohémienne.' The idea is not that you pity him but that you're saying 'I'm a nobody, too.' There are fifty points like this."

"Well, let's go over them," eagerly suggested Horne. With

one week to go, this was patently impossible, although Horne's buoyant full-steam-ahead attitude indicated that she had despaired of the efficacy of any more complaints. "Now or never, our only chance"—this unspoken motto emanated from her every gesture and comment today.

The tempo of the "Séguidille" was bound to be discussed. Bernstein said that without consulting Horne he had decided the day before to speed it up but that it had not worked any better.

"Nothing worked yesterday," summarized the mezzo.

"I want it to be slow enough to keep the kick, the guitar feeling," and when they started, Masiello having by now replaced prompter Altman at the keyboard, Bernstein felt that they had arrived at a beautiful tempo. Horne again mentioned how frustrating it was not to be able to tap heels on the carpet, but Igesz, emerging from a lengthy reserve, reasoned that although not heard, the taps could be seen.

"I'm running out of breath," Horne warned when they came to the second verse, but Bernstein went on, encouraging her with his comment that the "Séguidille" was now so sexy that it was giving him gooseflesh.

McCracken, too, put in his share of rooting: "She's creating as much excitement as she can." And when they sang at close quarters, he behind her, he whispered in her ear, "You do all the wiggling. Atta girl. Sensational!"

On the second verse Bernstein told Horne she could use more chest before her last "Manzanilla," which would take her into the forte ending. It *was* "sensational" finally, at least in this room, and even the thrown rope, which fortunately the carpet would keep from rolling—its one cast-acknowledged good deed—landed in the right spot when Horne aimed it at McCracken's feet.

"Terrific!" exclaimed the tenor, pure joy and a good deal of relief written across his face. "It's right!"

Bernstein too was enthusiastic, but seeing the dimensions, the possibilities of this *Carmen,* he remarked that he wished they had another orchestra rehearsal. "Why don't you call one?" prompted Horne, by now perspiring profusely.

"That's all I need to do." The tone of voice was not the lightest imaginable. Bernstein quickly returned to matters at hand, instructing Horne to increase the tempo of that "Prends garde à toi!" to Zuniga before her exit. "It was like the 'Liebestod' before." Horne agreed that it would be better faster.

Still following the order of the opera (although because Maliponte had to go off to a *Roméo* rehearsal, the Micaela-José duet would not be examined until later), the Act Two "Chanson Bohémienne" reappeared. Bernstein showed Boky and Baldwin how by giving tension to their "l's" in their tra-la-la's they could still sing piano and project and how he wanted Horne to break out on her repeated "montait" (a problem because this is where the girls have to begin their dance steps).

The first spoken lines after the "Chanson" concern Zuniga's invitation to Frasquita, Mercédès, and Carmen to go off with him for whatever remained of the evening. Bernstein had first decided that instead of turning him down with a "Non" they should do so with a typically Mediterranean "tsk" and a head movement. "For fifty reasons—lights, distance, focus—they do not work," he now allowed. "Say 'Non. Non.' That will be funny." (Actually in the case of Carmen's reply, a minor grammatical error crept in. Zuniga says, "Tu ne refuseras pas?" Her answer should, of course, be "Si.")

Krause retrieved himself unscathed from the Toreador Song, although because of some combination of forces he always fell behind on "Et songe bien, oui, songe en combattant" in the second half of the refrain. The quintet repairs concerned questions of direction—to whom individual lines were addressed, where people rose, where there was a "button" (Bernstein's Broadway lingo for sitting). The conductor found the whole piece a bit "general," and Velis, whom Valin instructed to reproduce Horne's tone of voice, but not her feminine adjectival ending when he declares that he too is "amoureux," thought spaces between the singers should be closed up for better communication. "I'm not satisfied with it completely," Bernstein concluded, but, given the work that had already gone into the quintet and the unlikelihood that any further fussing with it would extract positive results, he decided to let it rest. "The 'Dragon' was late yesterday," he told McCracken.

"There's an army backstage and you can't hear," Horne defended her colleague.

"It feels so spooky singing into those curtains," said the tenor about his offstage distancing effect. "It sounds like the opera's over and everybody's gone home."

Another acoustical quandary not yet settled centered on Horne's castanet-playing. As of the day before, two sets of castanets were in operation, one in Horne's hands, the other in the timpani section of the orchestra. "It's not working," Bernstein declared. "Both sets can be heard." McCracken put in a last plea for the plate as a substitute. "No," responded the conductor, "but I love your ideas." Should Horne play the castanets at all? She very much wanted to, claiming that she had not rolled them in opposition to those in the orchestra. How about rubber castanets for her? What about somebody stationed behind the bar to play them?

Bernstein did not like the idea of the sound of the castanets obviously coming from a direction where Carmen's fingers were not, but at the same time he was reluctant at this late date to burden Horne with the new task of coordinating fingers as well as feet and throat. "Oh, I don't know," joked McCracken. "It will give her something to occupy her time." Horne kept holding out for the job. Today she made it clear she could do anything, although up till then she had always had trouble just getting the damn things into position and keeping them there. Bernstein thought that maybe someone behind the bar was the best solution.

"I can do it, Lenny, at the beginning."

"Then we'll figure out something for the middle" (where the clickety-clacking becomes more intricate), supplied Bernstein. They decided that Horne would practice at home that night and see how accomplished she could be by tomorrow's piano dress rehearsal. They moved on to Carmen's mocking imitation of José ("Il souffre de partir"). "Jackie," said Bernstein, "you sang it like a recital yesterday. You must ham it up." Horne immediately got the point (but why wasn't it made earlier?), and she did the line, in her way, as if she were mocking a bad song recitalist. It was very effective, if, naturally, at this juncture, out of proportion.

McCracken felt that there existed also a problem with Carmen's throwing of the saber at his feet. "I have an idea," he helped out. "I'll place it forward on the bar when I come in so when Jackie goes for it she won't have to turn upstage and sing upstage."

"I sort of enjoyed singing upstage," laughed Horne. "It gave me a chance to rest." She would now not get that rest, no matter how humorously it had been wished for, nor would McCracken's execution of the Flower Song be made any easier by Bernstein's request for a more *sostenuto* attack.

"Yes," agreed the tenor, "and I've got to get closer to Carmen for that little sound I'm making at the end. Can they really hear me?" He was reassured that he was quite audible throughout the aria. "I wish I was capable of holding that B-flat longer," McCracken lamented.

"But you've been doing it exactly the way it was written," comforted Bernstein. One wondered if that was sufficient balm to a tenor where a high note was concerned.

"The tempo of the 'là-bas' yesterday was all right," Bernstein announced, "except, Jackie, you tend to hold back on the legato. It's a tendency in the voice." Horne acknowledged this but requested that they get a clear cutoff from Bernstein at the end of the duet (the last "Emporte-moi" for Carmen, "Tais-toi" for José). He agreed, countering with a direction for her to be certain to take time for her exasperated "Eh bien! pars!"

"OK, but why does he look away from me there? And do I hold that last 'Adieu' long or not?"

"It doesn't matter."

"You know," interjected McCracken, "we've been doing something different now when Zuniga knocks."

"Well, Jimmy my 'Tais-toi' there should mean," explained Horne, "that if you keep quiet, you schnook, you can still make it back to the caserne." This was again an illustration of a quick change in the mood of the gypsy: Where an instant before she is furious, dismissing her lover forever, she now turns protective, concerned about her charge, the corporal in trouble.

Later, during the final ensemble, and it's an exchange not often very clear, Carmen asks José, now in disgrace with the military, if he is at last finally one of them, one of the band of smugglers. His monotone reply is "Il le faut bien," or, essentially, "What choice have I got?" This, Bernstein, pointed out, was the real turning point in Carmen's feelings for the soldier. Without ever having consummated their relationship, she now regards him with the seed of contempt growing in her. Her reply to this is an ambiguous, "Ah! le mot n'est pas galant!" and she throws José a rifle, not too sweetly. This moment provides not only the link already mentioned to the mood of Act Three, but also a basis for Carmen's gales of laughter—they should be there, even if silently—in Act Four when José, in desperate pleading, vows that to please her he will remain a bandit. Bernstein paraphrased: " 'What a schlump you are,' the laughter says. 'You were even a failure as a bandit.' " All these points, although all marvelously insightful, were coming a bit late in the game. They were basic anchorings that should have been secured weeks before, not the day before the last true working rehearsal.

"Jackie," continued Bernstein with some anxiety in his voice, "what about your circus trick?" (The leap on "La liberté!") "You don't sing words. It can't be a cadenza. It's not Donizetti. It can't be ha-ha-ha."

"Lenny, I can't sing a "t" on a B. I practiced."

"Well, at least get the 'é.'" Why was he compromising here? Why did he not simply suggest that she cut it out and sing the words as written, either a sixth or an octave lower, as Bizet, or at least many editions of the score, had given the option to do? One wondered if there had been some kind of subliminal plea-bargaining at work here.

Maliponte, resurrected from her Juliette tomb in another studio, now joined McCracken for their Act One encounter. The soprano was told that her first spoken lines did not get past the prompter from her upstage position by the gates, and she promised yet again to say them louder. The idea of separateness during the duet could now be facilitated if the singers would make use of the wing monitors. This way they would have the possibility of not facing Bernstein in the same way. McCracken was especially pleased by this choice since there were certain difficult high *piano* notes he could dampen by directing them into the wings.

A small but crucial point, when José is to kiss Micaela, still hung in the air. McCracken got a full-throated "Awful!" from Bernstein when he suggested he might cross, kiss her, continue crossing—all the while singing a single phrase. Finally the kiss was set to be delivered behind her ear in a logical musical silence for José during which he could cross and get in position for the final section of the duet. But the postduet routine also contained some built-in stumbling blocks: Maliponte's maintaining of softness in her dialogue while projecting both character and words, McCracken's projection of a slight coldness toward Micaela occasioned by his troubled awareness of Carmen, and his holding taut the silence while he gives the letter from his mother at least a perfunctory glance.

These questions, however, did not dampen the tenor's spirits, for he suggested in an inspired moment that the reason nothing is seen or heard or referred to about Micaela between the time of Act One and Act Three is that, having wandered back onstage during the factory brawl, she is clobbered by one of the girls in the chorus and so has to go to the hospital, from which she is released just in time to go looking for José in the mountains.

Very few minutes remained for anything more than isolated spotting of questionable moments in Act Three—the matter of adjusting the length of the struggle between José and Escamillo, a troublesome phrase in Micaela's aria, and whether or not an actual physical deterrent should be introduced to keep José away from Carmen when the chorus tells him to "prends garde." (McCracken thought it would help the logic of his not moving on her, but Igesz, stepping back into the day, thought his lines of menace would be enough for José, and Bernstein agreed with the director). It was also questioned whether Micaela should physically tug José away from this highly charged confrontation with Carmen (no, said McCracken, he did not want to be pulled, which reminded Horne of a performance Giulietta Simionato was once supposed to have done of *Il Trovatore,* during which as Azucena, feeling herself too much handled by DiLuna's soldiers, she screamed a very carrying and *hors-de-texte*-motivated "Mi lasciate!").

Only a bit of the Act Four duet was looked at now. Masiello having left, Bernstein seated himself at the piano, and using his orchestral score, proceeded to deliver an on-the-spot piano reduction. He accorded Horne a requested extra beat before her withering "Non, je ne t'aime plus" and directed McCracken to be sure to think of his difficult phrase—"Cet homme qu'on acclame, c'est ton nouvel amant," which usually leaps out in imprecision—in four and to deliver it sinisterly and with great legato phrasing. And then Bernstein was off to the playing courts of the Yale Club, leaving Igesz to polish a few of the duet's positionings. Horne promised she would yell only in two places—her last "Non, non!" and, of course, on the most famous "Tiens!" ever set to music.

"I hated that long shriek I did on it yesterday," confessed the mezzo. "While I was doing it, I was thinking, 'Oh God, I hate it—what I'm doing.'"

September 13

This was it, the last real rehearsal, a "dress" that also served as a "photo call." There were, at quick count, at least eleven tripods set up in the auditorium. It was a rehearsal to be conducted as close to performance standards as possible (singers using full voice), except that there would be interruptions and a piano would substitute for the orchestra, this last condition one of the most difficult to understand, given the manifold complexities of grand opera.

Before the rehearsal actually began, Igesz relayed to the supers what had been discussed at yesterday's rehearsal concerning their disposition during Carmen's entrance in Act One. Bernstein arrived in a blue denim work shirt with an embroidered set of cigarette-smoking lips on its back, its front emblazoned with a rhinestone "LB" brooch. He told the photographers that naturally they would not be interested in snapping him in this "fun" getup. His mood seemed bright (the previous day's squash an antidote to operatic cares?), and he joked with Hawkins about certain misapprehensions in *The Times* article about the *Carmen* preparations which had appeared that morning.

Eleven A.M. Ready to start. At her amplified pit piano Alberta Masiello struck the D-minor tremolo of the fate motive, the curtain rose, the mystical half-light went on to reveal Don José, back to audience, *seated* on the platform. Conservation of energy or unannounced change in interpretation? The triple-forte diminished seventh chord signaled all lights on, although the *toldo* over the guardhouse looked dim and creased—quite a contrast to its leafy shadowings when Svoboda first set the light plan. And immediately Igesz was on his microphone with a plea to the chorus men to fan themselves more obviously, and before anyone in the chorus even opened a mouth Adler shouted at them to watch for their cues. Maliponte, still uncomfortable with her gesture of denial, forgot to interrupt the laughing of the soldiers, then remembering, did it too late. Igesz stopped the chorus: "Gentlemen, you're singing it like the *St. Matthew Passion*. Sing to one another," an instruction, Bernstein noted to Mauceri, that would keep them from maintaining ensemble.

The offstage trumpet splattered badly ("Oh well, that's the way they were in the army," rationalized the conductor), and the children seemed to sneak in to their positions—an en masse sneak. Some were missing. "Where are the kids on the fence?"

"In school," the maestro was told.

Igesz stopped them all again on the "Halte! Repos!" calls. Some of the men were doing their own individual brands of maneuvers. McCracken told Igesz that stylistically they were in error. "It's settled this way," replied Igesz with great evenness. Pause.

"Do you want to leave it?" Bernstein called into the dark middle distance where Igesz manned the directorial table.

"I don't want to take time now."

A resumption, and Masiello's fingers flew unerringly over the keys. The cigarette girls wandered through the gates, and it suddenly seemed a moot point, given the courtyard setup, as to just where they were supposed to be coming from. Where did they spend their lunch break? In spite of all efforts, Carmen was not especially left in the clear on her entrance. Igesz leapt to the stage, closely followed by Bernstein himself. There they argued, the conductor in favor of moving the chorus farther away from her, the director against it. Bernstein won the point.

The conductor returned to the podium after a few directorial words to Gramm concerning Zuniga and a remark to Mauceri about how little he felt the original lighting intentions had been carried out. Horne, her path relatively cleared, moved to midstage, rejecting the blandishments of the gentlemen pimps with gestures more redolent of a great lady's put-down than of a flirtatious gypsy. Igesz warned the chorus not to sway to the lilt of the "Habañera," and Horne and Bernstein exchanged winks when she remembered the grace note on "je t'aime." She also got out an "Oh, these shoes!" when she tried a little obviously uncomfortable pacing between verses and revenged herself on them by prolonging her low, trumpeted "Prends garde à toi!" much more than she and Bernstein had agreed to do.

No applause from the photographers, who were by now tripping over each other, or from anyone else watching greeted the end of the "Habañera." Horne called out for costume coordinator Caine to get her different footwear, Adler cautioned the chorus pimps not to run away with their "Réponds-nous" implorings after the "Habañera," and Igesz had Horne practice her flower-throwing. "It's a different weight flower every day," she noted as, much like a horseshoe pitcher, she aimed at McCracken's upper chest.

"Jackie," Bernstein interrupted, "make a contrast between 'peut-être jamais' and 'peut-être demain.'" Indeed, during this first appearance of the heroine, Horne's reactions seemed too consistent, too slow, too cautiously the same throughout. There were few of those points of change in evidence that Bernstein had so recently begun to discuss.

The chorus, instructed to watch José for his reactions on their laughing exit, left the stage to a Micaela in considerable initial difficulty with Bernstein's slow duet tempo. The separation effect in their duet worked well, however. In fact, the duet went superbly, with both Maliponte and McCracken in splendid form, Bernstein's only direction being to McCracken that he keep his mother's letter before him throughout. "It's the letter that makes you sing."

Oh, the catfight. *The* first-act headache, if any single one were to be selected. "Girls, don't run!" Bernstein yelled.

"Resistance! Put up a fight! Sopranos, yell!" came Igesz's voice over the microphone. The women, with their difficult syncopated lines, were taking a decidedly tame approach to their stage anger. Horne and McCracken were late coming from the factory, emphasizing rather than minimizing this dead spot, now even more greatly magnified by the soldiers' frozen lineup stance on the guardhouse roof.

Horne gave her all, however, and she attacked one of the chorus girls so enthusiastically that she found herself sitting on her favorite carpet. She said it was her own fault, having waited too long for her aggressive gesture.

They went back to her entrance. "Girls," Bernstein pleaded, "I know you're in twenty thousand positions, but try and sneak a look at me."

"Half of them have their backs to you," Adler chimed in.

The girls, hustled upstage by the super soldiers, were reminded by Igesz that they must not lose interest in what was happening among Carmen, José, and Zuniga. ("Jackie, piano on those first tra-la-la's," Bernstein advised.) A dropped signal to them, however, held up, as always, the cry and running attack from one of the girls. "Oui, c'est elle!" had almost never worked. McCracken, grabbing the battling and then suddenly cuddly Carmen, feared a new peril: that the buttons on the front of his uniform would hook onto Horne's laced bodice. That would really bring them together.

A half-hour break was called, Bernstein laying down his baton with grimness. Some friends approached the podium, and perceiving his mood, began to reassure him. At this point, no one could doubt, it was the staging that bothered him rather than anything that was not being realized musically. To a suggestion from one of these acquaintances that he jump in and take charge of this domain, he replied with a blank stare.

In his dressing room (only a temporary one; the more elegant S2, he was assured, would be available to him on Saturday), Bernstein remembered the beginnings of his involvement with this opening night. No, unlike Horne, McCracken, and Krause, he had been engaged *after* the bill had been changed from *Tannhäuser,* although he had first been asked for the Wagner opera and had turned it down.

"I had several meetings with Gentele, and we also had many transatlantic calls," he recalled. "We had a joint meeting that lasted long into the night with the librarian to set cuts. It was a joy to work with Gentele. I can't help thinking of him every time I hear the fate motive. I associate it with him. Maybe this is a doomed production." His voice trailed off suddenly. He probably had not wanted anyone with a pen in hand to hear him say this.

Asked about the research he had done on *Carmen* in order to arrive at the performing version now being prepared, Bernstein said that it went back more than ten years, to the time when he did a television program comparing the grand and the *comique Carmen*. He had seen the *comique* version some ten years before that and was taken by it. He had always wanted to do it, having at no time in his career, except for a childhood pastiche that was immediately dubbed *Carmen Bernstein,* conducted a performance of the opera. "I demonstrated in that television show, in which I used both actors and singers, how much more of the characters, especially Don José, comes through when the dialogue is used."

How closely was he keeping to the decisions that had been arrived at during those first sessions with Gentele? "I've tried, but, of course, some did not work out. You can set only so much in advance, but changes have to be made when you actually come to do it. For instance, the cross-fade in Act Four [the entrance of the children] has not proved possible. [A chord was restored.] No, I never had any discussions with Svoboda. In fact, I did not meet him until last week."

How did Bernstein now see his role? "When the Gentele tragedy came, it became a problem of time. I had several telephone conversations with Bodo and one long session. In the past I have been accustomed to a week of musical rehearsals that would be attended by the director, and he would have return privileges, a week of drama rehearsals that I would attend. But the incredible rehearsal schedule worked out by the previous administration prevented this. I was counting on that week. Bodo was counting on his week. Then we found out that we each had one day. As a result we have had to grab people as we could."

Was there ever any question in his mind about the practicality of dialogue in French in a house the size of the Metropolitan? "I know it's a problem, but neither Gentele nor I questioned the decision to use dialogue. It was, we felt, the basic way to take a new look at *Carmen.* We reached total agreement within our first two minutes as to the approach to the set and to the light—the lack of emphasis on 'local color,' for example. I do not want to discuss the degree to which I feel the carrying out of the original plans has succeeded."

The break ended and we were back in mid-fracas, everything the same, except that now Strasfogel manned the keyboard. Carmen's attack on the chorister was simplified to a spit and some restraining action from José. "Oui, c'est elle!" finally was uttered in time and with such accompanying physical conviction from the girl specializing in running and hitting that Horne reviewed her performance with an "Ouch, my arm. Jesus."

"Smile on that la-la, Jackie" (her last taunt, before which a delicious little hold had been inserted), Bernstein instructed. Horne, however, was showing some frayed nerves rather than smiles, especially when she found she could not get up, her arms bound, from her platform perch to vamp Zuniga. Again there was no reaction to Zuniga's order to carry out his first judgment, no change from smiles to pout to show that Carmen was disappointed that her way with this officer had not worked. Nevertheless, except for some rushing on "Je ne te parle pas," Horne sang the life out of the "Séguidille," thrilling even the flashbulb poppers and especially one of the kids from the chorus, who, having broken away from his peer group, sat in the first row, his eyes ablaze with pleasure.

The curtain fell slowly. Again. The photographers, with nothing before them but the gold curtain, turned their weapons on the only animation left to them—a conference between Igesz and Bernstein.

David Walker, if anything, looked even grimmer than Bernstein. The real difference between them, however, was that Walker was talking. He relished the act. "McCracken decided at the last costume fitting that he looked bad. But the principals have all been helpful. However, we have had very little time for really proper fittings. That would not be the case in Covent Garden. It all has to do with money. One is never allowed to forget that in this house. Also I find I have to cope with the families of the stars and the star entourages. They can be helpful or destructive or just time-wasting. It's a serious problem, and I got it all today. I mean, here I am, a designer faced with a bunch of people in a star's dressing room. I am not introduced but rather treated with familiarity as if I were a lady's maid. Mind you, Jackie's husband has been marvelous, but a strange jealousy seems to take hold of a husband or wife when the star gets near to the point of being before the public. And I always seem to have to deal with these relatives. Pilar Lorengar's mother, Rossano Brazzi's wife.

"If a star is nervous, the clothes get it first. Now Jackie, Jimmy, and Micaela have all been very conscientious. People here have all been terribly nice. I have to hand it to Bodo. He has been extremely ungrand, scrupulous in trying to stick to the original ideas of Gentele and Svoboda. As for me, I have had to stick to materials that receive light, the monochromatic idea that was Svoboda's. Yes, the clothes are somewhat based on Doré, but Doré's illustrations are lit with a warm light. There is no bleakness. Nothing in Doré is this bleak. It's strange, with the lighting here as it now stands, they have to use an old-fashioned follow spot."

The designer was now hitting his full stride. "This production has the kiss of death. I knew it when Goeran first asked me to do the costumes. The trouble is that the people in management don't know how to delegate responsibility. Bernstein, with all his 'charisma,' should have brought it all together. In this respect he has not been generous. And this way of doing *Carmen* is very foreign to Americans. The lavish, detailed Zeffirelli Italian method is better for them and for the singers, too, than the stark Central European way. Here almost no props are carried on. There is nothing for people to work with. Svoboda, mind you, is a fine artist who isn't a 'fine artist.'

He wants to make pieces of sculpture out of his setting, and the result is that people look deadly in them.

"Well, I did it for the money. That's the way it usually is. Maybe one in fifteen productions you do is a success. Here I did what I was told was needed." Thus one important pillar in this *Carmen* was apparently psychologically preparing himself for a critical disaster. Was he doing what everyone else was doing or should be doing to steel himself against what could easily be, if it indeed did fail, the biggest operatic debacle in New York in years, perhaps even more crippling than the opening of the house with Barber's *Anthony and Cleopatra?*

Masiello was back in the pit, but she did not get a chance to perform the entr'acte to Act Two. The curtain rose immediately on the "Chanson Bohémienne," which, this time, featured even more bare chests from "les boys." Paul Franke, as Lillas Pastia, got out his few lines, including a peculiar, ululating reading of "je suis obligé," which relied on an exaggerated rolling of the "o" in "obligé," that Mme. Valin had told him the previous day was meaningless and un-French. It was now longer than ever.

Although a glaring, harsh light hit the back entrance wall of the tavern against the white paint—it looked more like a work light than a plotted illumination—Escamillo, for his entrance, was in the dark until he strode all the way downstage. (Bernstein was more preoccupied here, however, with whether or not the onstage choral "Vivat!" cries could be heard.) Krause appeared master of the Toreador Song, except in that "Et songe bien, oui, songe en combattant," where his breath still ran out.

Gramm, too, was working well today. He obviously was going to be a completely supportive factor—a solid performer. Also quite solid was the quintet, although Velis was still saying an ungrammatical "des jolis," a spot on Carmen somewhat vitiated the ensemble nature of the piece, and Horne and Boky for the briefest of instants appeared to be on a blocking collision course. When it ended, that Bernstein well-wisher ran up to the podium with an opinion and a prediction that, if nothing else, the quintet alone would be worth the price of admission.

Horne's acting, however, in this part of Act Two, still exhibited a detachment that would pass muster at an earlier stage of rehearsing but seemed curious on this quasi-ultimate day. For instance, instead of trying somehow to make the correction a part of her action, she came out of character to put that barside chair in place when she found again that there was "pas de chaise." Of course, she made her point, although she could have helped the scene by not doing so right away and by waiting until the next halt, which came soon enough, and requesting, as she did anyway, that a mark be made for this troublesome prop. Another pesky prop, one that was to be the cause of great hilarity shared by thousands at the dress rehearsal (one wondered, incidentally, about Walker's assessment of this production as wanting in props), was José's sword, which unbuckled with the greatest of fumblings. It had to be taken off—logical, too, for a soldier to remove his weapon while tête-à-tête-ing with his gypsy—so that Carmen could later throw it at his feet.

"Jimmy, when you enter, keep smiling until you come downstage into the light and see Carmen's expression," Bernstein offered a quick direction.

McCracken nodded. "I haven't smiled very much today." And they went on with the long dialogue scene until they got into a plate crisis. Horne was supposed to select one of three real plates (instead of a breakaway as until now had been used in rehearsals) to shatter for her pre-dance castanetless rhythm beating. Today she did not know which plate to use. In a flash Igesz and a crew of prop people were at the bar puzzling out how the plate to be broken should be placed and designated. Bernstein called up from the podium that it should have an "M" inscribed on it, but McCracken with a genius for the solution of complex stagecraft, told them to put out one plate only and then there would be no question of which to use. Tuhrrific!

Although Horne still had difficulty getting her castanets

on in time, she almost got their playing right for her dance. Bernstein congratulated her. "I practiced," the singer acknowledged. "If I miss a beat, I'll miss it because I have to remember the dance steps." Bernstein, however, reminded her about the forte-piano passages, where she was still not making the indicated dynamic distinctions. Horne was visibly annoyed with this fault-finding after the great castanet success, one she had in all performances.

The offstage trumpet interruption got very much behind the beat. McCracken offered to draw out his phrases to bring everything back into phase, but Bernstein insisted that the trumpet had to be absolutely in rhythm. Assistant DiNunzio popped out from the wings with apologies and a vow that they were "trying like mad and watching." They repeated, and this time the trumpet got ahead and Bernstein diplomatically gave his forte-piano note to Mauceri's notebook.

From the end of the dance, however, the scene came alive. Horne suddenly was "on" in full force. Her anger was natural and convincing, her mockery of José devastating. The choking made a superb climax to the sequence. "Beautiful," remarked the conductor. "They got the feeling of killing into it." McCracken, however, was not quite able to support his piano high notes in the Flower Song, although the mood was very much there. The succeeding "là-bas" section also went well, Bernstein swinging in rhythmical sympathy on the podium, and the tenor got out one of his swattiest "soits!"

But the duel still looked a mess, and many quick but crucial reactions, it could be seen, had not been settled. For instance, what was Carmen's attitude to Zuniga here? Horne registered neither hostility nor patronizing disdain. She also registered nothing when José refused Zuniga's order to "decamp." Surely something should be seen. It was left in the air. Horne, to her credit, on her "circus trick" did sing "La Libeté!" that day, and her contempt, perhaps too underlined as it was on an only recently established bit of business, did read on "Ah! le mot n'est pas galant!"

The curtain fell, and Bernstein was immediately besieged by a phalanx of photographers and reporters asking questions he had responded to over and over again during the past several weeks. How did he stand it? Or was he by now so used to the press that he was able to adopt a protective covering from behind which his voice conveyed the requested words?

Margaret Carson, press representative for Leonard Bernstein: "There is a certain value in underrehearsing as opposed to overrehearsing. This the maestro understands. For instance, his letting the orchestra go early during the orchestra rehearsals was a masterstroke."

The opening chorus of Act Three went along with exemplary exactitude except for the phrase "La fortune est là-bas, là-bas," which, for some reason, refused to submit to the dictates of unity, and for the word "garde" (as in "prends garde") that about half the singers insisted on pronouncing without the "e." "I've given that note thirty times," Bernstein noted. Yes, and the lantern fell off the disk, which upset Horne not at all as she produced a marvelously focused performance of her section of the card scene. Bernstein was getting everything he wanted from her for this. But "Frasquita, I didn't hear your 'fortune,'" he had to say.

"I didn't sing it," the soprano admitted from her pocket of darkness, one that remained constant throughout the "douanier" chorus, but it did seem from what could be descried that much less was being done in the way of *cornuto* hand gestures by the chorus for José's benefit.

"What a long empty stage," Bernstein observed after everyone left on smuggling business so Micaela, somewhat marked today, could come in and do her big number. Bernstein signaled the horns for its beginning. Horns? "Where is my mind?" The conductor shook his head. His horns, like strings, reeds, and percussions, were today all in Masiello's fingers.

Maliponte backed out of the light and got off when the aria ended. No applause from the observers, a bravo from Bernstein, and an instruction from Igesz to assistant Melano that the soprano should be told not to make any gestures—"no gestures whatsoever." Krause also received a bravo from the maestro on his difficult new music before the José-Escamillo altercation, but the approval broke the baritone's concentration and he appeared to falter. The "bagarre" itself looked better, except that when McCracken fell against the wall of the tube, he bounced down it out of control, like a package coming down an air-terminal chute, a sliding action curiously paralleled by Horne a few minutes later when McCracken pushed her to the carpet in Don José's now acted-on anger.

Bernstein was tiring, the tremendous energy he always displayed consumed by the niggling and unresolved problems of the day. He forgot a ritard on Carmen's "Oui, tu devrais partir" that had been previously agreed to, and he apologized to Horne, who at the end, deserted by a chorus that had lost interest in the drama, remained alone in the lengthy blackout, alone with the slowly falling curtain and the echo of Escamillo's promise of glamour as a torero's concubine.

Purple plastic masking tape went around the now well-established prompter's box—apparently to reduce as much as possible its visibility in the strong lighting. The break also gave Bernstein a chance to tell Adler that chorus rhythms were still a problem and that he was tired of mentioning the dotted eighths he had first insisted on so long ago. Strasfogel reported that Krause was afraid that his offstage Toreador Song reprise could not be heard. The conductor smiled. "Tell him he's too loud, and he'll be happy."

A rumor was now circulating in the house to the effect that the chorus had turned down the offer for their services in the Deutsche Grammophon recording of this production, thereby putting the entire project in jeopardy.

Bernstein, again in his dressing room, addressing a young reporter from *Newsweek* who had asked him whether he thought *Carmen* was a singer's or a conductor's opera: "There's no such thing as a singer's or a conductor's opera. Take the example of *La Sonnambula* when I did it with Visconti and Callas. *Son-*

nambula is usually thought of as a vehicle for singing, but with us it developed into what opera should always be: theater."

The chorus again tripped over their hawking of "évantails." "Can't we get that right once?" Bernstein called up from the pit. "Don't run." They repeated, controlled, and did get it right, although on the greeting of the bullfighter, one member of the ensemble was still loudly and clearly pronouncing his name "Escameelyo." Escameelyo himself today did a good job in balancing his adoring looks at Carmen and his now-and-then cheating glances at the conductor. Outstanding problems: a lack of choral unity on the *a cappella* Alcade section, and the fight Boky still had to wage to get out of the crowd to warn Carmen.

Horne was going into the final duet with more reserve, cutting down on her finger-wiggling and fan-fiddling. A great improvement, and the duet itself proceeded at full tilt until she fudged the G-sharp on "Jamais je n'ai menti." "Dammit," she whispered in annoyance at herself.

"Say it! It was great up to there," Bernstein coaxed. They repeated to get the correction and went on, Horne doing rather too much with the laughter on José's avowal that for her sake he will remain a bandit. The business had not yet been honed down to proper scale. McCracken inadvertently stepped on her dress when she tried to move away—her first big movement of the scene—but the duet, as far as Horne and McCracken were concerned, now presented few problems. The chorus still had to give more, vocally and in terms of movement when those that could be seen in the upstage bleachers were supposed to react to the triumphs in the ring. They also were not well enough synchronized with the stabbing, which was supposed to occur to a backdrop of a shout of victory. Today Carmen had to die twice. Then those little heads on the balustrade turned on their spits and observed José's remorse.

Osie Hawkins called to Kuntner to turn off the stage lights and bring up the house. "We're burning up back here, Rudi," was his desperate plea. Were there going to be repeats? Is that why Kuntner had left the hot spots on? Riecker approached the podium. "Maestro," he inquired gently, "are you through?"

"Don't ask me. I'm not the maestro," Bernstein replied with considerable unhappiness as he surveyed the day just past. Riecker put his arm around the conductor's shoulders and led him away.

Horne, backstage, was in a much better frame of mind. She acknowledged that it had been a rough rehearsal. "What a day! What a role! Carmen, Isolde, Butterfly, Orfeo [a part she was to sing just a bit later in the season]—they're the killers." But she was scrubbing her makeup off with great energy, evidently not all that fatigued by the efforts she had had to make. She also indicated, when told about the chorus's rejection of the recording contract, that she was not upset about this stumbling block. "I'm glad they said no. I have enough to do right now. In fact, I haven't signed my contract with DGG either."

*

September 16

The house was nearly full, many in the audience having arrived at least an hour early to get a good unreserved seat for this late-Saturday-morning dress rehearsal. The section at the front of the orchestra was reserved for members of the company, and they were there in force: Sándor Kónya, Ezio Flagello, Peter Maag, Gilda Cruz-Romo, Martina Arroyo, Bonaldo Giaiotti, George Shirley, Placido Domingo, Sherrill Milnes, Matteo Manuguerra, Paul Plishka, Shirley Verrett, Nedda Casei, all the covers, naturally, plus Rafael Kubelik, the man designated to become music director of the company the following season, and a nonoperatic luminary, Van Cliburn. Interestingly, two prominent Carmens of the company were also in attendance: Regina Resnik down front amid her colleagues, and Grace Bumbry, who had created the title role in the just discarded production, alone, in the last row, just in front of the lighting booth.

It was a rehearsal in name only. Really more of a preview with an overlay of first-night excitement, for now it was not so much that for the first time what had been polished during the rehearsal period was to be revealed to musicians, a demonstration of how well the work had been done, but that members of the laity, Guild members and guests with no particular *partipris* except curiosity and a desire to be entertained, were sent as an advance wave of the great general public this production had to convince. Was it to be worthy of the Metropolitan? Of opening night? Of the memory of Goeran Gentele? Of the famous personalities who were connected with it? If the production could conquer this dress rehearsal, the path to opening night was clear. Excitement was intense. How close would one's impressions, hopes, doubts coincide with those of a full theater?

What would be the impact? And the biggest questions of all—would the snarls, sores, and unattended patches so evident up to now be absorbed in the face of performance? Would adrenalin conquer Bernstein's evident pessimism? Would Horne make it in a role few could visualize her in and in a production she had clearly not liked? And would the vocal risks McCracken was taking pay off? Would Krause's suavity carry? His breath hold out? All these questions would soon have replies.

Hawkins came before the curtain and in his orotund Southern senator's tones announced the pleasure with which the company was presenting this rehearsal of the Gentele *Carmen*. He also warned that there might be stops for corrections (there weren't; in fact, later that season when there were, atypically, several interruptions at a dress rehearsal of *Il Trovatore* with Mme. Caballé singing at half-voice, the Guild member guests, forgetting that they were attending a rehearsal, became vocally abusive). Hawkins next welcomed Leonard Bernstein back to the Metropolitan. These were housewarming sentences sufficient to bring a standing ovation for Bernstein when, red-shirted, with Mauceri at his side, he made his way through the pit to the podium. He quickly gave his first cue, and the crashing cymbals announced the brio and rhythmic snap that could be expected from him. The Prelude was clear, idiosyncratic, alive.

Don José was standing in his fate-motive light again, although the light itself appeared to arrive somewhat tardily. When full lights came up, no sound from the audience greeted the sets. It was a silence carrying wonder at the starkness of it all. The back curtains were visible. The soldiers smoked, those plumes of gray helping to fill up the spaces of the arid geometry. Maliponte got her gesture of rejection at long last, but Gibbs's voice was being swallowed up by something. Was it the carpet, giving off much dust, whose effects were possibly now, under performance conditions, to be known fully?

Some blocking bits still appeared arbitrary: Micaela's cross to the stairs leading to the top of the guardhouse, where she sits with considerable boldness, having made up her mind to wait for José. (Was the chorus's assurance that "il y sera" sufficient motivation for a rather uncharacteristic "making herself at home"? Maliponte also got off the beat when she announced she would come back at the changing of the guard.) And, unsurprisingly, putting the children in place meant the usual gear-shifting. Fortunately they sang absolutely in time.

Gibbs's dialogue exchange with McCracken was also disappearing, although the tenor did not seem to find it difficult to project his speaking voice. Gramm radiated assurance, even when he momentarily slipped away from the light, and infused life into the longueurs of the spoken French. The audience, however, did not respond to anything until that one wayward urchin, separated from his troops, was hustled offstage. Some chuckles greeted this.

The chorus girls wandered on, the haphazard checking by the guards at the gate not sufficiently specific to identify the action. They were on their toes for Bernstein's beat, only occasionally going awry on those quick sixteenth half-tone figures for "c'est la fumée." Was anyone paying attention to the new music? No turning heads or buzzing had yet been detectable.

Those sitting in the orchestra, of course, could not see Horne on her entrance, upstage and below stairs as it was, but applause came from those in the upper levels. The mezzo's very piano first verse of the "Habañera" was focused, careful, and somewhat tight, but it held the center of attention as it had to. She was worried about platform steps, but she gradually warmed and her voice bloomed. The low, broad, chesty "Prends garde à toi!" aroused in the audience a perceptible snort of pleasure, amusement, and enjoyment of her vocal instrument. The house, too, was beginning to loosen, the first signs since the curtain rose. McCracken was already perspiring and looked hung up on the frozen semi-blacked-out "fate" walk, which Horne could not enrich with enough intention to make the lengthy sequence hold.

Maliponte reappeared and promptly forgot a line ("C'est moi"). They did not stop. She was again a little off the beat during the beginning of the duet but recovered. In general, here, it seemed that either Bernstein was setting an even slower tempo or that nerves were making the singers want to pull ahead. With this phenomenon, plus McCracken looking awkward on his cross to get away from Micaela to muse on the "démon," and Maliponte's somewhat mincing sweetness, the duet had come across more successfully on other occasions. The applause was good, but it threw the two singers for their subsequent dialogue—one of those previously unexpected occurrences they would now be able to prepare for.

The battling factory women came on limply, leaving Zuniga quite deserted in his concern at their minimal agitation. There was still enough confusion for Miss Brewer to find herself for the first time at the bottom of the pile of bodies and for Horne to forget a cross that had been planned on. The mezzo was doing this scene quite gingerly, treating it, as was her option, as a rehearsal. She got a good laugh, nevertheless, on her shrug of denial that any of this strife had been of her doing. The "Oui, c'est elle!" cry was late again, and the dash by that chorus girl downstage to attack slowed everything up. The audience responded to words for the first time when Zuniga declared that Carmen had "la main leste." Laughter also was provoked by those held-off la-la's.

The tying-up of Carmen was clumsy, fumbled, and Horne's responses to Zuniga were likewise confused. Her dialogue with José before the "Séguidille," however, was infused with that largeness and earthiness of gesture ("Sans doute!" she roared) which was her particular capital in realizing the validity of Carmen. She did not tap her feet on the carpet, and gone too were the quick changes of mood in the lines of the "Séguidille" Bernstein had wanted. She appeared to thrive on the tempo and had the audience with her. In fact, by now she was playing fully for them, having subtly, perhaps even unconsciously, made the transition from a rehearsal with colleagues to a performance with watchers. Her untying of her bonds amused, although the tug-of-war looked like a bit of business rather than something that naturally happened between Carmen and Don José. The final push that frees Carmen and sends her lover-to-be to prison came off snappily. The curtain, with a little holding help from Bernstein on the last note, made it. The applause for this first act would have been rated as moderately warm.

The Guild ladies, wise in the ways of dress rehearsals, munched on trimmed-crust sandwiches in the recesses of the Grand Tier bar during the intermission, making it back to their seats in time to applaud the Act Two set. (Interestingly, the previously remarked-on echo that some of the woodwinds were making during the entr'acte was not absorbed by all these bodies.)

The torso show had been toned down, and so was the "Chanson Bohémienne," all three girls finding their choreography a source of disagreement. Horne held back considerably as if, as in the first act, she had yet to warm up. Paul Franke did his "o-o-o-obligé" with conviction, actually one of the few words of spoken French that could be heard during the hubbub before the arrival of Escamillo. Boky held her final "Vivat!" too long, but Krause came on in a stylish flourish that carried all before it. He was fully alive, a complete figure of the corrida today, even if the dotted eighths were not exactly in time and he grabbed the proffered cloth (the restaurant make-do cape) with altogether unconvincing improvisation. Once in hand, however, it was wielded with great style. The second verse saw an adjustment in the dotted eighth-note calculation, but he appeared to be having a slight breathing problem, just what had been feared.

Carmen whispered in Escamillo's ear to readable comic effect, and one of the ballet boys cleanly placed that without-which-nothing chair against the bar. Boky collided with the rear-end-scratching dancer, but finally all except the quintet people got off. It could now be seen that Velis's camping, which was calculated to indicate Remendado's homosexuality, was not achieving what he might have hoped. Finding not much response from the audience—no laughter, nothing he could put his finger on—he began to force, to broaden more than would have been necessary if an ensemble of characterizations for these supporting players had been fully worked out. The quintet itself had been more *tutti* in the past, the return to *a tempo* at the end being especially rough. Still, it was all basically there, and someone in that preview audience accorded it a sincere bravo.

Now came the real laugh of the day. José's "Dragon d' Alcala" was heard offstage, and he arrived to Carmen's petulant "Enfin!" which communicated nicely. The audience was with the scene. The long dialogue began with José simultaneously protesting his adoration and trying to remove his scabbard and its contents to place on the bar for later heaving by the heroine. McCracken could not get it to come loose. "Carmen, je t'aime, je t'adore" he protested, and Horne, not able to resist, replied in English, "Yes, after you take the sword off." The house exploded in roars of laughter and delighted applause. (Horne said later that she had not consciously been aware of the Freudian connection between the word "sword" and José's obvious intentions; it was just one of those fortunate verbal accidents.) At least a minute for this spontaneous demonstration passed before the two could continue. Horne herself had some difficulties coming up. She forgot to "croque les bonbons" so José could remark that she did so, and the castanes, which she found with an adorable "Tiens, les voici!" would not go on with ease, nor did they appear to want to stay there once donned, and she flatted during the dance. The interrupting offstage trumpets were only moderately in time.

But Horne did do something new and wonderful, and that came in her reaction to José's announcement that duty dictated he must return to the barracks. Her "Au quartier! pour l'appel!" was delivered with unbelieving, withering intensity. This was a tremendously effective change of mood. The not very readable mockery, however ("Il souffre de partir," etc.) was balanced by the very realistic-looking choking before the Flower Song, which McCracken began in a beautifully hovering *mezza voce.* He had some difficulty in support midway through, but the final scale to the pianissimo B-flat submitted to complete control. Bravos echoed throughout the hall. The gamble, at least today, had paid off.

Horne proved correct about the carpet, at least at one point, for the beginning of the "là-bas" section, which she sang on the floor, was quite swallowed up. She had to be careful to keep her head raised. The act continued with a confused "Qui frappe? qui vient là?" and a still disorganized duel, accompanied today by light projections on the back wall popping in and out of focus. Horne's reaction to the battle was unclear, as were the audience's reaction to her "circus trick." There was no mass intake of breath, no rustling of pleasure or surprise or suppressed giggles of admiration as had greeted that Act One tromboned "Prends garde à toi!" It was not making any particular point. In other words, it had been a lot of calculation and conflict for no real result. Bizet knew where all the really socko moments were, and one could not really manufacture any others. The massive ritard on "Comme c'est beau la liberté" went off perfectly. Horne, no doubt trying to hammer home her point concerning her extraordinarily wide range, took a brilliant high C in the finale, marred by that glaringly lit back wall but responded to by the audience, which chuckled at Carmen's contemptuous presentation to Don José of the rifle.

One Guild lady to another: "The dialogue is coming across beautifully. I do wish I understood French."

Another Guild lady to still another: "But Horne is so unsexy."

One cover announced to another that the recording had definitely been canceled.

Members of the company excitedly discussed the almost completely negative reception given the night before to the New York City Opera's new production of *Don Giovanni.* The booing of conductor Bruno Maderna and director Frank Corsaro particularly impressed them. One wondered how the Kolombatovich duels for this earlier set-in-Seville drama had fared.

Bernstein, in clean turtleneck, came out for Act Three. The entr'acte was played angelically and the set received with applause. The tube really had everyone taking notice. Still, now seen somewhat from the side, the stage picture made a strange impression. The inclined tube area was fine, but there were acres of space on either side that, by not being defined, became a sort of no-man's-land, at least until filled by moving figures.

The chorus got off the beat in its "Ecoute, compagnon" but recovered, as did Horne and McCracken from a slight hesitancy in their first round of dialogue—a rather truncated bit involving José looking down into a village in the valley where his mother lives, an action that becomes an object of Carmen's scorn. Baldwin and Boky also had difficulty staying with the orchestra on the reprise of their trio tune ("Parlez encore"), and Horne's contribution seemed even slower than ever. Could it now be at less than half the speed of the first part? Had Bernstein forgotten the ratio he had emphasized so early in the rehearsals? Horne was clearly not finding it easy, and on the crescendo phrase "Recommence vingt fois," etc., she gave one the feeling that she might be nearly at the end of her generous breath reserves. That, with the other two again not anchored during the second "Parlez encore" reprise, indicated that a little conference here might be in order. At the end Horne stood, the first time she made this move at a rehearsal. It seemed suitably emphatic.

Russell Christopher, who initially had great trouble with his spoken parts—pronunciation, pace, focusing—was now showing the results of the work he must have put in. His words as Dancaïre were all extraordinarily clear, as clear as the shawls the three girls snatched from the smuggled casket and wore gleamingly around their shoulders as they moved in the darkness around the disk, taunting Don José. Indeed, it *was* very close to Woglinde, Welgunde, and Flosshilde baiting Alberich.

Bernstein manifestly was enjoying this "douanier" chorus, but he was making an awful lot of ritards, even in places where he had previously said he would not. But it was "his" passage, and he should be allowed his way, one felt. This ended,

Maliponte appeared at the apex of the funnel and Micaela's air began. "What, no recitative?" whispered Gilda Cruz-Romo to Shirley Love, the Mercédès cover who was sitting next to her, this particular cutting of recitative evidently making an impression because it involved a sequence this singer had probably never questioned. How startling.

Maliponte did not have a good day with it. The tempo was too slow for her own inner rhythms, and she was gesturing all over the place—face, shoulders, everywhere. (Had Melano delivered Igesz's note on this subject?) Furthermore, she was finding it hard to keep the legato going, and those pesky upper note supports were buckling. She no longer backed offstage.

Krause, crystallinely fresh, reappeared, but McCracken, his nerves betraying him, like most everyone else at least at one time or another today, jumped a cue and crossed to engage Escamillo in knife thrusts. Krause recovered but again showed that the scene taxed his capacity for breath control. The tenor, surprisingly, now grew in his capacity for dramatic, lyric outpouring, and the finale made its impact, especially if one were able to overlook that senseless mass chorus exit.

"I don't like the way they're treating Don José," said Placido Domingo to a companion. "No, I don't approve of making fun of him that way."

"Well, do you like it, Alvin?" someone inquired of choreographer Ailey. A straight-on stare was the answer.

Yes, he was in still another shirt, a fresh one to lead the musicians through the dynamically pulsed rhythms of the entr'acte to Act Four. Gilda Cruz-Romo, her Mexican blood coming to the surface, bounced in her seat in sympathy with the pseudo-flamenco cadences. It was a spectacular miniature, almost as dazzling as the lights that burned into the Act Four set. No applause for this, but enough stirring (puzzled admiration?) to indicate that by now the audience was in touch with the Svoboda intentions, operating on his wavelength.

"A deux cuartos" began shakily, but fortunately those

"éventails" were hawked rhythmically and with conviction. The same could not be said about the wrenching running-in and getting-in-place that was required of the urchins, who then went on, in their downstage bit of trying to fix in space the movement of the unseen "quadrilles," to point in all directions. The "A bas" rejection of the Alguacil still puzzled, of course, but on the whole the chorus today was showing that it had heeded Igesz's long-ago win-one-for-the-Gipper speech and was meticulously acting through on his directions. Many of them, nevertheless, did forget to look back at the much vivaed and bravoed Escamillo, a direction given to them that superseded their first instructions to turn their backs entirely on him and Carmen.

Krause today sported some red in the capelet around his shoulders, almost the only strong color on the entire stage, which was soon emptied of everything save Carmen by, for the first time that day, the voice of Igesz over the microphone. Resnik, in her orchestra seat, raised her head to check the light on the character she had played for so many years and was now beginning to direct in productions far from home base. The light struck Horne and her immobility full force. Resnik could not have found it anything but effective. The opera's powerful final scene moved right along, one's only reservations being centered on the still unintegrated "bandit" laugh and the feeling here, perhaps more than elsewhere, that Horne wanted, needed to be told more, would have welcomed an exploration of Carmen's character and specific applications of it to business—more than there had been time for.

The knife was drawn out of José's belt, and the audience gasped as he drove it home, McCracken slightly cheating upstage so that the bullfight fans would not have to crane too far to observe this other slaughterer. The curtain fell and the house erupted into exuberant applause and *bravi.* For them it was a triumph. Opening night was three days off, but the cast now could believe with reason that it was on its way to a critical success. Details? Oh, well. Time would take care of those.

*

September 19, A.M.

In the fifth-floor design shop David Reppa, the man charted with the actual execution of all sets seen at the Metropolitan, discussed his *Carmen* assignment.

"With a local man, Boris Aronson or Robert O'Hearn, for example, you can always hold consultations. That was not possible with Svoboda. Last April for three days, after he brought me the models and the ground plan, we talked about materials and textures. The big problems here were that of large flat areas with, hopefully, minimally visible seams, and that of the sweep from the walls into the carpet. We made up samples after he left and elevations that he could look at when he returned in May. After converting his meters, we did these elevations on the scale of one-half inch to the foot."

Very few changes were made, he said, one, however, being that a section of the stage-right wall in Act Four, although originally there, was removed when it was thought Acts Three and Four would be done without intermission. When this was changed, the wall was put back. Again, in the Act Four set the top section of the stage-left bleacher wall originally continued at an angle to its upper limits. It was found that this was not possible, so that wall ends in a somewhat snub-nosed cutoff. Of course, the very minor changes, such as the prompter's box and the ancillary steps in the platforms, could be expected. Such adjustments never came as a surprise.

Well, yes, there were a few other changes. After a *Bauprobe* in April it was seen that the Act Three tube, as designed, would be too small for the Met's dimensions. It was made higher and deeper and consequently more awkward to handle. It had to be dropped down and rolled out to the side stage, where it would wait to be dismantled by the night crew. In contrast the Acts One and Four sets, with their wide-based walls, needed no bracing and therefore took up less space. He expected that by the time of *Carmen's* reentry into the repertory the following March the crew would be accustomed to the sets sufficiently to cut down in the time required to handle them. In general Reppa found that this was a simpler, a "lighter" show to do than many of the Met productions. While those undecorated plains meant that the execution and placement had to be perfect, the absence of moldings, columns, and decoration of all kind cut down on the weight.

"This *Carmen* design is typical of the school of Svoboda," Reppa pointed out. "Oh, he has done scenery-style productions: a *Rigoletto* in Prague and a *Don Giovanni* there that reproduced on the stage, like a mirror-image, the interior of the auditorium. He has even done a Baroque *Waiting for Godot.* I expect the reaction to him in New York to be split. People here tend to like pretty pictures. That is why the second and third acts were applauded Saturday and the first and fourth not. The question is, are we going to move into the twentieth century or not? Can we accept, as Europe has done, his kinetic approach to design?"

Reppa went on to compare Svobada's pure and minimal style with the traditionalism of Aronson and the overwhelming conceptions of Franco Zeffirelli—without necessarily indicating which sort he favored. He did say, however, that he found Svoboda's *Carmen* an intellectual conception which might not sit very well with people's preconceived notions and 90 percent emotional response to stage pictures. Reppa was, one suspected, less candid about the lighting side. He claimed that the post-Svoboda experimentation with projections came about because Svoboda had decided he did not like them in the first place. Reppa did admit that the equipment of the house may have been basically at fault. "In Prague he has the best equipment. We do not have it here. For instance, we cannot do mirror projections. Yes, Svoboda had made initial lighting specifications, but they could not be set until he arrived. He was, of course, disturbed by those proscenium surfaces bouncing light into the auditorium." Was Svobada returning to check up on his work? "Oh, he might drop in in November when he comes back for a lecture tour." But Reppa's mind was already on next season, this one being an easy one for him with only one other new production, the adaptation of the Salzburg *Siegfried.* He was already concerned with next year's *Die Götterdämmerung,* and by January he expected to be well launched into *Les Troyens, Don Giovanni, L'Italiana in Algeri, I Vespri Siciliani,* and *Les Contes d'Hoffmann,* the other new productions for 1973–1974.

*

Opening Night

If there had been photographers inside for that piano dress rehearsal, they were now outside, in the lobbies, on the staircases, lugging their ungainly lighting equipment around, to record the traditional opening night ritual, which for many seasons had been shedding the stigma of aged debutantes kicking up their heels and which this year was definitely an occasion that concerned the Metropolitan Opera Company, what went on onstage and in the pit, and what this augured for the immediate future.

The personalities one recognized immediately—Eleanor Steber, Blanche Thebom, Maria Jeritza resplendent in emeralds and her eternal majesty, Joanna Simon, Pauline Trigère, Bess Meyerson, Betty Comden, Norman Singer—projected anticipation of an artistic event, and those one did not know followed their lead. The customary electricity in the air for such an evening was so strong that a kind of numbness to ordinary observations and manners set in. One could easily say, "Look, there's so and so," be overheard, not be embarrassed or think that the designated personality would react any way but positively. And others of the famous were there in abundance, one read later: Mayor and Mrs. Lindsay, Mrs. Edward Kennedy, Norman Vincent Peale, Roger Stevens, Laurance Rockefeller, Jim Nabors, Connie Stevens.

"The Star Spangled Banner!" Indeed, that did make it a special occasion, the cutting of a very big ribbon or the opening of a very big bottle (something that one cheering celebrator had apparently already taken care of). Hawkins appeared this time only briefly to introduce Lowell Wadmond, Chairman of the Board, who, although mispronouncing some key names—Igesz, Svoboda, and Gentele—made a short, graceful speech about how the show must go on in spite of all adversity. "Ladies and gentlemen, we bring you Goeran Gentele's *Carmen.*"

It was 8:15. The audience was primed to like what it saw and to not quite settle down during Bernstein's pomp-and-pride-rich Prelude. The "fate" light went on slowly and then full to the Seville square, which, seen from a new angle—the distance of the balcony—looked surprisingly different. The drabness was there, in fact a kind of battleship gray seemed to conquer the intense light, but more important, a geometric monumentality imposed its laws. One might have thought oneself in the Seville of a good, clean German production of *Fidelio.* The seams in those flat planes were not noticeable. Reppa had done his work well, as had the crew tonight.

Gibbs could not perk up the first vocal lines, and the problematic early scenes ran rather true to form, including Maliponte's lazy gesture of rejection and that cross to sit on the steps, which one realized now seemed at fault because it was not infused with any sense of its being executed by a shy, albeit knowing, peasant girl in the rough company of soldiers. The action looked dull, the set sparsely inhabited, but Gibbs brought his Morales back to *a tempo* laziness nicely after Micaela's departure. Curiously, the kids' arrival was the first touch of life. They were filling out space, and they stayed in time. As some climbed to the guardhouse roof, one realized that the *toldo* above it, with or without projections, was almost completely invisible from this angle.

Both Gibbs and McCracken boomed their first spoken lines of the night. This first indication, this first evidence of the textual newness of the "new" *Carmen,* although it had been well publicized, generated no tangible stir. The audience chuckled at the wayward child, but once these gamins were off, the stage returned to a statically rigid state. The second bit of dialogue between Zuniga and José showed that McCracken was tense. He jumped Gramm's line—the dawning realization and accusation of a past murder—so that his denial made little sense.

The "fumée" chorus did not have this tension. It badly needed more precision, especially when one took into consideration the meticulousness of the work in the pit. Horne appeared at the back of the stage and went through her slow, confident, but ultimately unexciting entrance. The "Habañera" caught fire, predictably, on her chested, emphatic "Prends garde á toi!" but elsewhere it was somewhat tight and off-pitch (to be expected under these circumstances; Caballé later in the season sang the entire Act One of her first Metropolitan *Norma* off pitch) and not in total accord with what Bernstein was doing rhythmically. She was vociferously bravoed when it ended (yes, there was a boo). From this new distance the long "fate" cross held and Horne's look back at José from the factory door as she ran off read effectively.

Again, dialogue sounded shaky, this time the few lines exchanged between Micaela and José, but the duet itself was lovely, Maliponte, working from strength, with only the most fleeting signs of those awkward areas of her scale. McCracken helped, too, of course, but he seemed not quite warmed up, occasionally slipping under the note and at the top somewhat constricted. Naturally, he was perspiring profusely, and he appeared almost to forget the buss he administers to Micaela. Was he going to have an off night, one wondered. The applause for the duet was solid.

Some rhythmic confusion reigned during the factory squabble, but visually it was a very controlled ruckus, again reminiscent of a Germanic way with crowds, specifically the riot in the old stylized mid-fifties Wieland Wagner *Die Meistersinger.* And where was the "couteau" José refers to when he explains the origin of the dispute to Zuniga? It was on the ground, out of McCracken's reach. He did not stop to pick it up. Horne reaped the hoped-for laughter on the la-la's, but not on her shrug with its "c'est pas ma faute" implication. Perhaps it was lost to this particular crowd, a differently complected one from that of the dress rehearsal. Impossible to gauge these things. They chuckled, however, at Horne's surprising of José with kisses and ear nibblings, which tonight she timed exactly, better than she managed the beginning of the dialogue that introduces the "Séguidille." This she anticipated, and this might have started a chain reaction because the play with the rope between them did not work smoothly, and this was reflected in the lack of freedom she was able to find in her singing. The rope did not have its space, and the "Séguidille" did not have all the abandon one knew Horne, in spite of her concern about the killingly, sensuously slow tempo, could give it. Act One ended. Many bravi. Three curtain calls for the ensemble. Omens positive.

The naked torsos returned for Act Two, and the back of the down-front center one offered a gleaming plain to set off Carmen's long nails in an astute bit of live prop employment. Boky improvised like mad for the dance steps, which none of the three girls were conquering tonight. Horne, however, projected well, including the spoken words that follow, tending only once in a while to a fishwifey volume that worked against the illusion of the sexy gypsy. Projection tonight was a problem for Tom Krause, whose Escamillo visually had all the élan it needed but was vocally lightweight at this distance. Was he too to have an off night? Was the carpeting ironically affecting the male voices and not the female ones? No, it could not be a question of masculine registers, because Gramm's voice was hitting all targets. The Toreador Song was coolly applauded, although Carmen's whispered response to Escamillo was quickly seized by the audience as something worthy of laughter.

From the balcony the quintet took on an isolation in space as the stage around the participants grayed out. It went well, with only the slightest hint of too much pressure of speed at the end, marred a bit by a squeaky high A-flat from Miss Boky. One also, even at this distance, could detect McCracken's fear of not getting his sword off in time. He rushed through showing Carmen the coin she had sent him in prison so, taking no chances, he could get at that unbuckling. Horne, however, seemed to be slowing up in her reactions. Some of her lines—still making a charming impression in this eating scene—emerged almost as afterthoughts. The dance, too, sounded tired, and unlike McCracken tonight, she was unable to get rid of a prop—her castanents—which have to be thrown at José's feet when he tells her that he's not staying for the rest of the planned entertainment. Those castanets that previously did not want to stay in her hands now were sticking there like glue, and when you can't throw in anger, when the emotion seizes, you can't throw later very convincingly. As a result the mocking of José was somewhat undercut, and Horne generally pulled in her Hornes, toppling only one chair when previously two or three had to receive the impact of Carmen's annoyance. The viciousness of props particularly attacked Act Two tonight, for later, in the duel, at last much improved as to vigor, Zuniga's sword broke off at the hilt.

McCracken made a positive impression with the Flower Song, although he and Bernstein did part company briefly toward the middle of the aria, getting several bravos before the orchestra could finish its postlude. This was no surprise, certainly nothing like the shock of Horne's ha-ha-ha on her circus trick—"La liberté!" On opening night the lady was taking no chances.

Intermission eavesdroppings:
"Jackie is a divine Carmen."
"It's a catastrophe, except for Horne."
"I miss the old *Carmen.*"
"I'm tired of *Carmen.*"

The audience drifted back into the hall for Act Three, the regal Jeritza just making it to her first-row orchestra seat in time to shake warmly the hand of conductor Bernstein as he reached the podium. Tonight he conducted an entr'acte whose crucial flute solo lacked the ultimate smoothness of legato the conductor wanted. Never mind, it would be better another time. The set was applauded, Act Three, like Act One, looking better from straight on above and at a distance than from close by in the orchestra. Unfortunately, however, for balcony and other upper-reach patrons, the uneven ridges of the tube top suggesting mountain silhouettes had gone the way of the Act One *toldo.* Some grumblings from the older devotees (those who after twenty years had still not adjusted to the Bayreuth lightbulb shortage) about how dark it was.

Sore thumbs: McCracken still saying "Carmen" with the accent on the first syllable and giving "village" a feminine "une"; Horne turning up neither "carreau" nor "pique"—red and black, even if not suits, can be seen from a great distance—as she read the cards and her forgetting to turn up a new card every time she sang "Encore!"

The *cornuto* gesture from chorus members appeared to have returned, *malheureusement,* but Bernstein was getting tremendous mileage out of his beloved "douanier" chorus culminating in that extraordinary modulation back to G-flat Major and the hammered-out repetition of the original melody.

Maliponte, too, rode high. Micaela's aria came through accurately (although the first "Seigneur" was arrived at a shade too soon), smoothly and with splendidly supported tone, which she called on later for a brilliant forte *portamento* (high B-flat to E above middle C) in her plea to José to have pity on his mother. It made such a favorable impression that when someone began mood-breaking applause before the postlude was concluded, he was promptly shushed. Only when Bernstein hit the last triple-piano chord and the soprano had backed completely offstage did the house erupt in approval.

Krause seemed more at ease for his reappearance, and the fight with José looked relatively real and under control, more so than the later hurling of Carmen to the ground by José. Where, however, was the light on him for his exit?

Again, a boo mixed in with all the tumultuously warm reception. The artists now took solo curtain calls (Micaela was through for the night), and it was clear that Maliponte and Horne were garnering the major share of the house's favor.

The customary applause for conductor and orchestra meted out before the last act of any performance at the Metropolitan was tonight long and loud when Bernstein returned to the podium. He immediately rejustified this approval with a taut, controlled, yet excitingly sensual entr'acte to Act Four. But, as at the dress rehearsal, the raising of the curtain elicited no response from the audience. The chorus proffered their "lorgnettes" and "évantails," and with the addition of the kids, who rushed forward on Stivender's very audible command after the two G Major chords Bernstein had reluctantly restored to allow for more stage action time, the stage took on a dynamism that surpassed anything that had yet been seen this opening night. The combined greeting to Escamillo, with the drums and cymbals and the cutting tones of the children, which could be heard above the fortissimo efforts of everyone else, added up to a terrific impact for the entering Escamillo (again without a red touch on the cape) and Carmen. One old problem still persisted for our bull-baiter, that is, getting hung up stage left in a frozen reception of the Alcade and his wife while Frasquita (still somewhat blocked by the crowd), Mercédès, and Carmen conferred about the José threat.

Horne tonight made more extensive and more telling use of her fan, opening it with a flourish to chase away José's overtures, but if one's ears did not deceive, did Bernstein not cut her off on the held A-flat of "que je l'aime!"? Was this revenege for ha-ha-ha two acts back? Well, be that as it may, the moment passed and fury took over. Carmen lay dead in a pool of light. The mythic death, the apotheosis of the workings of fate. From the balcony it looked the way one hoped and one expected it should. The house received it wildly and, later, Maliponte, Horne, and Bernstein on their solo calls. Alvin Ailey, David Walker, and Bodo Igesz joined the lineup in front of the curtain, the last of these not taking a bow of his own.

The production was written about with general euphoria by the press. Harold Schonberg, next day in *The New York Times,* thus treating this event as much as a news item as a musical happening (for the past few years this paper has pursued a policy of running notices *two* days after a performance), dubbed the previous evening's *Carmen* "daring and provocative . . . a brilliant conception." He commented favorably too on Horne's "earthy quality," her humor, and her attempt to make Carmen a woman "eternally fascinating. And she sang it magnificently. . . . Probably not since Bruna Castagna has New York heard this kind of sung Carmen, so secure in the lower register, so smooth in the scale, so subtle in phrase." The man from 43rd Street also lauded Bernstein for his "emotional control" and "elegant line from beginning to end, unorthodox as some of the tempos were." Praise went to McCracken for his pianissimo ending of the Flower Song and for the "real grandeur" of his acting in Act Four. Maliponte he found a "real comer" with "a good deal of authority," and he liked Krause's acting although "one would have welcomed a little more velvet in his voice." Schonberg barely mentioned Igesz, almost as if no stage director except the ghost of Gentele had been at work.

Harriet Johnson in *The Post* seemed somewhat more in touch with the specifics of this production when she commented on its "mood of Greek tragedy." "Rhythm is the life of music," she wrote, "and last night Bernstein was its Atlas." She continued: "Many who had thought of *Carmen* as a great but overworked score realized that under Bernstein it had thrown off its shackles as surely as Carmen rid herself of the rope which bound her hands behind her back." She praised the production, the work of Igesz and Svoboda but, amazingly, did not bother to mention the singers.

The third New York daily, *The News,* next to a wrongly captioned photograph (*Time* a few days later made the exact same mistake in attributing a shot of some Act One action to Act Two), also called on nothing but positive adjectives in Douglas Watt's summary of what had been seen and heard. He liked Horne's "sluttish authority and heartiness" and McCracken's "robust, dull-witted but immensely appealing Don José." He liked the use of the broken plate as ersatz castanets, apparently under the impression that this was a directorial touch rather than an *opéra-comique* given.

If anything, the weekly critics went even further. *Time,* concentrating on Horne's contribution (a five-paragraph mini-bio was appended to the review), asserted that this *Carmen* allowed one to "begin to believe again in opera itself." Alan Rich in *New York* magazine called the production an "overwhelmingly brilliant accomplishment" and he sanctified Igesz as "one of the great stage directors of our time," Horne's Carmen as "one of the most remarkable minglings of endowments and intelligence I have witnessed on any stage," and McCracken as "the first of a new breed, a tenor who can take stage direction." The reviewer clearly viewed the event as a watershed separating what went on during the, for Rich, deplorable Bing years and the epoch inspired by the vision of Gentele. Leighton Kerner in *The Village Voice* also viewed *Carmen* as a landmark.

Newsweek, amid all this reporting on what was shaping up as an historic event in one of the major institutions of American culture, strangely refused to lose its head. Although critic Hubert Saal greatly liked many elements—Bernstein's "powerful" conducting, Svoboda's "stark and startling" sets, Horne's "baked from Spanish clay, earthy and knowing" Carmen, and McCracken's "unflagging mixture of strength and sweetness," he wrote that "the whole . . . does not equal the sum of its parts. The Gentele vision is never unified. . . . The production suffer[s] from overkill. Agitation rather than excitement overtakes the stage." He went on to mention Igesz's lack of preparation time and quoted him as saying that getting the production ready was "like trying to fit a jigsaw puzzle together."

Perhaps the coolest of all reviews was that written by guest critic Andrew Porter as his debut contribution to *The New Yorker.* This immensely knowledgeable commentator, who is never caught without a full panoply of information, appeared the only one who reviewed the evening as a musical occurrence uninfluenced by considerations concerning the Gentele real-life drama or the changing of the guard this *Carmen* marked. He liked some things, disliked others. Among the former, McCracken's "forceful and passionate" José and Horne's Carmen, which he implied had succeeded in spite of the unsuitability of her looks and voice. He deplored, however, her spoken dialogue in which he felt she came through as "disconcertingly apt to suggest a big jolly girl, as refreshingly harmless underneath as any Micaela. She won many laughs." He found Maliponte "conventional" and Krause's singing "monotonous and imprecise, and his French barely intelligible." He kudoed Gibbs and Gramm and most of Bernstein's work, except for the Prelude which he said was "all battery and brass, where what matters is that we should hear vigorous string articulation." He spent the rest of his space questioning Svoboda's efforts ("a fluent, versatile designer . . . but the cut of his sets is often awkward and crude") and the advisability of calling upon so many musical restorations. He concluded most surprisingly, considering the startling effect it makes, by damning the end of Act Four. "The alternatives here are numerous, and the version chosen by the Metropolitan Opera is disastrously less effective than the familiar ring of fanfares cutting into José's 'Eh bien! damnée!'"

Mr. Porter had got his New York career off to an independent start.

All six *Carmen*s that fall sold out as soon as tickets went on sale, and the series in the spring, although, of course, Bernstein was no longer conducting, did just as well. *Carmen* was as big a hit with the public as any the company had produced, and naysayers were few. One heard mostly remarks about the startingly clean sweep this *Carmen* made of all past conceptions and how it would now be impossible to accept the old grand-opera version and its usual "Best Wishes from Seville" incarnation.

For a direct confrontation of the two styles, a visit was paid shortly after opening night to the offices of Amberson Productions, Bernstein's own company, to view a cassette tape of the conductor's 1962 television show entitled "The Drama of Carmen." This was the earliest evidence of the maestro's thinking about the work, the earliest testimony to his understanding of how the dialogue enhanced the viability of the opera as a stage work and to his likemindedness with the later thinking of Gentele. It's a curious tape to watch at a ten-year remove: advertisements for out-of-date cars, a Bernstein with only a touch of gray in his hair, singers and actors one now thinks of in other contexts.

Bernstein conducted the New York Philharmonic in the Prelude much as he was doing now at the Met, perhaps a little faster, but with the pronounced dotted eighths and the ritard leading to the return of the first statement very much in evidence. He then addressed the viewers directly, mentioning the color and abandon, wit, irony, humor, mockery, and fun he found in this overture to a tragedy. The conductor's exuberance led him to some tautologies the man today would never be caught trapped in, for example, a reference to the fate motive as a harbinger of the "final dénouement." This doom, he said, is the other side of the *Carmen* coin, Carmen's bullfighter like flirtation with death. He illustrated how her Act One entrance music is really only a speeded-up modification of that same fate motive.

He then introduced the singers, Jane Rhodes and William Olvis, both ex-Metropolitanians in a traditionally staged and costumed run-through of the "Habañera," a segment that showed the French soprano as a markedly gayer interpreter of the scene than Horne, a gaiety Bernstein underlined by quoting Nietzsche's words on the "tragic humor of Carmen—short, sudden, without forgiveness." The conductor clearly thought this element a keystone to any successful essaying of the part.

Then Bernstein went on to demonstrate how the Guiraud recitatives, written for the first Vienna production in 1875, the same year as the first comique performance, abbreviated and distorted the burden of the original dialogue. "The depth of the characters is revealed in the dialogue, and further layers of meaning by the music after the dialogue," and he illustrated this by showing the same scene, the José-Zuniga exchange in Act One, first in the recitative version (with English subtitles), then in an English translation of the *opéra-comique* lines. "You see, Don José is a ninny without the dialogue, but with the words he is not prissy." He also had the post-"Habañera" dialogue spoken to prove that Carmen's interest in José is more likely to be aroused by these lines that it would be by what she is offered as a love object in the recitative.

The spoken Carmen of this telecast was Zohra Lampert, the dusky-voiced, highly individualistic actress known for her work with the Second City Review, from small but telling character parts in several films (*Splendor in the Grass*), and from the early days of the Lincoln Center Repertory Theater. Miss Lampert, whose engagingly off-center delivery of lines marks her as a true original (ripe for imitation if she were recognized by a wider audience) approached the gypsy in her own quasi-Actor's Studio fashion, but after a few scenes one's amusement at the notion of these two ever getting together on common turf subsided and Miss Lampert's sincerity took over. "She's a true beatnik," Bernstein summed up in a time-fixing judgment on Carmen as painted by Lampert in the here much less cut dialogue scenes between the cat fight and the "Séguidille."

Bernstein acknowledged the overwhelming popularity of the grand-opera version but lamented the loss of depth that accompanied its supplanting of the original. He compared *Carmen* to a Broadway musical in its canny alternation of words and music, and he referred to the "hit-tune" quality of the "Séguidille" whose composition he described as "water off a duck's back." He even took some time out from his main *comique*-versus-grand thesis to make an analysis of Bizet's way of handling harmony, what he called Bizet's slinking around the key of B minor in the "Séguidille." "It's the twenty-fifth bar before he states it. This has a titillating effect." He similarly pointed to the "kife like" modulations in the "Chanson Bohémienne," which he cited for its intensity as a nonplot number. He then conducted it quite a good deal faster than he was to do ten years later.

It was very entertaining to watch the eating scene as delivered by Lampert and James Congdon; Horne's voluptuary "de tout, de tout, de tout" was now transformed into the actress's manic "everything, everything, everything." This segment Bernstein held up as a paradigm of the quick-change artist that Carmen was emotionally; thus her childlike joy in food and in taking the trumpet sounding from the caserne ("danser sans orchestre") for accompaniment suddenly derailed into a vixenish taunting of her lover. Rhodes took over for the dance itself, no better a terpsichorean than Horne, but she was wonderfully effective in the drama that followed. The mocking phrases of "Il souffre de partir" were not there, nor were any of the restored passages; this part of Bernstein's approach had apparently not yet entered his consideration, nor had the emphasis on José as a protagonist equal to Carmen or as a figure of violence. The German researcher of the middle 1960s and the return to Mérimée still lay ahead. Interestingly, though, some bits of the Met staging could already be sampled: Carmen's curtsy to Zuniga (William Chapman both singing and acting) as she flounces the "Habañera" refrain at him just before the Act One curtain falls, Bernstein's statement that Carmen at the end of Act Two already despises José ("he's a goner") for his weakness, and Carmen's laugh in Act Four at José's promise to continue his career as a bandit.

Act Three, Bernstein said, was where we first see the tragedy of the opera, and he contrasted the darkness of Carmen's part of the card trio (faster in 1962) with the scherzo of Lee Venora's and Janis Martin's Frasquita and Mercédès (slower; the 1:2 ratio thinking was also saved for the future). Rhodes smiled through the desperate action at the end of the act, dropping the cards, not clutching them to her bosom as Horne did in her different way with the forces of fate.

"Carmen is complex and subtle. She's rich in contradictions in this opera so rich in paradox." Bernstein set her acceptance, her fatalism about death, against her compulsion for freedom (life). The contradictions, he indicated, came together in the final duet of the opera, "the crux of the drama." Rhodes, here, showed herself a much more fidgety figure of destiny, but she managed a quite wonderful expression of insight when she sang "Je sais bien que c'est l'heure," and wonder of wonders, she also appeared to hold on to that A-flat "que je l'aime" for as long as the present lady of the Met. However, she concentrated beautifully, so that when she decided to throw her ring at José it seemed a completely spontaneous idea or, perhaps even more, an idea that was working through her, moving her without her being able to resist: to hurl the object, to produce the action that would engender the reaction of murder. She did not scream "Tiens!" but sang accurately the E as scored.

Here then was visible testimony to the genesis of Bernstein's thinking about the opera, one crucial stage of development, when he actually had the opportunity to take charge of a microcosm of a production that would show him and show others the viability of his claims for the dialogue, the strength of his views on *Carmen* as music drama.

THE RECORDING

Photo: Beth Berg

The changing of the guard (Act One).

"L'amour est un oiseau rebelle . . ."

Photo: Beth Berg

Photo: Beth Bergman

.ll eyes on la Carmencita as she sets off
n her fateful stalking of Don José.

'he battling heroine flirts with her captor.

Photo: Beth Bergman

Photo: Beth Bergm

"La Séguidille."

Photo: Beth Bergman

Carmen entertains her admirers (Act Two).

Photo: Beth Bergman

Escamillo (Krause) hypnotizes the clients of Lillas Pastia.

The Quintet (Boky, Baldwin, Velis, Russell Christopher, Horne).

Photo: Beth Bergman

Adriana Maliponte
as Micaela holds
center stage
in the lonely
mountain pass
(Act Three).

Photo: Jack Mitchell

The fight down the tube.

Photo: Beth Bergman

Photo: Jack Mitchell

The crowd points out an advancing *quadrille* (Act Four).

"Si tu m'aimes . . ."

Photo: Beth Bergman

Photo: Beth Bergman

"Ah! ne me quittes pas, Carmen!"

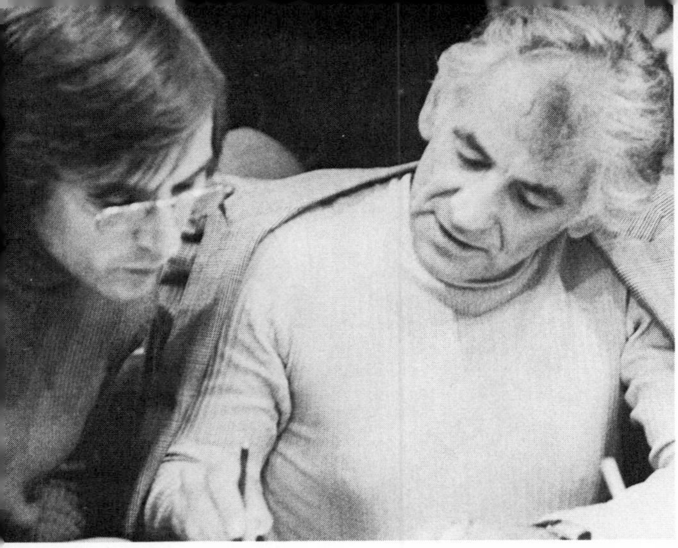

Bernstein and DGG producer Thomas Mowrey consult.

Horne listens to a playback.

The artists concentrate around the console.

*

The Recording

No change had occurred in the resistance of the Metropolitan chorus to the terms of the DGG contract, but this obstacle was not going to sink the project. At the eleventh hour, on September 15, in fact, contracts between DGG and the Met were signed and with the Thomas Pyle Chorus. This group, New York's most important jobbing singing ensemble since the disappearance of the Robert Shaw Chorale (and often a halfway point for young singers on the rise), was used to taking on the identity of the organization that hired them. The name Thomas Pyle means little to the public, even the public that is used to hearing it, and hearing it often, in performance.

Of course, this new ingredient meant extra work for Bernstein, extra rehearsal sessions with assistant Mauceri, extra expenses ($5,000) for DGG, but on Friday, September 22, another curtain rose, that on the first session of the first important commercial opera recording to be done in the United States since the Boston Symphony *Lohengrin* of 1965 and the first one involving the Metropolitan since the (again Leinsdorf) *Macbeth* of 1959. For years it has been economic folly to contemplate opera with its expensive soloists, chorus, and orchestra as a suitable investment for recording companies unless the recordings were made abroad, where union scales have as yet not been leaping about in the high coloratura ranges found in America.

Deutsche Grammophon had not, of course, gone in for profit shaving. Thomas Mowrey, American artists and repertory chief, producer of this *Carmen,* emphatically declared that "although we are budgeted at approximately two-hundred-seventy-five thousand dollars—the equal of a five- or six-disk Wagner recording of European origin—we feel that with such luminaries as Leonard Bernstein, Marilyn Horne, and James McCracken involved, we will make money." Also, Deutsche Grammophon is probably the only company in the world, with the exception of EMI and Philips, to have the distribution facilities to reach markets all over the globe, markets where classical recordings account for 20 percent of sales as opposed to the 4 percent current in the United States. An official of London Records—a company which issues a substantial share of new opera recordings these days—with something like tremulous awe in his voice, estimated that 125,000 of the Metropolitan *Carmen* would have to be sold for DGG to turn a single red peseta.

The Met and DGG, whose mutual courtship began with the Bing gala taping of spring 1972, hoped that if *Carmen* made it, this would mark the beginning of a new period in domestic opera recording. In the back of everyone's mind, too, was the undeniable fact that costs of recording in Europe are quickly approaching prohibitive American dimensions.

Mowrey also spoke further of the chorus problem. He negotiated the basic contract with the Metropolitan and with each solist. The Met in turn bargained from its own position with the orchestra, children's chorus, and adult chorus. The first two accepted terms offered, but the third group balked at what it called "after scale"—or $40 per singer per session. The Met, knowing full well that any chorus in the city would work at this rate, feared setting a dangerous precedent if it gave in to the chorus's demands for parity with the orchestra, whose members were to receive $90 per session. Now that the possibility of local recording activity presented itself, the chorus likewise did not want a precedent unadvantageous to itself established. It turned down Schuyler Chapin and his representatives but lost a job and obviously failed in making its point.

The first two recording sessions, both that first Friday, in the seventh-floor ballroom of the Manhattan Center on West 34th Street, were closed to all observers. But this grimy realm of peeling plaster, depressingly démodé decor, inch-thick dust, debris-strewn floors, *and* great sound for engineers, opened its doors to a few the following Tuesday. The Prelude, entr'actes, Flower Song, Act One Micaela-José duet, Act Three José-Escamillo scene, and Micaela's aria had already been taped (although it developed that some of these had to be repeated), and that day Stivender and the kiddies were on hand, in addition to the Pyle people (henceforth to be referred to officially in all Deutsche Grammophon publicity releases as "the Manhattan Opera Chorus"), for Act One and Act Four scenes.

Six hours of choral rehearsal had preceded this session, four yesterday with Mauceri and two today with Bernstein himself. This was to be the piecemeal method followed throughout—rehearsals for particular choral segments held just before they were scheduled for taping. The choruses were deployed on a platform at one end of the ballroom, adults in back, children in front of them at the side, with the soloists on a separate platform in front of all. White acoustic hangings, looking somewhat like emblemless fascist banners, billowed from the balcony (the eighth floor) that ran around three sides of the room. Over the great space of the ballroom area itself the orchestra spread out, most of its sections commanded by an individual track boom microphone. Under the players' feet snaked every imaginable gauge of cable. These ropes of power, paralleled somewhat by the overhead strands of floodlights, also appeared to concentrate their greatest convolutions around the conductor's fluorescent-lit podium, which nestled cozily among the instruments but which was also the depth of at least two orchestra pits away from the edge of even the frontmost platform. At any rate, the players could not complain about lack of space here.

Tuesday's three-hour session was intended to produce some forty minutes of usable recorded material, roughly a one-to-six ratio. At 2:29 P.M. the orchestra tuned up, Bernstein appeared, and immediately put the children through their paces. The youngsters were followed in the acoustic spotlight by the adult chorus and finally by playbacks in the control room, an equally dingy lair transformed into a sound factory by a maze of intricately outfitted consoles, decks, piles of one-and-a-half-inch-wide tapes, and four huge speakers (this was to be a quadraphonic as well as stereo release).

Bernstein, sitting at the coffee-cup-and-ashtray-decorated center table, listened. "It's like a male chorus, that whole last take" (the beginning of Act Four). The women were weak. Could they give more? No, Bernstein was told. Their track was played separately, since the efficient German engineer, Gunter Hermann, and his helpers, imported specifically for this project, were immediately able to rewind to the right spot and press exact levers. Bernstein shook his head but made a choice. Time already was running out. More takes for the chorus, with the demonic red eye signal staring everyone in the face, that light the symbol of the inhuman delicacy of all this machinery, machinery that had no respect for anything, even when Bernstein himself scraped a chair, in its lust for perfection.

For the next session Bernstein was again wearing his LB brooch on the denim shirt, that of the smoking lips, which he described as having been fabricated "by a hundred blind nuns." Spirits high then as he began with the "Notre métier" ensemble. The light went on. A chair scraped in the observers' balcony, and the culprit received a sharp look from the maestro. Again. The chorus was almost inaudible to the naked ear, but one assumed it was the right level for the microphones. The take ended, but another was immediately requested. Some things had to be corrected: McCracken had to come in closer to the microphone (Horne, in contrast, Mowrey later said, had a tendency to "creep" into the mike), some string articulation had to be clearer, and the chorus itself was warned about extraneous, inadvertent noises.

"This is it!" Bernstein announced. The silence while waiting for his downbeat deafened. A ticking watch, not one's own, could be detected, and so could the B-flat hum of the lights. The overhead illumination suddenly failed, then blinked back again. Start. Stop. Chorus then behind. Start. Buzzer (rather like Beckmesser's chalk) from the control. McCracken was ahead on both takes at the very beginning. Horne looked a little bored. Again.

The voice of Mowrey: "Mr. McCracken's ahead."

The voice of Mr. McCracken: "Are you sure they aren't all behind?"

"Habañera" time. "Good old entrance sixty-nine," Bernstein announced and dove into a rehearsal of the strings that slash into the notes of Carmen's entrance. Mowrey himself was adjusting Horne's music stand. The mezzo, equipped with her Rethberg watch, a very ungypsyish gray print dress and sensible low-heeled footwear (reminding one of Birgit Nilsson's dictum that all one needed to sing Isolde was a pair of comfortable shoes), noiselessly turned, without looking at them, the pages of the score in front of her as she somewhat tightly delivered the first verse. She sounded slightly overeager. It ended; the chorus applauded. Horne bowed to them, and acknowledging the strain of the situation, did a demicollapse into her chair.

In the control room, head in hand, Horne, seated in the center of the room, concentrated on the playback. Once in a while she looked up at Bernstein or Mowrey, pouted Gallicly to show she found a certain effect "pas mal," and at the *moment juste* threw a flower (a crumpled piece of paper) at the maestro. Bernstein loved the take, even to a few wheezes, which he thought contributed reality. "It sounds as though you've been sampling too many of your own cigarillos." He did want to redo the first verse. "The second is perfection. It has fire, it's hypnotic."

Back in the ballroom Bernstein announced: "This is *the* take." Horne looked pleased and more relaxed this time, hands on hips, then at the pit of her stomach for the "Prends garde à toi!" "Great, Jackie! Fantastic!" The postaria "sur tes pas" had to be redone ("Let's be together—by eye, not ear") again and again and again. Late flutes. Rushing. Again. "I'm going crazy now," Bernstein mourned. "I can't rely on my own judgment."

"They're pushing," Mowrey reported.

"They sound behind to me," said Bernstein. Again. "If that's good, I'll shoot myself."

Complete quiet in the hall for two minutes as those in the control room listened for distortion. Bernstein smoked and gazed into the middle distance. For technical reasons the end of the "fate" walk and the flower-throwing girls' chorus had to be taped again. The ladies were not together. "It was terrific the other time when the tape was bad," Bernstein lamented as he left the podium.

"I like the second "Habañera" even more," he told Horne in the control room, and she wondered which take had the better recitative. She half shut her eyes in concentration on the playback, screwing up her nose in distaste on a "je t'aime."

"You don't like it?" Mowrey seemed startled.

Bernstein remarked on her question-and-answer way with the words. He did not think the second verse this time was smoky enough. "Tuhrrific 'Habañera,'" he concluded, however. Carmen's final laugh was left to be dubbed later, and it was also provisionally decided that the take of the recitative up to the "re-" of "rebelle" would start the "Habañera," the rest to come basically from the second complete run-through.

"As far as I'm concerned, the rest would be nitpicking," concluded a very satisfied mezzo. Since the Act Two finale was scheduled next, Horne said, again in a dead-accurate imitation of Nilsson's speaking voice, "Ooh, then I must go warm up my high notes."

McCracken pointed out, when everyone had reassembled in recording position, that on Zuniga's Act Two knocking entrance his first "Qui frappe? qui vient là?" should be loud to make sense of Carmen's subsequent, protective "Tais-toi." He had been half whispering up to now. "You're right, Jim," agreed Bernstein. "It's not often I learn something from a singer." Much laughter and some rude gestures from the platform. They started with a take, right through to Horne's ha-ha-ha's, which now would be preserved for posterity. "Well, let's do that all over again," Bernstein announced. "Jackie, watch me on 'Au diable le jaloux.' You're late. Also 'le mot n'est pas galant' drags. Andy, you're singing wrong notes." Everybody retuned and rewarmed.

Another take, this time with a somewhat quavery Gramm, Velis again singing wrong notes, and a slightly shorter lingering on the high B from Horne. Bernstein beamed his approval but allowed only a verbalized "Pretty good." Mowrey, at the playback, remarked on his dislike of Horne's joining of Guiraud's interpolated soprano and Bizet's mezzo lines.

"I'll never give you one the other way," Horne laughed with iron in her chuckle. "You might use it." (In fact, Horne in the Lewis-led performances did sing the passage somewhat "the other way." Instead of Guiraud's E—F-sharp—G—B sequence, she went back to C—D—E for the first three notes before shooting up to the B. This seemed to enable her to sing all the words.)

October 4 was another big day, beginning with the end of Act Three. Here Maliponte had a chance to make love to her music stand, filling the air around it with caresses. Her *portamenti,* as usual, were chillingly effective. Krause backed off to simulate distance on the Toreador Song reprise of his exit, shrugging his shoulders to express uncertainty as to whether or not this movement was sonically correct. Actually, of course, such details could always be taken care of by the big machine. Gone are the days when opera singers moved about among numbered squares to indicate positions that would show up as action in stereo reproduction. The consoles can do it all.

"Well, there were wrong notes, wrong tempi, wrong dynamics. Otherwise we could have used it," Bernstein gallows-grinned in the control room. But when the segment was played back, he found much of it "exciting as hell," shaking the baritone's hand on the elegant invitation to the Seville bull-fight.

Horne indicated to Mowrey which one of her two discoveries of Micaela she wanted used, and remarked on what she considered Maliponte's heightened presence. "She sounds like Brünnhilde compared to the rest of us." Mowrey immediately appeased her by saying that they had merely turned down the orchestra in order to hear her better. They all gazed at the magic machine that could perform such wonders, and

McCracken, perspiring even here without benefit of stage heat and contemplating the dancing columns of lights, asked, "Which one is me on that thing?"

After another go at the same terrain the principals reassembled around the console.

"Well, do you have a nice patchwork now?" Horne jokingly asked Mowrey.

McCracken was not quite so amused. In fact, he was visibly upset when he heard what he thought was a very weak Don José after Micaela's entrance. He rose quickly from his console seat and declared darkly that he was leaving. "Choose something you like. I'm going." He was growing very red with anger, but instantaneously Mowrey and Bernstein calmed him, the former assuring him that his level could be adjusted, the latter grabbing his hand and kissing it like a mother with a hurt toddler. McCracken was appeased. He thanked Mowrey.

"Thank *me* for the psychotherapy," the conductor wryly insisted.

"Gee, you can really bring things up and down like that?" McCracken, wide-eyed and transformed, took his seat again.

"We're going to spend hours putting this together later," Mowrey explained.

"I want to be here when you do it." The voice of Horne.

Unlike his other colleagues, Krause was repeating an assignment. This was to be his second complete Escamillo on records, his first having been done for London in a performance led by Thomas Schippers. Nevertheless, he rolled up his sleeves for *his* big number, the Toreador Song. Bernstein rehearsed the chorus men on the *a cappella* "Vivat!" cries that bring Escamillo on. "You forgot the diminuendo at the end, schmucks!" he laughingly rebuked them. They waited for the red light signal, the conductor singing a snatch of Marguerite's "Jewel Song" in his inimitable croak. "Let's go." He was in superb coping shape. Krause worked very hard, his hands performing their customary ear-cupping and tempo-keeping functions. He turned his pages noisily, almost gasping during his few measures of rest. The suave dotted eighths were there, but the end came across with a good deal of hard breathing, Boky shrill on her high C. Bernstein rounded off the take with the *Nachspiel*, as he called it, and a "Just tuhrrific!" verdict.

He told Mowrey before the playbacks that this was one bit he would very much like not to have to do again. He found the chorus "fantastic," and he almost leapt from his console table chair on the lift of the fortissimo string upbeat to the aria itself. Krause sounded infinitely stronger here than either in the ballroom or in the house. Bernstein even wanted his volume taken down a notch on the first refrain. The second, with a knowing sense of contrast, Krause had brought down himself.

"It's so sexy," Horne smiled with enthusiasm. Bernstein grunted in recognition of her own very earthy "L'amour!" punctuation.

"Tuhrrific!"

"Let's do one more take to cover this and that." Krause also seemed pleased, although he thought his tone on the second refrain had been too diffuse. Bernstein liked the contrast but cautioned him that he would continue to distort tones if he sang "tor*i*ador." Everybody joined in on a verse of everyone's favorite childhood operatic parody ("cuspidor"-"floor," etc.; Adrinana Maliponte even knew an Italian equivalent), and deciding they had just recorded the most famous tune ever written, returned to the ballroom to do it again.

The opening of Act One came up to the block, Maliponte and Gibbs called on plus, of course, the men's section of the chorus. Gibbs used no score but, instead, leaned on his music stand in a nonchalant pose, paralleling somewhat the lazy gestures and tone he was supposed to use on stage. One hand in pocket, the other toying with a soft drink can, he was a model of cool confidence. One could not help remembering, although it now seemed years ago, the sweat-soaked shirt of this young man as he self-consciously participated in that first day's run-through.

Maliponte, at the playback, noticed a frog in her throat on

her first line, and she got slightly away from the beat later on. Her excuses for this tended to the florid—"I had my head in the score. The *tessitura* bothers me. I have *Orphée* and *Flute* in my throat, everything but Micaela."

Bernstein said, "Watch me." They returned to the floor to make an insert. Gibbs had pitch trouble. Another insert take. Maliponte hovered, elbows shoulder level, over her stand. In the can.

"We made three takes of the Prelude the first day, and none was any good." Bernstein stood on the podium, and now with everyone dismissed from the platforms, he faced only the orchestra. "The tendency is to play late in this hall. The acoustics have been adjusted, but we must emphasize lightness and staccato—the French 'whack' instead of the German 'whock.' Let's do both parts of the Prelude, including your favorite *tremolo*, your favorite and mine."

Bernstein appeared resigned to interruptions, and to lift the spirits of his players he told them a possibly apocryphal story about Mike Nichols tongue-lashing Walter Matthau at a rehearsal of *The Odd Couple.* According to the maestro, when the director was quite done, Matthau took a beat and asked if he could have his balls back, to which request Nichols replied (*without* taking a beat) with a snap of his fingers and a one-word shout: "Props!" The men loved it—the ladies, too, one should add.

Again the Prelude and a reminder to the trumpet and trombones to copy Krause's double-dotting on the Toreador statement. "I liked that." The phone rang. "Oh, no," wailed Bernstein. They had to do the fate *tremolo* again. The strings, of course, hate all that sawing, but they did it and the conductor was able to tell them that he had never heard a *tremolo* like that, "especially with your arms falling off." The orchestra was dismissed.

"This was one of the best recording sessions I can remember," Bernstein allowed in the playback room. He certainly seemed to have enjoyed it; none of that weariness that sometimes covers his spirits had been in evidence. "It's time to change my shirt and have some Scotch. Look, I smoked all these," and he showed the empty state of his gold cigarette case.

Krause and Maliponte waited for playbacks of their most recent efforts. When the freshly attired conductor returned from his improvised dressing room, the second take of the Toreador Song was set spinning. The maestro sipped his drink and munched on a pear. "Sen-a-hors, sen-a-hors!" he exclaimed. "What's that?" For some reason Krause had distorted "señors" into three strange syllables. "The chorus repeat is not good either. Again a splice-up job." The aria went on. He liked the "Tout d'un coup" attack. "Terrific. It sounds a little Finnish, but everybody's French in this production is unbelievable. Nevertheless, Tom, you've got across the feeling that the whole world is yours. I could listen to you forever." The end came. "See, no accelerando on the end. That's taste."

Maliponte still waited ("With a maestro 'si aimable,' I don't mind"), but Bernstein grew ever more relaxed and was inclined to reminisce about past recording experiences, specifically about his Vienna *Der Rosenkavalier,* which he felt had not been sufficiently rehearsed, the sessions occurring three years after the Staatsoper performances, and the great *Fidelio* he had conducted for the Beethoven bicentenary at the Theater an der Wien and regretted very much never having put on disks. He even repeated for everyone's enjoyment a *New Yorker* story about Mark Spitz. It had been a good day.

But Bernstein, the following day, complained of ill health. Nevertheless, he launched into the first item of business: "Let's do one really lousy take of the 'Séguidille' and get all the mistakes out of the way—heavy, and no one together."

"That will be easy," observed Carmen.

Actually, Bernstein was able to say, after it was done, that it wasn't "so lousy" at all, but, phone receiver in left hand, his right simultaneously clutching his baton and pinching the bridge of his nose, he listened to Mowrey's comments. "OK. Let's make another one. That wasn't horrible enough. This one will be a little faster." It was for everyone an improvement on an already rather praiseworthy run-through.

In the playback room Horne heard the first phrase of take two and immediately said, "Keep it!" Unfortunately, she flatted on "mis á la porte hier" and went sharp somewhere else. Bernstein wanted more of a breathless quality from McCracken on his excited interruptions, and he and Horne agreed that she too should get a little breath, a little smile in the sound of her first three notes—"Près des rem-."

All was to be done again. Bernstein's jacket came off, his towel made ready and, after he reminded the orchestra about Carmen's whispered opening, Horne sharped badly in the "Séville" of the first phrase; still this was the loosest and sexiest take yet. Horne concentrated hard on giving an impression of casual flirtation; she held her hands tight and folded in front of her at shoulder level, letting them go into a free swing only at the very tossed-off ending. Tenor McCracken applauded her.

Instead of any further repetitions of the "Séguidille" ("too delicate to do over and over again at this point"), Bernstein wanted to go straight on to the Act Two dance, for which he felt that Horne was now properly "oiled up." Castanet players retreated behind baffles, trumpeters to an alcove at the end of the hall opposite the platform. Bernstein reminded Horne about the forte-piano alternation of those la-la-la's (a dynamic indication Horne seemed to drop in the *Carmen*s of the second half of the season), and so with the basic setup fixed, another break was called to listen to "Séguidille" number three.

"I want the beginning still more breathy."

"I can't do more."

"I can do the breath but not sing."

"More breath and I'd be back in *Carmen Jones*."

Bernstein reached across the table and held his mezzo's hand on what he thought a particularly successful effect. "Set up 'je chante pour moi-même' so that 'il n'est pas défendu' will contrast. I can see you shaking your head on that." The conductor showed McCracken where he went flat.

"That's because I had no breath left. That's something new."

"He sounds so much closer than I."

"They're bringing me up because I'm hardly singing."

"I think this 'Séguidille' is good enough for release," Bernstein concluded.

Horne agreed. "Except for the shmear in the third bar."

The dance sounded even slower than it did in the house, but the take was going well, Horne using gestures to work into the mood of her angry mocking of José. She was perspiring. Elevator rattlings could be heard from the corridor, but the musicians went on with the post–Flower Song section. Their soft "Tais-toi/Emporte-moi" ending was not together, and the conductor wrinkled his nose in disappointment. With the violent "Adieu pour jamais," it ended. Bernstein gave it an audible raspberry. "That's a hard bit to record—one problem after another. For the purposes of the recording I think that the dance should be a little faster" (to compensate, apparently, for the living-room audience not having anything to watch).

The first part (up to the beginning of the Flower Song) was repeated with Horne unfortunately singing "mon âme" instead of "son âme" in her mocking imitation of José, a mistake she occasionally later still made in performances. "I would like to do one page by itself," she announced when it ended, that which included the phrase "Va-t'en donc, canari! Tiens!"

"Jackie, we'll have to start further back because it's hard to splice right there."

Again. The rough spot was smoothed. Bernstein then wanted to repeat immediately the "Séguidille." Horne protested that she had just done, for her, the most fatiguing part of the opera.

"Let's make a dash at it anyway," he cajoled and got his way. He crouched down, almost behind the podium, to convey the delicacy he wanted, and Horne responded with the breathiest, most piano opening yet of the four takes. McCracken mistimed his "Tu le promets" entrance, however, and he signaled recognition of his mistake to the conductor. They stopped. Bernstein took the hold-up lightly. "Follow me no matter what I do, whatever I may happen to decide," he half-joked.

"OK. Sure! Fine!" McCracken shot back.

Bernstein found Horne's announcement of her dance, "Je vais danser en votre honneur," rather "like Donna Anna," but he approved of the "snakiness" of the slow tempo. She occasionally sang sharp in this difficult section, but her astounded reaction to José's announcement that he had to return to barracks was terrifically effective. Bernstein loved it. Still he told Horne she was dragging on the cadence "Voilà son amour." "It's 'voilà!' Deliver it and get off. You're dismissing him. That's the idea." The second "Au quartier! pour l'appel!" was even stronger in outline. "Elle est stupéfaite," declared the conductor. The wrong word in the mockery was noted and Bernstein decided that the sighing, leering violins here had to be brought up. That little section was to be done again.

And now they listened to the last "Séguidille." Bernstein dubbed it fabulous, although Horne did not like one note in her first phrase, the E at the top of "Séville," and Bernstein pointed out that an F-sharp in the end of the opening cadence was better in other takes, "but I love the quality. It's like you're turning a new trick every minute." He grabbed fistfuls of peanuts from a console-top bowl and gulped them down with delight.

Certain passages in the "Séguidille" are repeated note for note for the singer, and Horne, finding that a first statement had been better than its later one, wanted the engineers to use the first one twice. Unfortunately, differences in orchestration would not allow this. And now everyone got into a discussion of which "Près des" was best, which had more atmosphere. For the last take, McCracken's "Tu le promets" pleased him, but Horne's ending displeased her. She thought there were better endings that could be spliced on.

"Well, patch me up something nice," McCracken sighed. "Maybe with something from *Bohème*."

Back in the hall the "Il souffre de partir," more slowly, therefore more exaggerated in its scorn, was taped after many false starts, but a minuscule number compared to those necessary to get the post–Flower Song section. They started at least eight times, but finally, with Horne's right hand held high to remind her visually to keep the pitch up on "si tu m'aimais," they got as far as the pianissimo "Tais-toi/Emporte-moi," where mezzo and tenor parted rhythmic company.

"It was divine up to there," Bernstein told them.

"As long as we're going back, can we go back to 'surtout'?" (a high G), Horne requested.

"Then let's start at the beginning."

"No, that's the problem. The little girl is getting tired."

But the end was still not right, and again back they went three more times until finally they agreed, all and one. Only now, McCracken did not like his tone quality, which had been quasi-falsetto. And again. Bernstein was looking very fatigued. The pianissimo end still did not work. The conductor suggested that they were not breathing together. They repeated the final cadence, but was Horne on pitch? McCracken thought his voice had quivered too much. "Maybe it will sound like emotion," he rationalized.

Then Horne taped the first phrase of the "Séguidille" twice, almost crooning it the second time. "The first one was dynamite," Mowrey reported from the control tower.

"And the second wasn't bad either," added Bernstein.

All this footage had now to be listened to. "That duet will have to be a patch." Horne eased herself into her customary console position.

"Of course it will," Mowrey agreed.

"Is it conceivable we will do 'Tais-toi' again?" questioned an apparently still not pleased Don José. Both he and Horne were surprised at the difficulty they had found in recording this small but important moment, for in performance they stand ready to embrace to sing it. Here, separated by several yards, each on his own track microphone, that kind of breathing contact was impossible.

"It's inconceivable," Mowrey shook his head.

"OK, let's hear that dynamite take," Bernstein urged bemusedly. He pursed his lips and announced that he had heard takes of "chez mon ami" that he had liked better. Then the second insert went on, and the conductor declared it "double dynamite." However, the two were replayed and it was generally agreed that the "Près des rem-" of the first insert should be joined with the rest of the second insert. Then, this as a whole would be grafted onto a complete (although probably not any entire one of the four "Séguidille" takes) version. McCracken looked dazed by the prospect of all this surgery and remarked that he wanted himself recorded in long stretches. He felt that some people could not help but hear the differences in tempo between takes, infinite though they be. "But these boys know what they're doing." He later stated that he had originally been under the impression that the recording was to be based on the house tapings of the six performances Bernstein was conducting rather than on studio work. He thought that this would have been a better idea, although, naturally, sonically the results would not be so brilliant.

The session was going into overtime, at least a half hour, possibly a whole one. The maestro ran in place on his podium, bent to touch his toes, and called out: "All right, let's make the entr'acte to Act Four, the *Zwischenspiel.*" This again was a repeat of work that had been scheduled for the first day of recording. McCracken watched from the platform as Bernstein attacked take one: fine until the very end when a tambourine went awry. "Oh, for Christ's sake," snapped the exasperated leader. Again from the top, with Bernstein's flamenco footsteps definitely on the weary side. It ended. "Good shabbus. I thank you."

It was 5:55 of a long day's afternoon, but McCracken still had work to do. He moved back to the chorus riser, where baffles were readjusted for this *a cappella* "Dragon d'Alcala" effort. A piano in the pit between the two platforms offered the tenor his initial note, a G, but to sound it the large man had to squat down on all fours and reach to the keyboard himself. Alone in the huge room, he took his instructions for starting ("Wait till the echo of my voice stops") from the unseen Mowrey. McCracken found it difficult to maintain correct pitch, and both verses of the short passage were repeated.

In the control room Horne and Bernstein waited for the balance of the day's playbacks. Bernstein, a scotch already in hand ("It's my end of day reward"; "Mine is food," countered Horne), reassured McCracken about his pitch problems, which he felt would not be of any importance since the effect of "Dragon d'Alcala" was meant to be that of someone singing in the street, and the notes themselves were sung against an animated discussion among the quintet people onstage.

"It doesn't matter if you slip from pitch," he said. "Only those smart asses with pitch pipes will mind, people like Andrew Porter." Nevertheless a pitch pipe was passed around the table for an impromptu check. Horne played a G and found that McCracken had gone a whole tone sharp at the end of one take. John McClure, a free-lance recording consultant for the conductor, always by Mowrey's side during these sessions, then checked the pipe with the piano, not believing that such a variation was possible. He jocularly accused Horne of blowing wrong. "Do you mean to say I don't know how to blow?" was her foot-in-mouth mock-indignant response to that. Then Bernstein blew, and the best "Dragon" take had the tenor slipping his G to an F-sharp at the end of the first verse and sharping to an A-flat at the end of the second.

"I like the spirit. We'll keep it," announced the conductor.

McCracken was relieved. "I'll never get it better."

As for the "Tais-toi/Emporte-moi" end, the best one had McCracken singing falsetto and he would have preferred one with a real, sung pianissimo. All those which he did do "in his voice" had something wrong with them—pitch, rhythm—and again he mentioned that he wanted to do another take of the phrase the following Tuesday. Again McCracken's motion was denied, and he settled for the falsetto version with assurance that his track would be brought up to give him more presence.

"I love splicing in the springtime," sang an amused Horne.

After this long day of work everyone's mood seemed improved by the lifting of a burden. After all, some of the opera's knottiest problem spots had been passed. It was late, but Bernstein and the two principals wanted their moments of anecdote-swapping: McCracken told about how during one performance's Act Three fight he took a header under the disk and couldn't find his way out. Horne relayed a remark her sister heard opening night when the curtain went up on Act Three. Someone seated near her had loudly whispered to a companion: "My God, it looks like a gynecologist's nightmare."

"Especially with that disk," contributed McCracken.

"Well, Svoboda is very Freudian-oriented. I wouldn't be surprised if he had something of that order in mind," Bernstein commented seriously.

Back in the playback room on October 6, Bernstein noted that they had spent the first hour and a half of that day's session on eight minutes of music. He shook his head incredulously. His spirits were lifted, however, when Horne made her entrance, a rose between her teeth. "I have to do it once," she giggled, this Carmen caught in an antitraditional period. They listened to the kids bouncing along on the tape, giving their full-throated Act Four tribute to Escamillo. "I love them when they're flat," smiled Horne.

"Otherwise you wouldn't know them from sopranos at the Metropolitan Opera," Bernstein riposted. He was very tired, although one suspected he could only thrive on the kind of fatigue that a week such as this engendered: recording sessions, rehearsals for them, performances, and work on his upcoming Norton lectures at Harvard. Subject? Transformational grammar.

After three encounters with the "douanier" ensemble—plus an insert—and several battles with the girls' Act One quarrel chorus, the maestro listened to the results.

The Ballantines was waiting for him, as well as a black, German-speaking friend of Maestro Maag who gave the shirtless conductor a lengthy message as he judged his work. He thought that the big moment of the "douanier" modulation to the first statement was overblown, "too Rockettes," as he put it. He was also disturbed when he found out that the percussion instruments were on the same track as the strings, elements he would have preferred to separate for better control. Mowrey and McClure explained the distribution of the sixteen tracks (three for soloists, three for the chorus, etc.) and how it was impossible to divide the orchestral ones any differently. The maestro deferred to their expertise.

He did love that chorus. "I'm sorry when it's over and Micaela comes on. What a plot. Here they are in the middle of the mountains, and everybody dropping in like Times Square."

On Columbus Day the weather turned brisk, a great contrast to the summer heat in which the *Carmen* rehearsals had begun, now almost two months before. It was a day on which the singers agreed that the *Carmen* the previous Saturday, one attended by another Jackie, Mrs. Aristotle Onassis, was the best yet (ex-manager Bing had dropped in on the second performance and visited dressing rooms after depositing, finding no other place to leave it, his coat with Winnie, the *doyenne* of the switchboard), a judgment that held a quotient of irony for baritone Christopher, who said that he had come up with his worst flub yet. It happened during the quintet. He simply had forgotten to sing his second line, and when the silence got to him the question of "who the hell made that mistake?" quickly faded into the alarm of "Shit! It's me!"

But to work. Bernstein lifted his baton for a run-through of the quintet. The coldness in the hall brought on a slow, plodding, sluggish trial. "Orchestra," Bernstein cautioned, "as light as possible—not only for aesthetic reasons. I can't hear the soloists." A second, recorded, attempt seemed to have more life as the five, eyes glued to the maestro, got through to the end, their score pages turned automatically and silently.

In the playback domain Bernstein complained of the temperature and of fatigue, the result of what he called "pushing," but he was immediately ready to listen. He found fault with a trumpet and with Carmen's handling of her announcement that she is in love. "That's too long," he reasoned. "It stops the show." He found that the return to the first theme, when executed more rapidly, was better than the initial statement. "Is it easier for you faster?" he asked.

"Yes!" they chorused.

"Well, it's not logical, but it may be true." Horne was worried about not hearing the dynamics (Velis was concerned about not hearing the women at all) and her vocal line not coming through. Bernstein reminded her that when they sang *tutti,* all voices had to be equal. "For me, it's all too heavy," he summed up.

On the podium Bernstein addressed his troops. "We have a lot of notes on tape. No spirit, no lightness. I have had most comments about the way the quintet went in performance. Now we have to put the performance on tape."

"We know how bad it is," acknowledged Horne. And this time the opening had what the conductor was after, but there was some confusion on the intricate "de nous-de vous" syncopation.

The buzzer went off. "Oh, I have already stopped them," Bernstein reported, not altogether mirthfully. Again. Boky forgot to sing her first line. (Christopher: "Oh gee, and that was my best opening so far.") "From the top." Bernstein raised his arms and increased, barely perceptibly, the tempo. Again Horne made a big moment out of "amoureuse à perdre l'esprit." The conductor shook his head but went on. A buzzer. The men were late. "I can't hear them," Bernstein moaned. They repeated all for safety. Ah, but they weren't finished yet with this tongue twister. The second exchange of "de nous-de vous" had to be corrected.

"It's going to be a thing now," baritone Christopher groaned.

"Listen, kids, we've got to get this straight," Bernstein urged. He led them through a words-only rehearsal, the girls instructed to listen, the boys to count. It appeared to be solidly understood. The orchestra cheered. The light went on and the insert went on tape.

The voice of Mowrey: "OK. That'll do it."

The voice of Bernstein: "Or blew it."

Instead of a break to listen to the quintet, they went on to the card scene. Bernstein's jacket came off. "Lights!" he called out, but there was no light. He brought his baton down and the strings made a hash of their rapid sixteenth-note introductory pattern. "I'm glad there was no light on that." It was tentative all around, even for Horne, who for some reason sounded unusually unsteady. She shook her head, disapproving of what she was doing. The tempo was at below-normal speed. But in spite of everything, even Bernstein's decision to sing along, they finished, Horne including a big vocal and physical gesture for her dramatic "répètera: la mort!"

"I forgot to watch during the slow section. I had my eyes closed," Horne admitted as she took her seat at the console.

"And there was a cough," McClure noted.

"Yes," Bernstein nodded. "A viola player was having a fit, stuffing a handkerchief in his mouth." Mowrey told Boky that she had been moving her head too much for the microphone to catch her voice evenly. They listened.

"The orchestra is not spooky enough," Bernstein analyzed.

"And I'm not loud enough," Horne analyzed.

"Oh come on. . . . The first bar is critical," he went on and underlined some passages he thought the mezzo was rushing, although at the pace he set the word hardly applied. "Not bad for the first time," the conductor allowed.

"That had some good things in it," Horne agreed. "Don't throw it out. It had a monotonous quality."

"'Egalement,' as it says," he concurred.

"We're on recording time, now," McClure cautioned.

They resumed at the very beginning of the card scene. Again the starts and stops, buzzers and lights, chased each other dizzily. The strings could not get their sixteenth notes right ("smearing and rushing," the maestro judged). Then, when these were finally sufficiently clean, Boky, although she was at one with the conductor, was again moving her head from side to side. In fact, Baldwin was now accused of doing it too.

"But if I stand like a statue," Frasquita remonstrated, "I won't have any expression." Horne, too, one noticed, now that one's attention was drawn to it, moved her head away from a position directly in front of the microphone, but presumably the rich, all-powerful color of her normal tones prevented any distortion that might be caused by the slight variation in position.

"That had a lot of good stuff," Bernstein approved when the scene finally ended. He conferred on the phone. Evidently Mowrey had liked it this last time, for Bernstein smiled and told the ladies, "When they say pretty good, we know it's fantastic; and when they say very good, it's lousy."

Oddly, Horne did not listen to the card scene playback. Bernstein had grown somewhat prickly, his typical, somewhat skeptical side glances at those around him a shade harder than normal. He reserved a few of his better ones for Mowrey when the string introduction to the scene was put on. "That's supposed to be good?" He also noted for the record that he did not think that Boky's head movements had in any way harmed the microphone pickup.

But the final take still had to be heard. Bernstein approved of Horne's otherworldly, hypnotized first line. ("We had to struggle for that one. She should hear this.") But, incredibly, he, yes, even he, found the tempo too slow and thought that one of the mezzo's "la mort!" outbursts had been sharp. "And there should be more brass and bassoons." Well, all those details, except tempo, of course, could be adjusted by picking, choosing, boosting, or suppressing.

Bernstein and Mowrey next discussed which "douanier" chorus they could use. The difficulty in selecting one lay not only in its internal merits but in its relationship to Micaela's aria, which follows. In the rerecording of the aria today (Maliponte was waiting to do her bit) the end of the "douanier" was fed to Bernstein so he could set his tempo.

The aria introduction itself poses a few problems of its own —horn entrances for one, today augmented by extraneous noises in the hall—but on the third try they made it and got into the aria proper. This initial starting and stopping may have unnerved Maliponte somewhat, for she lost pitch on her first phrase and she rushed elsewhere. The quality of the voice, however, seemed full. She cracked on her held G before the beginning of the second verse, and with a look of disgust on her face signaled her displeasure to Bernstein, who nevertheless went on to the end, where he again faced problematic horns. Cold may have been affecting them; some of the players had donned overcoats as the late afternoon chill invaded the interior. The phone message dictated another complete take.

"Maestro, je ne m'entends pas," Maliponte proffered from her platform.

"Mais je vous entends," Bernstein settled the complaint. "What was that tempo again?" And again the end of the "douanier" chorus was fed. This time Maliponte stayed with the maestro throughout, although some pitch uncertainties remained. The soprano concentrated intensely; her hands were first fisted and held high, elbows straight out from her shoulders, then moved expansively in the broad gestures Igesz had wanted her to omit. Breath at the end of the first verse was not overly copious, and again that held G, although more focused, proved questionable. It ended, but Bernstein did two final takes of the last word, "Seigneur", and of the quiet horn cadences.

He even wanted to do a third, but Mowrey overruled (!) him. "We have it, maestro." Maestro smiled.

"Well, that was a photo finish!" exclaimed McClure, the session not having gone into overtime, but only just, thereby saving DGG a few dollars in this glitteringly expensive venture. Bernstein, with his instinctively beautiful manners, apologized to Maliponte ("Oh, maestro, I was trembling with fear") because he was going to ask her again to wait while he listened to the last take of the quintet. *"Oi vays mir,"* he sobbed when he heard the beginning. But after that he mostly liked what he found. He scowled, however, at Horne's overlong "amoureuse" (*"Bella voce,"* whispered a smiling prima donna–wise McClure), especially after he had just mentioned to her how he wanted it simplified. Nevertheless, "A tuhrrific performance" was his ultimate verdict.

The examination turned to Micaela's aria. The playback of the first take excited almost unanimous head-shaking, mostly from Maliponte herself, who nevertheless thought that perhaps boosting her low notes might help, a suggestion the maestro turned down. Extraneous noises could be heard. Mowrey looked worried because material from the earlier session, before the change in the acoustical setup, according to him, could not be used. The second take also revealed some bad intonation from the soprano, but on the whole it seemed more acceptable. Bernstein promptly suggested some patch possibilities from take number one. Mowrey and McClure had stopped looking negative, but Maliponte continued gloomy.

"You're going to have to do some copying with this," commented the conductor. It was decided to hunt for those first-session tapes and listen to them anyway. No doubt about it, Maliponte had been in altogether better form that day. They all listened intently. After the first of last week's two was played, Bernstein stated that he preferred her voice in the old acoustic ambiance. "It's rich, sumptuous, totally different." Mowrey said that the same effect could be achieved with today's recording if rear-channel reverberation were boosted. He then had the levers pulled to demonstrate this truth, Bernstein groaning, however, that he could not bear to hear that tune again.

Maliponte was not going to be shortchanged. She firmly urged that take *two* from session one be played. "I don't like my voice today." Not right away was her request granted. Today's work with the reverberation boost was played, the young soprano slapping her forehead in frustration every time she found a fault.

Bernstein was not far behind her. "Look, why the fuck, if the acoustics can be altered, can't the two sessions be spliced? This time it's driving me crazy." But Mowrey was not sure if all four channels could be spliced simultaneously. "Do it!" the maestro laughed. "It must be left in their hands," he reassured Maliponte.

"Je m' excuse, maestro."

"For what?" And he reached for the hand, the one that had assaulted her head, and touched it with reassuring lips.

October 10 brought the final day of recording, exclusive of dialogue, which was to be postdubbed in the case of melodramas and fitted in for the unaccompanied sections. Bernstein insisted that Igesz be present for this work, saying, too, that he was "shocked" that Mowrey had not invited him of his own accord. The conductor himself was not to be there. A new diction coach, Edward Beck, had been hired for any questions the recording's spoken portion might raise.

As a sort of foretaste of this extraoperatic dubbing business, the day's session began with a taping of the bell that calls the working girls back to the factory in Act One. While Horne and McCracken warmed up on their platform for their final duet and shared a green apple, the percussionist got ready. Silence, and then thirty seconds of indescribable clatter. The ringer took a bow to unanimous applause. His, it was true, was the only contribution so far that had not had to be repeated.

Then the light went on for the final duet of the opera, but it developed into a test run very quickly when various mishaps took place. Horne flatted quite early, sticking out her tongue in self-disapproval. McCracken, physically, maintained his usual form, his hands held high, thumbs up, other fingers pointing into his breast bone, elbows well away from his torso, flapping slightly in rhythmic support. Bernstein, working hard, was making a lot of two-handed baton gestures, and Horne, warming to her task, found a moment to slip off her fur coat for a reproachful "A quoi bon tout cela?" McCracken muffed a line, but Horne and the man on the podium were in complete accord on that oft-disputed cutoff on "que je l'aime!" Mauceri, stationed in an alcove under the far side of the balcony, was in charge of the "offstage" chorus and trumpets, Bernstein turning 180 degrees to throw him his cue. The final Toreador Song reprise, now with Carmen's orchestra death moans slower than ever and accompanied by some trumpet accidents, brought the take to an end. In spite of everything they went off to hear it.

"Well, I hated that," announced Horne, entering the room.

"It's a miserable thing to begin with before the adrenalin gets worked up. Let's look at this as a rehearsal," said Bernstein, and they began to listen. "Slow, draggy," he remarked to Horne, and he told McCracken that it should "move a little more."

McCracken seemed alone in liking much of the duet. His pronunciation of the phrase "sauver avec toi" was challenged, however, since he was making a broad elision between the final "r" of "sauver" and the "a" of "avec." He also had persisted, as he did in many performances, in replacing "du passé" with an ungrammatical "*de* passé."

"You're taking too long with 'je ne t'aime plus,' Jackie," Bernstein remarked, and she shook her head on an overquivery "Libre elle este ñee." Her hard-hitting "c" added to that violent "donc" in "Frappe-moi donc" brought a smile to the maestro's lips. He suggested, when, the playback finished that Carmen's death gasps be recorded at the dialogue session and be dubbed in later rather than risk recording wrongly timed ones today. As he accompanied Horne downstairs he urged her to endow the duet with a more spoken quality. "It's too Wagnerian now."

They began again, McCracken now clutching a pen in one of those tense hands, Horne flatting ever so slightly on the "fini" of "tout est fini." However, there were no stops until that disputed "sauver avec toi." Bernstein said there was no elision.

"Could it be either way?" inquired the tenor.

"No."

"Now he's a French expert," McCracken murmured coolly to Horne. Coach Beck suggested that he hit the "r" slightly rather than roll it. Horne, who was no friend to French "r's" herself, bet them it would come out like a flat American one.

They rolled again from just before this knot. Horne again had pitch troubles, this time with the low A of "céderai pas." She shrugged her shoulders, but McCracken, coming up again against "sauver avec toi" in the concerted section of the duet, disliked the way he coped with it, slapped his thigh in impatience, and signaled so to Bernstein. The conductor went on, and McCracken turned a bit red. One wondered if perhaps Bernstein calculated that the tenor might be most exciting here if just a bit pricked by annoyance. In any case, this Don José was all there, alternating the gestures of the stage with a precise beating of time during that tricky, agitated "Où vas-tu?/Laisse-moi" exchange. Both singers were in full flight until the very end when a horn splat underlining Horne's "Tiens!" ruined the effect. Inching to the climax, Bernstein double-clutched his baton, visually tightening his control, and McCracken, in spite of some rough brass ringings again, got to sing his final line.

The podium verdict? "That was good."

Referring to her unsatisfactory low A ("céderai pas"), Horne confected an apt simile: "My voice is like a blanket: pull it up and the toes get cold; pull it down and your chin freezes."

Bernstein was happy. "It's alive now." He listened. "Wonderful!" (a compliment to Horne on her handling of "inflexible"). He found that McCracken was ahead at one point, but his "du passé" was grammatically above reproach.

"Can we get more volume without more presence on the offstage chorus?" the conductor inquired. Mowrey replayed the first offstage outburst, achieving exactly what Bernstein asked for, except that he still could not hear the chorus's words. This, too, could be adjusted, he was told. Getting in on the dial work, McCracken asked to be brought up. Granted, because Mowrey felt that McCracken in his excitement had been moving his head somewhat out of mike range.

These chorus and tenor adjustments meant that the tape

kept rolling back to Horne's fierce "donc!" She enjoyed this. "I love the way I come in on 'Cette bague.'"

"Me too," agreed her vis-a-vis. The "Tiens!" was so wild — wild, not sung, of course—that Horne recoiled and joked that she was "going for the throat operation tomorrow."

"We're on recording time." An anxious McClure tried to prevail, hoping to get these people, enjoying what they heard, back to their positions, for Bernstein had decided that there were things to retouch.

Horne put in a die-hard request to redo "que je l'aime!" and hold that A-flat a bit longer. She was denied. "No," said Bernstein, dealing with this old dispute. "It's too long already."

The mezzo bristled, smiling nonetheless. "I'm a musician but I'm still a singer."

"But, Jackie," he reasoned, "it's for dramatic reasons. 'Je l'aime!'—and off. That's it. You've said it."

On the soloists' platform, where the two were to repeat the first half of the duet (up to "Libre elle est née"), McCracken did some bending to loosen for the battle. Again Horne had trouble with "fini" pitch. She wrinkled her nose and delivered a sigh when "je ne te cederai pass" also would not yield to improvement. But the conductor continued until McCracken went back to his "de passé" mistake.

"I think we should do it over," Horne announced. "I ran out of steam." This time she liked her "céderai pas," indicating so to Bernstein with a decisive nod of her chin. Bernstein, mouthing everyone's words, worked like a demon to get this half-a-duet on tape. And he got it.

"You know, Lenny, this was really a very easy recording job. Only seven sessions." Horne was feeling good.

"Seven for you. You forget there were three more *without* you."

The "Chanson Bohẽmienne" was still outstanding. Bernstein conducted a dry-run of the orchestral introduction and found it acceptable. When the light went on for the real thing,

Horne could be seen tensely working for a light touch for her beginning, Baldwin nodding in concentration to assimilate the ever quickening tempo before she had to enter, Boky stiff at attention to the conductor's wishes.

"That was terrible!" Bernstein groaned when he brought his baton down. "It was as though we had never done it before," he continued in the playback room. "It was like the first read-through. It will be a misery to listen to, but we have to." He reminded Horne about the "in-and-out" quality he wanted from her, a mysterious toying with the words. He thought she was doing too much, too big, also the verdict for Frasquita and Mercédès, who should be "staccato with a little accent." "Jackie, it's not spicy enough." Boky could not hold back her bitter giggles when she heard the yelps the Frasquita and Mercédès tra-la-la's had become.

"Print it. It's heaven," hooted Horne, but Bernstein's look of disgust mollified. "You know, it's not as bad as I thought. It's not all a nightmare, although the orchestra at the beginning of the first verse is." He again turned to his mezzo, who was then in quest of her favorite libation, a warm Diet Pepsi. "Can you do the first verse piano and not have pitch problems?"

"I'll try, but I don't want it to sound like the beginning of the 'Séguidille.'"

"No, no. It's a whole other thing."

Horne understood what Bernstein meant and sang her first words, "Les tringles des sistres tintaient" quietly but with through-the-teeth control. He nodded. "But it's so easy to go off pitch that way," said the worried mezzo, who, when she regained her platform position, told Bernstein she did not really think she could sing it that softly.

"OK," he acquiesced. "They'll bring it down, but keep the intention." Horne, now like many of her colleagues, held her hand up to her ear to check her own pitch, working hard again on the light "in-and-out," but relaxed and spirited enough to produce a few gestures and even an occasional foot tap. But something happened to another area of her concentration, and after she reached the crescendoing "Cela montait, montait, montait, montait!" she simply forgot to sing the tra-la-la's that followed. She buried her face in her hands.

Mowrey was more than understanding. His voice came over the intercom. "Very nice, though, Jackie."

"Jackie, would you like another shot at the beginning?" Bernstein queried.

"Love it."

"The misery of this piece is that it's almost impossible to splice with its almost, or supposed-to-be, imperceptible accelerando."

Back to Carmen's entrance. Horne shook her hips with the music, got slightly off the beat before the high held G-sharp on "tourbillon," and sipped some more Diet Pepsi during the wild postlude, smiling in the knowledge that they were inches from a musical finish. The phone rang.

"He says he's got it."

"I think so too," nodded Horne.

"But it's chancy because of the *più mosso.* I think we should do a complete take, whatever happens." And that is what happened, the "Chanson Bohémienne" from beginning to end, with the spirit there, the rhythmic feel more unified than ever, the postlude very unleashed, with Bernstein in a fierce, excited baton duel with the players before the *tutta forza* trilled climax.

"Tuhrrific!"

Not over yet? Well, no. There was still the entr'acte to Act Three to redo. Bernstein started this delicate interlude, with its harp accompaniment to long flute solo. But the latter instrument's player, Mr. Politis, was in trouble, gasping loudly for breath. "Just relax," coaxed the conductor as he went back to the beginning. This time some noise from somewhere in the area of the orchestra intruded, but Bernstein got through the last bar. "Not bad at all. Once more." Harp fingers slipped, but the leader went on, Mowrey buzzing them to a halt. The conductor looked annoyed, addressing the unseen producer. "We have that. Let's just make another take, Tom, please."

The flute quality was exceedingly breathy on the second go-around. He consulted the engineering oracles by phone. "They'd like another take." The flutist, suffering because of the cold in the hall, still found it hard going, but in any case, Horne, who had retreated to the balcony to observe, suddenly shifted weight and her chair legs noisily ground against the gritty balcony floor. "Be quiet, upstairs." Bernstein's eyes fiercely made no allowances for leading mezzos.

A take. "It was so close I'd like to do it again."

This time (and the last!) the flute flubbed less, but some of his fellow wind instruments, also reacting to the temperature (in cold weather winds sharp, strings go flat), broke breath, which roused a frown or two from Bernstein. It ended. The phone. "Now right away," announced the conductor with whatever energy remained to him, "the melodrama." That Act One violin solo under Zuniga's address to the rebellious Carmen had never been really good, and now concertmaster Gniewek played it twice. It's over! The orchestra applauded the maestro, who, smiling tiredly, reached forward and shook the hands of as many of the players as he could reach.

Bernstein quickly ran off for his absolutely final shirt change of this DGG *Carmen* and returned to hear the last "Chanson Bohémienne." "It's the closest thing to a performance we have, and the first two verses were marvelous," Bernstein said upon the take's ending. Horne questioned, however, her "tourbillon" notes. "The first one is dubious," agreed the conductor, but some possible inserts were played, Mowrey cautioning them against too much optimism in the infallibility of this operation since they did not know if something could be matched until they actually tried to do it.

One of these insert candidates had Horne's forgotten "montait" follow-up. "Well," she cracked, "if I ever fell in love with a note, it would not be an E."

Another take. "No sock," said Bernstein. Another take. Everyone nodded. Horne shook her head no.

Another take. Horne preferred another tra-la-la upward scale passage. "After this, can we hear the last complete one again?" she asked.

"We have time," Bernstein told her, "but we may all go insane."

"I think maybe that's the one all the way through," she argued. It was played.

Bernstein nodded. "This is the mother with some replacements."

The mezzo held her ground. "For me it's the whole thing. It has a sex thing basically. Basic sex." Bernstein smiled somewhat enigmatically, and the subject changed to a light discussion, now that the issue was no longer a moot one, of Horne's interpolated high notes grafted onto the mezzo line. "Oh, Richard Bonynge found them for me in some obscure Paris edition," she joked. "But seriously," she asked Bernstein, "what did Bizet mean about the heaviness of that last duet?"

"He meant for Carmen to be singing like a bull calf."

"But they must have had a forty-piece orchestra for her to sing against."

"And a *tenorino.* Here you have a mensch."

"He ain't no *tenorino.* That's for sure."

And now they listened to the bull calf–mensch ensemble, at least those takes after the cold first one. "Oh what contempt," said Bernstein admiringly to Horne about the tone she established.

"I like this," she agreed, but the "je ne te cederai pas" was not good. Nevertheless, McCracken was coming through powerfully, so much so that Bernstein now expressed regret that he had stopped him on the mispronunciation of "du passé." "It's so alive. Fantastic!" Horne too acknowledged that McCracken had been extra special in the "de [sic] passé" take.

"You can splice the 'du,' can't you?" she urged, and thinking only then of herself, she added, "and find me the best G for 'Libre elle est née.'"

The flute gasps proved rather painful in the entr'acte, but McClure suggested they could be "dipped" out. They decided that after all it *was* the first take that would be the mother here. "I want to experiment with extra reverberation, taking both instruments [harp and flute] down and putting echo in." Bernstein had suddenly gone over completely to the technical side. "We need to get atmosphere." Several mixes were tried, one apparently pleasing. "Work with that take, but let's not settle on any tired choices now, Tom," he cautioned. "You will listen to all again." Indeed every one of the 261 takes would be considered, including the ones summarily rejected here in New York, during the work of splicing that would be done in Germany, when Mowrey would be joined in this task by a DGG expert recording engineer, tape editor, and razor blade handler, Gernot Westhäuser.

Two hundred sixty-one takes. Actually a not excessive total, considering *Carmen*'s complexity. Bernstein's *Falstaff* and *Der Rosenkavalier* (the latter admittedly one disk longer) had both passed the seven-hundred mark, but then these New York sessions had enjoyed the symbiotic relationship of taping and performing at the Metropolitan during the same period. In return, the opera house and the public at the performances benefited from the polishing that went on in the studio. It was a truly unique situation, and seemingly, there was no reason why this *Carmen* should not emerge as one of the finest operatic recordings of recent years.

"Well, good-bye, everybody." Bernstein was ready to leave and was going to do it casually. "It's been a ball. Tuhrrific." Hands shaken, some eyes decidedly misty, and he was gone.

*

Final Notes

"It was dreary being all alone without orchestra, chorus, Lenny, and all the others," reported Remendado Velis about the dialogue-dubbing session that took place the following Friday. "The hall was deserted and dark, and we were placed in specially constructed booths that eliminated mike spillover. Bodo sat upstairs, and Beck cleared up many pronunciation problems that had never previously been settled." In these booths some of the singers, most importantly Donald Gramm, because he had more of the melodrama scenes than anyone else, sat wrapped in earphones through which they heard the underpinning music, their spoken words therefore being dubbed, but dubbed with more exactitude than if lines had simply been read and then forced to fit in by stretching or contracting.

In no booth, however, sat Paul Franke, the original Lillas Pastia. His agent had asked for a singer's fee to read those three lines in Act Two, a fee coming to a flat $1,500, which is what such supporting artists as Velis and Christopher collected. Mowrey offered Franke $750, and the tenor turned DGG down. What to do? Velis would not read the lines, because, as another character tenor with the Met, he did not want to antagonize a colleague. Mowrey, the day of the session, tested coach Beck in the part, but his nonoperatic throat sounded out of place. Looking around him, the producer's eye lit on Russell Christopher, the Dancaïre, and the baritone was elected, collecting a very neat $750 for this minuscule effort.

The artists had been very cooperative, McClure reported. Christopher and Velis, as old-hand character types, found it easiest, Horne was conscientious, and Krause demonstrated that his spoken French was far superior in clarity to his handling of the language when sung.

In the wreckage of the control playback room, the Diet Pepsi cans, dirt, oddly glitter-sprinkled faded draperies having survived, the equipment brought down from Boston (where DGG records the Boston Symphony) already sent back, Mowrey and McClure gathered their possessions together for a final vacating of this unlikely *Carmen* scene. The producer spoke of various problems connected with this project: the tough contract negotiations (the chorus and Paul Franke had not been alone in holding out; they were alone only in *losing* out, but the Met and Horne had driven hard bargains), which he handled exclusively; the acoustical setup change, which he said had been effected mostly for the benefit of the musicians so that they could hear better, not for the machines; scheduling changes (three different ones had been drawn up, the first scuttled because of the switch in choruses, the second because of a day's indisposition of Miss Horne).

"When I return to Hanover," said this young Eastman graduate, who in 1968 began experimenting with quadraphonic sound, and in 1969 joined DGG, and who reluctantly admitted that he had never before supervised an operatic recording (!), "we will spend three weeks listening, determining splicing points. As you know, some splicing can't be done until you try. Only *transient* points can be spliced. Our criterion in fitting details into a mother take is not only that the splice will not be audible but also that we choose what is artistically most exciting. It cannot be out of context. It will be as perfect as possible, but with nuances kept in mind. In our consideration excitement can outweigh technical imperfections, although now, it is true, many of them can be eliminated—bad attacks by clipping, and even pitch can be altered, but this is complicated and we try to avoid it.

"After the listening period come eight or ten days of the actual physical splicing, and the mixing [the musical balancing of the sixteen tracks into four tracks for quad and two tracks for stero] after that will take from three weeks to a month. Then about the first of the year we will have a version to propose." Bernstein, of course, would hear everything; the major singers, those parts that concerned them. Mowrey, whose operatic inexperience is impressively outweighed by his work with other musically complex recordings and multitrack sound (he at one time had been chief producer for Vox), stated that he had never received a request for a take substitution. "There's a good reason for that. There simply is no other possibility." He allowed, however, that in the case of *Carmen* he at least expected that this pattern *might* be broken. A February release date, after a final disk approval from Bernstein, was anticipated (ultimately the album appeared in late April), and then the fight would be on to retrieve DGG's investment.

What would be the aural temper of this *Carmen?* "Well, with sixteen tracks, each singer usually on a separate one, there are unlimited possibilities for action. The orchestra in quad will be made to sound wider than the speakers. That is what quad [Mowrey was speaking then of conventional quad, not the still controversial 'surround' sound] can do—provide a widening, an opening up. The chorus, too, will also be in these expanded areas, but the soloists' voices will almost always be between the two front speakers. Offstage voices will come from behind. The nonmusical sounds, the sword-throwing in Act Two or dueling, will be kept to a minimum, perhaps ten places in all." Mowrey believed these "effects" were impressive the first time a listener heard them but afterwards, on later auditings, grew annoying. He cited a relatively recent *Carmen* recording from a competing company as a good example of this kind of overindulgence.

The record world watched with interest as the release date approached. DGG itself went in for extensive promotion, even toying with the idea of a mass junket to Seville for stars and press to kick things off. This did not happen, but advertising was going to be heavy and no stone was to be left unturned. Members of the Metropolitan Opera Guild, for instance, several months before the release, were offered the privilege of placing orders at a reduced price. This was immediately countered by advertisements for orders at an even more reduced price from several of New York's many discount houses. Fifteen classical-music stations throughout the United States programmed the DGG *Carmen* during the week of April 22 to April 29, radio spot promotions were devised, the advertising in such trade and special-interest papers as *Record World* and *High Fidelity,* in addition to broader-based consumer publications, reached generous proportions, dealer co-op advertising was not neglected, a billboard was rented in Los Angeles, advance copies were rushed to key reviewers, and Horne herself agreed to personal appearances at major retail outlets in cities the Metropolitan visited on its spring tour.

Billboard reported on jumping-on-bandwagon plans made by other companies: CBS would rerelease some orchestral excerpts from the opera that Bernstein had done several years before, London would increase its promotion of that one-disk *Carmen* starring Horne and conducted by Bernstein's Met successor, Henry Lewis, and RCA was planning to fiddle with its *Carmen Jones* soundtrack recording, also of course, featuring Marilyn Horne. It was interesting that although *Billboard* called these promotions the battle of the *Carmen*s, what these companies were doing was not attempting to confront DGG with their Resnik, De los Angeles, Bumbry, Callas, or Price versions but hoping to profit from spin-offs involving the DGG personnel. Apparently everyone in the industry recognized at this point that the Bernstein-Horne-McCracken *Carmen* might just be the kind of blockbuster the makers of classical recordings always pray for.

At the time of this writing it is impossible to say whether the gods of merchandisers and consumers are working for mutual profit and enjoyment. The critical—much less the financial—verdict has not come in. The package is handsomely and expensively produced, lavish with color photographs of both the stage performance and the recording sessions. Unsurprisingly, the DGG sound is vividly full-dimensional. A lifelike quality has been preserved, especially in the orchestral clarity Bernstein worked so hard to achieve. Indeed the orchestra emerges as the star, very "front" and very dominating. Horne and McCracken are superbly captured, and one never has an inkling that the splicing is as intricate as modern engineering would allow.

Nevertheless, one can anticipate reservations: The overall pacing does seem too attenuated for living-room listening, the French diction at this close a range is occasionally embarrassing, and there exists a perceptible difference between the acoustic ambiences of the musical and the spoken segments. On the other hand, the fact that one can also detect Maliponte's off-form mid-aria sustained G or Mr. Politis's heavy breathing in the flute work of the Act Three entr'acte—both causes of concern to the technicians—contributes a rather pleasant touch of human scale. Within the slick and hoped-for definitive *Carmen* exist people who aren't machines, whose life-giving imperfections can't be surgically destroyed.

Carmen returned to sold-out audiences for the special Metropolitan June season, and it has been retained for the 1973–1974 repertory. With the public, at any rate, the live performance can be counted a winner; the sure-fire combination of a known quantity and a proven favorite work receiving a drastically different treatment insures an appreciative reception from the traditional audience and from those who can be flattered by a return to authenticity and the application of unorthodox sensibilities.

Of course, to call this the Goeran Gentele *Carmen* is a simplification, yes, even a mistake. We will never know what that *Carmen* would have been. What we have instead is a production that's partly Gentele, partly Igesz-Bernstein-Svoboda, and partly the talents of all the people who participated in it. Whatever one felt about the Metropolitan *Carmen,* there can be no denial of its existence as an example of international musical know-how, its totality the end result of a struggle to blend talents to bring forth an opera. Our evening in the theater, our perception of the genius and gifts of composer and artists, our moments are the distillation of months of labor: perspiration, anger, ego, inspiration, sacrifice, compromise, eagerness, boredom, frustration, resignation, determination—and not one element could be subtracted, not one conflict or exultation-worthy discovery could be omitted. We leave the opera house with our opinions, our pleasure or disappointment, but on the other side of the curtain the chronicle never stops.

Index

Adler, Kurt: in August rehearsals, 15-16, 16-17, 25-26, 43, 44, 51, 54, 72, 73, 91, 93, 112ff., 117; dissatisfaction with Altmeyer, 113; in September rehearsals, 127, 133, 134, 136, 138, 145, 147, 153-54ff., 174, 177, 194ff., 204
Altman, Millard, 74, 165-66
Amara, Lucine, 70, 72, 122, 123, 126, 146, 147, 149
Altmeyer, Jeannine, 41, 51, 68, 70, 76, 80, 98, 111ff., 121, 123, 126, 127; Adler's dissatisfaction with, 113; taken off first cover, 146, 179
Anthony, Charles, 26
Ailey, Alvin, 13, 18, 21-23, 28, 59, 116, 152, 161, 163, 177, 215, 226; and costumes, 28-30; and Horne, 56-57, 69, 118, 140-41, 150, 160, 164, 168
Arroyo, Martina, 207

Baldwin, Marcia, 31-32, 33, 61, 68, 124, 153, 166, 170, 187; and dancing, 56, 59, 140, 175; at dress rehearsal, 214; at recording sessions, 266, 273
Barrault, Jean-Louis, 15
Beck, Edward, 269, 270-71, 279
Behr, Jan, 125-26
Benzi, Roberto, 138
Bernstein, Leonard, 8, 13, 15, 31, 58, 82, 130, 159ff., 170; birthday party, 65; discusses *Carmen* project, 196-98; ill, 158, 163; Masielle on, 33; and opening, 221, 224ff.; press representative on, 203; quoted on "singer's" or "conductor's" opera, 204-5; and recordings, 245, 247ff., 280-81, 282; and rehearsals (August): *21,* 38-49; *22,* 50, 51, 53ff.; *23,* 59, 61, 62-63; *28,* 66-67, 69-70ff.; *29,* 77-78ff., 85ff.; *30,* 89-90ff.; *31,* 111ff., 116-17ff.; and rehearsals (September): *1 (Sitzprobe),* 121ff.; *5,* 131-32ff.; *6,* 142-43ff.; *7,* 153ff.; *11,* 171ff.; *12,* 182-83ff.; *13,* 193ff., 200ff.; *16* (dress rehearsal), 208ff., 213-14, 215; TV *Carmen,* 197, 229-33; Walker criticizes, 199
Bing, Sir Rudolf, 8
Boky, Colette, 31; August rehearsals, 38, 40ff., 45, 46, 56, 59ff., 68, 70, 72-73, 85, 96, 97, 118; and dancing, 56, 59, 140, 141, 175, 223; at dress rehearsal, 211, 214; learns Maliponte to do Micaela, 80; on opening night, 223; and recording, 253, 264, 266, 273; and *Romeo and Juliette,* 166; September rehearsals, 124, 132, 133, 140, 141, 153, 154, 170, 175, 187, 200, 205, 211, 214
Bronson, Michael, 34, 118
Buckley, Tom, 161
Bumbry, Grace, 207

Caballé, Montserrat, 208, 222
Caine, Charles, 29, 51, 141, 195
Carson, Margaret, 203
Casei, Nedda, 207
Castel, Nico, 124
Cehanovsky, George, 56
Chapin, Schuyler, 9, 66, 182-83, 246
Chapman, William, 232
Christopher, Russell, 31ff., 39, 76, 125, 127; and dialogue, 18-19, 26, 27, 60, 61, 72, 133, 170, 214, 279; and recording, 263, 264, 279
Cliburn, Van, 207
Comden, Betty, 220
Congdon, James, 231
Corena, Fernando, 147
Corsaro, Frank, 213
Cruz-Romo, Gilda, 207, 215

De Nobili, Lila, 35
DiNunzio, Gildo, 84, 180, 202
Dobriansky, Andrij, 64
Domingo, Placido, 71, 207, 215

Elias, Rosalind, 44, 47, 68, 85, 98, 132, 133, 137, 143, 173

Felsenstein, Walter, 147
Flagello, Ezio, 207
Foster, Don, 50, 51, 113, 132, 135
Franke, Paul, 60, 93, 118, 124, 165, 200, 211, 279

Galli-Marié, Célestine, 166
Gentele, Goeran, 7-8, 13, 15, 16, 36-37, 54, 86, 115, 124, 136, 161, 162, 196-97, 207, 221, 228, 283; Ailey and, 22; and interpretation of Remendado, 41; and interpretation of Micaela, 44-45, 146; McCracken and, 81; Svoboda and, 128, 129; Walker and, 34-35, 199
Gentile, Stella, 55
Giaiotti, Bonaldo, 207
Gibbs, Raymond, 42, 111, 112, 121, 136, 144, 171, 172, 183, 209, 221, 229, 253, 254
Giulini, Walker describes, 36
Gniewek (concertmaster), 275
Goodloe, Robert, 75ff., 84, 89, 93
Gramm, Donald, 38, 52, 59, 62, 64, 96, 114, 147, 158ff., 177, 185, 194, 200; and dialogue, 47, 48, 51, 60, 74, 75, 93, 123, 145, 158, 165, 174, 209, 279; at dress rehearsal, 209; and opening, 221, 223, 229; and recording, 251, 279; at *Sitzprobe,* 122, 123,
Guthrie, Tyrone, 32

Hawkins, Osie: August rehearsals, 50ff., 55, 69, 70, 72, 73, 80, 84, 93ff., 112; at dress rehearsal, 208; September rehearsals, 132, 135, 136, 143, 148, 151, 174, 177, 180, 193, 205-6, 208
Hermann, Gunter, 248
Horne, Marilyn, 8, 13, 163; and birthday party for Bernstein, 65; and card scene, 45-46, 68, 126, 178, 203, 214, 225, 266; and carpet, 51, 63, 67-68, 71, 72, 74, 78, 118, 212-13; and Cehanovsky and Rethberg, 56; and dancing, 56-57, 59, 69, 118, 140-41, 149, 150, 160, 164, 166, 168, 175, 184, 202, 224; daughter's illness, 58; Gentele and, 37; imitates Nillson, 98, 250; and opening, 222ff.; and recording, 246, 248ff., 256ff., 264ff., 268ff., 279, 280, 282; rehearsals (August): *21,* 38, 39, 42, 43, 45-46ff.; *22,* 51ff.; *23,* 58ff.; *24,* 64; *28,* 67-68ff.; *29,* 76ff., 85ff.; *30,* 93, 95ff.; *31,* 113ff.; rehearsals (September): *1* (Sitzprobe), 122ff.; *5,* 133, 235, 137ff.; *6,* 142, 145-46ff.; *7,* 153ff.; *8,* 158ff.; *9,* 169, 170, 172-73ff.; *12,* 184ff.; *13,* 194ff., 200ff.; *16* (dress rehearsal), 208ff., 216; reviewers on, 227, 228; on Valin's problems, 165; Walker on dressing, 35

Igesz, Bodo, 9, 36, 129, 197, 216, 226, 279; August rehearsals, 33-34, 43, 44, 47, 48, 50-51ff., 59, 61, 62, 68, 70ff., 76ff., 83ff., 89, 91, 93ff., 112ff., 118; lunch with newsmen, 161-62; reviewers and, 227, 228; September rehearsals, 120, 128, 131, 133ff., 143-44, 145, 151, 152, 153-54ff.; 159, 164ff., 170, 172, 178, 179, 183, 184, 192, 193ff., 198, 201, 203; Walker on, 199

Jeritza, Maria, 220, 224
Johnson, Harriet, 227

Keene, Audrey, 28, 29
Kennedy, Mrs. Edward, 220
Kennedy, Jacqueline. *See* Onassis, Jacqueline Kennedy
Kerner, Leighton, 228
Klein, Maureen Ting, 116
Kolombatovich, Oscar (and son), 62, 75, 130, 140
Kónya, Sándor, 207
Krause, Tom, 13, 38, 78, 116-17, 118; arrives for rehearsals, 115-16; at dress rehearsal, 211, 215, 216; and opening, 223, 225, 227, 229; and recording, 251ff., 279; at September rehearsals, 123, 124, 126, 127, 134, 135, 137, 148, 152, 153, 156, 157, 165, 170, 175, 179, 187, 200, 204, 211, 215, 216
Kubelik, Rafael, 207
Kuntner, Rudolph, 25, 27, 33, 34, 36, 52, 113, 120, 121, 128, 131, 132, 148, 180, 205-6

Lampert, Zohra, 231-32
Lawson, Nina, 29
Lear, Evelyn, 76
Levine, James, 27-28
Levine, Stanley, 27-28, 53, 55, 69, 91, 93, 180
Lewis, Henry, 46, 80, 138, 142, 165, 176, 282
Lewis, William, 169
Lindsay, Mr. and Mrs. John, 220
Love, Shirley, 46, 70, 215

Maag, Peter, 164, 207
McCracken, James, 8, 13, 160; discusses *Carmen* project, 80-82; and end of Flower Song, 54, 79, 125, 149, 163, 176, 212, 227; and opening 221ff.; pants rip, 156, 173, 174; and recording, 246, 248ff., 252, 256ff., 269ff., 276, 282, 283; rehearsals (August): *21,* 38, 40, 44, 45, 47ff.; *22,* 51ff.; *23,* 60, 62, 63; *28,* 67, 68, 70ff.; *29,* 76, 78ff., 86ff.; *30,* 94ff.;

31, 112, 114, 115, 118-19; rehearsals (September): *1 (Sitzprobe),* 123ff., 127; *5,* 132ff., 138ff.; *6,* 142, 143, 145, 148ff.; *7,* 153, 156, 157; *8,* 158ff., 162ff.; *11,* 172ff., 179, 180; *12,* 182ff., 188ff.; *13,* 194ff., 201, 202, 204; *16* (dress rehearsal), 208ff., 212, 214ff.; reviewers on, 228, 229; Walker on costuming, 198-99
McClure, John, 261, 263, 265, 267, 268, 272, 276, 279, 280
McCourt, Bill, 121
Maderna, Bruno, 213
Maliponte, Adriana, 66, 74, 80, 134ff., 142-43, 146, 154, 172, 173, 178, 179, 182, 183, 191, 194, 195, 203; arrives for rehearsals, 131; at dress rehearsal, 209ff., 215; goes to *Romeo* rehearsal, 187; and opening, 221, 222, 225ff., 229; and recording, 251, 253ff., 267ff., 283
Manuguerra, Matteo, 207
Martin, Janis, 232
Masiello, Alberta: and August rehearsals, 19-20, 26, 31-33, 38, 48-49, 53ff., 68, 113, 117, 118; and September rehearsals, 144-45, 160, 163, 169-70, 186, 194, 200, 203
Matthau, Walter, 254
Mauceri, John, 43-44, 54, 144, 147, 150, 154, 155, 159, 163, 194, 202; at dress rehearsal, 208; and recording, 245, 247, 269-70
Melançon, Louis, 27, 112, 148, 150
Melano, Fabrizio, 47, 53, 72, 76, 98, 116, 120, 152, 172, 203
Meyerson, Bess, 220
Milnes, Sherrill, 149, 207
Moffo, Anna, 166
Morel, Jean, 32
Morris, James, 38
Mowrey, Thomas, 151, 245, 246, 248ff., 256, 259ff., 263, 265ff., 271, 274, 277, 279ff.

Nabors, Jim, 220
Neidlinger, Gustav, 32
Nichols, Mike, 254

Oeser, Fritz, 8
Olvis, William, 230
Onassis, Jacqueline Kennedy, 71, 263
O'Horgan, Tom, 8
Owen, Irving, 57, 141

Peale, Norman Vincent, 220
Plishka, Paul, 207
Politis (flutist), 274-75, 283
Porter, Andrew, 228-29, 261
Probst, Leonard, 157
Pyle, Thomas, 245

Reardon, John, 41, 42, 44, 84
Rennert, Günther, 161
Reppa, David, 129, 217, 221
Resnik, Regina, 132, 207, 216
Rethberg, Elisabeth, 56
Rhodes, Jane, 138, 230, 232-33
Rich, Alan, 228
Riecker, Charles, 50, 55, 63, 64, 66, 74, 118, 131-32, 141, 162, 164, 206
Robbins, Jerome, 9
Robinson, Francis, 13-14, 50, 64, 66, 161, 162
Robinson, Gail, 70
Rockefeller, Laurance, 220

Saal, Hubert, 228
Schippers, Thomas, 252
Schonberg, Harold, 226-27
Shirley, George, 207
Simionato, Giulietta, 192
Simon, Joanna, 220
Singer, Norman, 220
Steber, Eleanor, 220
Stevens, Connis, 220
Stevens, Roger, 220
Stewart, Thomas, 76
Stivender, David: August rehearsals, 14, 15, 17, 24, 43, 50, 55, 83, 91, 114, 115; at opening, 226; and recording, 247; September rehearsals, 122, 126, 136, 145, 147
Strasfogel, Ignace, 38, 43, 46, 48, 54, 73, 80, 94, 113, 143, 152, 159, 165, 179, 198, 204
Stratas, Teresa, 13, 38, 66, 146
Strehler, Giorgio, 8, 35, 162
Svoboda, Josef, 8, 13, 14, 63, 74, 85, 128ff., 161, 175, 197, 215, 262; comments on carpet, 130; DiNunzio on, 180; at rehearsals, 25, 27, 33, 111, 117, 118, 120, 131, 136, 145, 148; Reppa on, 217ff.; reviewers on, 227ff.; Walker on, 199

Thebom, Blanche, 220
Thomas, Michael Tilson, 137-38
Trigère, Pauline, 220

Ulfung, Ragnar, 36, 37, 161

Valin, Danielle, 18-19, 26-27, 58, 60, 61, 98, 182, 187, 200; at rehearsals, 38, 40, 42, 47, 48, 68, 123, 128, 132-33, 134, 145, 150, 160, 165
Velis, Andrea (Andy), 31, 32, 39, 61, 76, 78, 97, 125, 169, 187-88, 200, 279; and dialogue, 26, 27, 41, 60, 63, 80, 96, 178; and dress rehearsal, 211; and homosexuality of character, 41, 82, 96, 148, 178, 211; and recording, 251, 264, 279
Venora, Lee, 232
Verrett, Shirley, 207

Wadmond, Lowell, 220-21
Walker, David, 28-30, 34-36, 72, 111, 162, 198-200, 226
Watt, Douglas, 227
Weidinger, Christine, 19, 27, 31, 33, 68, 70
Westhäuser, Gernot, 277

Zeffirelli, Franco, 35, 149